SCIENCE FICTION TRAVEL STORIES

NOT THE ONLY PLANET

COMPILED BY DAMIEN BRODERICK

LONELY PLANET PUBLICATIONS
Melbourne • Oakland • London • Paris

Not the Only Planet: science fiction travel stories

Published by Lonely Planet Publications
Head Office: PO Box 617, Hawthorn, Vic 3122, Australia
Branches: 150 Linden Street, Oakland, CA 94607, USA
10a Spring Place, London NW5 3BH, UK
71 bis rue du Cardinal Lemoine, 75005 Paris, France

Published 1998

Printed by SNP Printing Pte Ltd, Singapore

Designed by Margaret Jung

National Library of Australia Cataloguing in Publication Data

Not the only planet: science fiction travel stories.

ISBN 0 86442 582 1.

1. Interplanetary voyages - Fiction. 2. Time travel - Fiction.
3. English fiction - 20th century. 4. American fiction - 20th century.
5. Australian fiction - 20th century. I. Broderick, Damien, 1944-.
(Series: Lonely Planet journeys)

823.0876208

Introduction, selection and notes on contributors © Damien Broderick 1998
Additional copyright information appears on pp. 249–50.

*To Eric Van
for generous Readerly hospitality
and Christina Lake
for Boston and New York*

Contents

Introduction

DAMIEN BRODERICK

New worlds are waiting, in time and space. These are the places we will travel to, once the earth is paved over.

Consider this poetry of the scientific imagination, penned by the late Carl Sagan a quarter century ago in *The Cosmic Connection*:

> *There is a place with four suns in the sky – red, white, blue, and yellow; two of them are so close together that they touch, and star-stuff flows between them.*
>
> *I know of a world with a million moons.*
>
> *I know of a sun the size of the Earth – and made of diamond.*
>
> *There are atomic nuclei a mile across that rotate thirty times a second . . .*
>
> *There are stars leaving the Milky Way. There are immense gas clouds falling into the Milky Way . . .*
>
> *There are, perhaps, places outside our universe.*

This is not fiction, but simple reality. Tomorrow's travellers will go into that void, and gaze upon the diamond stars and the million moons. Today, long before that wonderful era opens, we can accompany these future voyagers in our imagination. Science fiction allows us to travel to all the worlds of the solar system, and beyond. Its palette blends romance and gritty science, whimsy and satire; the possibilities are boundless, because there is no passport control.

The best science fiction writing is about people. There is an underside to the human soul that finds its shadow in strange places, walking with us as we step from the airlock of the starship, through the portal of the time machine. Human nature, however twisted by difference and technology, is the vital touchstone in an alien world.

The human factor is also the key to this collection of trips into the unknown, to places not yet on the schedule of any earthly travel agent. In making my selection, I trawled through thousands of science fiction stories from recent decades – the period when sf finally grew up – seeking those writers who in some special way caught the experience of travel. Of course, it isn't difficult to find sf tales dealing with travel. If anything it's too easy, because travel is the strongest theme in the genre. Science fiction and travel have always gone together . . . like a cyborg and a spaceship, like an explorer and a time machine, like a high-tech wanderer and an unmapped globe of never-before-seen creatures living under a green sky and three suns.

Science fiction writers are attracted by the mystique of the outlandish. The disorientation they provide is part of the thrill; coupled with the addictive zing of travel, their art makes us tingle with anticipation at the prospect of heading out into the unknown. It's what makes life piercingly poetic, for if we're to believe that wise old Russian, Viktor Shklovsky, 'art exists to make us recover the sensations of life; it exists to make us feel things, to make the stone *stony*'.

Nothing makes a stone more stony than having one stuck in your shoe in the middle of nowhere. Especially in the Pleistocene, or on Mars.

Even if our entire planet sometimes seems doomed to a future of polite and phoney tourism, other places – Carl Sagan's astonishing planets and stars among them – lie in wait to bite. Some of them hide in the depths of space where our machines have just begun to venture. Other places, no less peculiar, quiver in the long-lost past and the far future, or peer at us sideways from the shadows of worlds that might have been. But even this apparently familiar world of ours isn't so easily subdued. Away from the secure pathways, strange and slightly twisted locales wait to seize us, to make us tremble or sigh. Think of the deep desert's profound solitude which increasingly evades us today, snug in our cities. Earth has a history measurelessly deeper and more mysterious than any sacred writing has glimpsed: floods thousands of years in duration, landscapes broken into fire by comets smashing down from frigid space, animals we know today only from bones and scraps of DNA.

The ten stories gathered together in *Not the Only Planet* range across an Earth oddly transformed by the traveller's eye, through planets and galaxies, and time itself twisted sideways (consider Garry Kilworth's cruelly hilarious package tour to the Crucifixion). They stretch from the *Twilight Zone* absorption that snares Lisa Goldstein's tourist and the troubled near-future Africa of Greg Egan's privileged visitor, to John Varley's glittering high-tech Venus with its casual life-support miracles and carefree sexual mores, and the nearly incomprehensibly strange deep future of Britain's Paul McAuley. Gene Wolfe's visitor to a ruined America of the near future shiveringly reverses an entire tradition of the westerner adrift in an Orient he or she cannot begin to grasp. For Brian W. Aldiss's astronauts on Mars, confronting the loftiest, most numinous mountain humans have ever seen, the apparently simple act of taking photographs of the trip becomes a voyage into inward dread and courage. We must hope that it never becomes necessary to enter as tourists into Stephen Dedman's world of the future, but we are nevertheless grateful for this glimpse into it. While Joanna Russ makes us laugh with her demented alien phrasebook ('That is my companion. It is not intended as a tip.'), Robert Silverberg's endless voyages into parallel possible Earths teach us that we ourselves are no less alien – and, finally, lovable.

Each story carries its special frisson: of startlement, or laughter, of rueful irony, or hard political realism. They make up a kind of scrapbook of traveller's notes and snaps, a jumbled backpack of imaginary memories. A set of exotic postcards from worlds that don't exist. Yet.

Tourists

LISA GOLDSTEIN

He awoke feeling cold. He had kicked the blankets off, and the air conditioning was on too high. Debbie – Where was she? It was still dark out.

Confused, he pulled the blankets back and tried to go to sleep. Something was wrong. Debbie was gone, probably in the bathroom or downstairs getting a cup of coffee. And he was – he was on vacation, but where? Fully awake now, he sat up and tried to laugh. It was ridiculous. Imagine paying thousands of dollars for a vacation and then forgetting where you were. Greece? No, Greece was last year.

He got up and opened the curtains. The ocean ten stories below was black as sleep, paling a little to the east – it had to be east – where the sun was coming up. He turned down the air conditioning – the soft hum stopped abruptly – and headed for the bathroom. "Debbie?" he said, tentatively. He was a little annoyed. "Debbie?"

She was still missing after he had showered and shaved and dressed. "All right then," he said aloud, mostly to hear the sound of his voice. "If you're not coming I'll go to breakfast without you." She was probably out somewhere talking to the natives, laughing when she got a word wrong, though she had told him before they left that she had never studied a foreign language. She was good at languages, then – some people were. He remembered her saying in her soft Southern accent, "For goodness sake Charles, why do you think people will understand you if you just talk to them louder? These people just don't speak English." And then she had taken over, pointing and laughing and looking through a phrasebook she had gotten somewhere. And they would get the best room, the choicest steak, the blanket the craftswoman had woven for her own family. Charles's stock rose when he was with her, and he knew it. He hoped she would show up soon.

Soft Muzak played in the corridor and followed him into the elevator as he went down to the coffee shop. He liked the coffee shop in the hotel, liked the fact that the waiters spoke English and knew what an omelette was. The past few days he had been keeping to the hotel more and more, lying out by the beach and finally just sitting by the hotel pool drinking margaritas. The people back at the office would judge the success of the vacation by what kind of tan he got. Debbie had fretted a little and then had told him she was taking the bus in to see the ruins. She had come back darker than he was, the blonde hairs on her arm bleached almost white against her brown skin, full of stories about women on the bus carrying chickens and temples crumbling in the desert. She was wearing a silver bracelet inlaid with blue and green stones.

When he paid the check he realised that he still didn't know what country he was in. The first bill he took out of his wallet had a 5 on each corner and a picture of some kind of spiky flower. The ten had a view of the ocean, and the one, somewhat disturbingly, showed a fat coiled snake. There was what looked like an official seal on the back of all of them, but no writing. Illiterates, he thought. But he would remember soon enough, or Debbie would come back.

Back in his room, changing into his swim trunks, he thought of his passport. Feeling like a detective who has just cracked the case he got his money belt out from under the mattress and unzipped it. His passport wasn't there. His passport and his plane ticket were missing. The traveller's cheques were still there, useless to him without the passport as identification. Cold washed over him. He sat on the bed, his heart pounding.

Think, he told himself. They're somewhere else. They've got to be – who would steal the passport and not the traveller's cheques? Unless someone needed the passport to leave the country. But who knew where he had hidden it? No one but Debbie, who had laughed at him for his precautions, and the idea of Debbie stealing the passport was absurd. But where was she?

All right, he thought. I've got to find the American consulate, work something out . . . Luckily I just cashed a traveller's cheque yesterday. I've been robbed, and Americans get robbed all the time. It's no big thing. I have time. I'm paid up at the hotel till – till when?

Annoyed, he realised he had forgotten that too. For the first time he wondered if there might be something wrong with him. Overwork, maybe. He would have to see someone about it when he got back to the States.

He lifted the receiver and called downstairs. "Yes, sor?" the man at the desk said.

"This is Room 1012," Charles said. "I've forgotten – I was calling to check – How long is my reservation here?"

There was a silence at the other end, a disapproving silence, Charles felt. Most of the guests had better manners than to forget the length of their stay. He wondered what the man's reaction would be if he had asked what country he was in and felt something like hysteria rise within him. He fought it down.

The man when he came back was carefully neutral. "You are booked through tonight, sor," he said. "Do you wish to extend your stay?"

"Uh – no," Charles said. "Could you tell me – Where is the American consulate?"

"We have no relations with your country, sor," the man at the desk said.

For a moment Charles did not understand what he meant. Then he asked, "Well, what about the British consulate?"

The man at the desk laughed and said nothing. Apparently he felt no need to clarify. As Charles tried to think of another question – Australian consulate? Canadian? – the man hung up.

Charles stood up carefully. "All right," he said to the empty room. "First things first." He got his two suitcases out of the closet and went through them methodically. Debbie's carrying case was still there and he went through that too. He checked under both mattresses, in the nightstand, in the medicine cabinet in the bathroom. Nothing. All right then. Debbie had stolen it, had to have. But why? And why didn't she take her carrying case with her when she went?

He wondered if she would show up back at the office. She had worked down the hall from him, one of the partners' secretaries. He had asked her along for companionship, making it clear that there were no strings attached, that he was simply interested in not travelling alone. Sometimes this kind of relationship turned sexual and sometimes it didn't. Last year, with Katya from accounting, it had. This year it hadn't.

There was still nothing to worry about, Charles thought, snapping the locks on the suitcases. Things like this probably happened all the time. He would get to the airport, where they would no doubt have records, a listing of his flight, and he would explain everything to them there. He checked his wallet for credit cards and found that they were still there. Good, he thought. Now we get to see if the advertisements are true. Accepted all over the world.

He felt so confident that he decided to stay the extra day at the hotel. After all, he thought, I've paid for it. And maybe Debbie will come back. He threw his towel over his shoulder and went downstairs.

The usual people were sitting out by the pool. Millie and Jean, the older women from Miami. The two newlyweds who had kept pretty much to themselves. The hitchhiker who was just passing through and who had been so entertaining that no one had had the heart to report him to the hotel management. Charles nodded to them and ordered his margarita from the bar before sitting down.

Talk flowed around him. "Have you been to Djuzban yet?" Jean was saying to the retired couple who had just joined them at the pool. "We took the hotel tour yesterday. The marketplace is just fabulous. I bought this ring there – see it?" And she flashed silver and stones.

"I hear the ruins are pretty good out in Djuzban," the retired man said.

"Oh, Harold," his wife said. "Harold wants to climb every tower in the country."

"No, man, for ruins you gotta go to Zabla," the hitchhiker said. "But the buses don't go there – you gotta rent a car. It's way the hell out in the desert, unspoiled, untouched. If your car breaks down you're dead – ain't nobody passing through that way for days."

Harold's wife shuddered in the heat. "I just want to do some shopping before we go home," she said. "I heard you can pick up bargains in leather in Qarnatl."

"All we saw in Qarnatl were natives trying to sell us decks of cards," Jean said. She turned to Millie. "Remember? I don't know why they thought Americans would be interested in their playing cards. They weren't even the same as ours."

Charles sipped his margarita, listening to the exotic names flow around him. What if he told them the names meant nothing to him, nothing at all? But he was too embarrassed. There were appearances to keep up after all, the appearance of being a seasoned traveller, of knowing the ropes. He would find out soon enough, anyway.

The day wore on. Charles had a margarita, then another. When the group around the pool broke up it seemed the most natural thing in the world to follow them into the hotel restaurant and order a steak, medium-rare. He was running low on cash, he noticed – he'd have to cash another traveller's cheque in the morning.

But in the morning when he awoke, cold sober, he knew immediately what he'd done. He reached for his wallet on the nightstand, fingers trembling a little. There was only a five with its bleak little picture of a shrub left. Well, he thought, feeling a little shaky. Maybe someone's going to the airport today. Probably. The guys in the office aren't going to believe this one.

He packed up his two suitcases, leaving Debbie's overnight bag for her in case she came back. Downstairs he headed automatically for the coffee shop before he remembered. Abruptly he felt his hunger grow worse. "Excuse me," he said to the man at the desk. "How much – Do you know how much the taxi to the airport is?"

"No speak English, sor," the man said. He was small and dark, like most of the natives. His teeth were stained red.

"You don't – " Charles said, disgusted. "Why in God's name would they hire someone who doesn't speak English? How much," he said slowly. "Taxi. Airport." He heard his voice grow louder; apparently Debbie was right.

The man shrugged. Another man joined them. Charles turned on him with relief. "How much is the taxi to the airport?"

"Oh, taxi," the man said, as though the matter were not very important. "Not so much, sor. Eight, nine. Maybe fifteen."

"Fifteen?" Charles said. He tried to remember the airport, remember how he'd gotten here. "Not five?" He held up five fingers.

The second man laughed. "Oh no sor," he said. "Fifteen. Twenty." He shrugged.

Charles looked around in desperation. Hotel Tours, said the sign behind the front desk. Ruins. Free. "The ruins," he said, pointing to the sign, wondering if either of the men could read. "Are they near the airport?" He could go to the ruins, maybe get a ride . . .

"Near?" the second man said. He shrugged again. "Maybe. Yes, I think so."

"How near?" Charles said.

"Near," the second man said. "Yes. Near enough."

Charles picked up the two suitcases and followed the line of tourists to the bus stop. See, he thought. Nothing to worry about, and you're even getting a free ride to the airport. Those taxi drivers are thieves anyway.

It was awkward manoeuvring the suitcases up the stairs of the bus. "I'm going on to the airport," Charles said to the driver, feeling the need to explain.

"Of course, sor," the driver said, shrugging as if to say that an American's suitcases were no business of his. He added a word that Charles didn't catch. Perhaps it was in another language.

The bus set off down the new two-lane highway fronting the hotels. Soon they left the hotels behind, passed a cluster of run-down shacks and were heading into the desert. The air conditioning hummed loudly. Waves of heat travelled across the sands.

After nearly an hour the bus stopped. "We have one hour," the driver said in bad English. He opened the door. "These are the temple of Marmaz. Very old. One hour." The tourists filed out. A few were adjusting cameras or pointing lenses.

Because of the suitcases Charles was the last out. He squinted against the sun. The temple was a solid wall of white marble against the sand. Curious in spite of himself he crossed the parking lot, avoiding the native who was trying to show him something. "Pure silver," the small man said, calling after him. "Special price just for you."

In front of the temple was a cracked marble pool, now dry. Who were these people who had carried water into the desert, who had imprisoned the moon in pale marble? But then how much had he known about the other tourist spots he had visited, the Greeks who had built the Parthenon, the Mayans who had built the pyramids? He followed the line of tourists into the temple, feeling the coolness fall over him like a blessing.

He went from room to room, delighted, barely feeling the weight of the suitcases. He saw crumbling mosaics of reds and blues and greens, fragments of tapestries, domes, fountains, towers, a white dining hall that could seat a hundred. In one small room a native was explaining a piece of marble sculpture to a dozen Americans.

"This, he is the god of the sun," the native said. "And in the next room, the goddess of the moon. Moon, yes? We will go see her after. Once a year, at the end of the year, the two statues – statues, yes? – go outside. The priests take outside. They get married. Her baby is the new year."

"What nonsense," a woman standing near Charles said quietly. She was holding a guidebook. "That's the fourth king. He built the temple. God of the sun." She laughed scornfully.

"Can I – Can I see that book for a minute?" Charles said. The cover had flipped forward tantalisingly, almost revealing the name of the country.

The woman looked briefly at her watch. "Got to go," she said. "The bus is leaving in a minute and I've got to find my husband. Sorry."

Charles's bus was gone by the time he left the temple. It was much cooler now but heat still rose from the desert sands. He was very hungry, nearly tempted to buy a cool drink and a sandwich at the refreshment stand near the parking lot. "Cards?" someone said to him.

Charles turned. The small native said something that sounded like "Tiraz!" It was the same word the bus driver had said to him in the morning. Then, "Cards?" he said again.

"What?" Charles said impatiently, looking for a taxi.

"Ancient playing set," the native said. "Very holy." He took out a deck of playing cards from an embroidered bag and spread them for Charles. The colours were very bright. "Souvenir," the native said. He grinned, showing red-stained teeth. "Souvenir of your trip."

"No, thank you," Charles said. All around the parking lot, it seemed, little natives were trying to sell tourists rings and pipes and blouses and, for some reason, packs of playing cards. "Taxi?" he said. "Is there a taxi here?"

The native shrugged and moved on to the next tourist. It was getting late. Charles went toward the nearest tour bus. The driver was leaning against the bus, smoking a small cigarette wrapped in a brown leaf. "Where can I find a taxi?" Charles asked him.

"No taxis," the driver said.

"No – Why not?" Charles said. This country was impossible. He couldn't wait to get out, to be on a plane drinking a margarita and heading back to the good old USA. This was the worst vacation he'd ever had. "Can I make a phone call? I have to get to the airport."

A woman about to get on the bus heard him and stopped. "The airport?" she said. "The airport's fifty miles from here. At least. You'll never find a taxi to take you that far."

"Fifty miles?" Charles said. "They told me – At the hotel they told me it was fairly close." For a moment his confidence left him. What do I do now? he thought. He sagged against the suitcases.

"Listen," the woman said. She turned to the bus driver. "We've got room. Can't we take him back to the city with us? I think we're the last bus to leave."

The driver shrugged. "For the tiraz, of course. Anything is possible."

If Charles hadn't been so relieved at the ride he would have been annoyed. What did this word tiraz mean? Imbecile? Man with two suitcases? He followed the woman onto the bus.

"I can't believe you thought this was close to the airport," the woman said. He sat across the aisle from her. "This is way out in the desert. There's nothing here. No one would come out here if it wasn't for the ruins."

"They told me at the hotel," Charles said. He didn't really want to discuss it. He was no longer the seasoned traveller, the man who had regaled the people around the pool with stories of Mexico, Greece, Hawaii. He would have to confess, have to go back to the hotel and tell someone the whole story. Maybe they would bring in the police to find Debbie. A day wasted and he had only gone around in a circle, back to where he started. He felt tired and very hungry.

But when the bus stopped it was not at the brightly lit row of hotels. He strained to see in the oncoming dusk. "I thought you said – " He turned to the woman, hating to sound foolish again. "I thought we were going to the city."

"This is – " the woman said. Then she nodded in understanding. "You want the new city, the tourist city. That's up the road about ten miles. Any cab'll take you there."

Charles was the last off the bus again, slowed this time not so much by the suitcases as by the new idea. People actually slaved in the same cities that the natives lived. He had heard of it being done but he had thought only young people did it, students and drifters and hitchhikers like the one back at the hotel. This woman was not young and she had been fairly pleasant. He wished he had remembered to thank her.

The first cab driver laughed when Charles showed him the five note and asked to be taken to the new city. The driver was not impressed by the traveller's cheques. The second and third drivers turned him down flat. The city smelled of motor oil and rancid fish. It was getting late, even a little chilly, and Charles began to feel nervous about being out so late. The suitcases were an obvious target for some thief. And where would he go? What would he do?

The panic that he had suppressed for so long took over now and he began to run. He dove deeper into the twisting maze of the city, not caring where he went so long as he was moving. Everything was closed, and there were few streetlamps. He heard the sounds of his footfalls echo off the shuttered buildings. A cat jumped out of his way, eyes flashing gold.

After a long time of running he began to slow. "Tiraz!" someone whispered to him from an abandoned building. His heart pounded. He did not look back. Ahead was a lit storefront, a store filled with clutter. The door was open. A pawn shop.

He went in with relief. He cleared a space for himself among the old magazines and rusty baking pans and child's beads. The man behind the counter watched but made no comment. He took out everything from the two suitcases, sorted out what he needed and repacked it and gave the other suitcase to the man behind the counter. The man went to a small desk, unlocked a drawer and took out a steel box. He counted out some money and offered it to Charles. Charles accepted it wordlessly, not even bothering to count it.

The money bought a meal tasting of sawdust and sesame oil, and a sagging bed in an old hotel. The overhead fan turned all night because Charles could not figure out how to turn it off. A cockroach watched impassively from the corner.

The city looked different in daylight. Women in shawls and silver bracelets, men in clothes fashionable fifty years ago walked past the hotel as Charles looked out in the morning. The sun was shining. His heart rose. This was going to be the day he made it to the airport.

He walked along the streets almost jauntily, ignoring the ache in his arms. His beard itched because last night, in a moment of panic, he had thrown his electric razor into the suitcase to be sold. He shrugged. There were still things he could sell. Today he would find a better pawn shop.

He walked, passing run-down houses and outdoor markets, beggars and children, automobile garages and dim restaurants smelling of frying fish. "Excuse me," he said to a man leaning against a horse-drawn carriage. "Do you know where I can find a pawn shop?"

The man and horse both looked up. "Ride, yes?" the man said enthusiastically. "Famous monuments. Very cheap."

"No," Charles said. "A pawn shop. Do you understand?"

The man shrugged, pulled the horse's mane. "No speak English," he said finally.

Another man had come up behind Charles. "Pawn shop?" he said.

Charles turned quickly, relieved. "Yes," he said. "Do you know – "

"Two blocks down," the man said. "Turn left, go five blocks. Across the hospital."

"What street is that?" Charles asked.

"Street?" the man said. He frowned. "Two blocks down and turn left."

"The name," Charles said. "The name of the street."

To Charles's astonishment the man burst out laughing. The carriage driver laughed too, though he could not have possibly known what they were talking about. "Name?" the man said. "You tourists name your streets as though they were little children, yes?" He laughed again, wiping his eyes, and said something to the carriage-driver in another language, speaking rapidly.

"Thank you," Charles said. He walked the two blocks, turned left and went five blocks more. There was no hospital where the man had said there would be, and no pawn shop. A man who spoke a little English said something about a great fire, but

23

whether it had been last week or several years ago Charles was unable to find out.

He started back toward the man who had given him directions. In a few minutes he was hopelessly lost. The streets became dingier, and once he saw a rat run from a pile of newspapers. The fire had swept through this part of the city leaving buildings charred and water-damaged, open to the passers-by like museum exhibits. Two dirty children ran toward him, shouting, "Money, please, sor! Money for food!" He turned down a sidestreet to lose them.

Ahead of him were three young men in grease-stained clothes. One of them hissed something at him, the words rushing by like a fork of lightning. Another held a length of chain which he played back and forth, whispering, between his hands. "I don't speak – " Charles said, but it was too late. They were on him.

One tore the suitcase from his hand, shouting "El amak! El amak!" Another knocked him down with a punch to his stomach that forced the wind out of him. The third was going through his pockets, taking his wallet and the little folder of traveller's cheques. Charles tried feebly to rise, and the second one thrust him back, hitting him once more in the stomach. The first one yelled something and they ran quickly down the street. Charles lay where they left him, gasping for breath.

The two dirty children passed him, and an old woman balancing a basket of clothes on her head. After a few minutes he rolled over and sat up, leaning against a rusty car up on blocks. His pants were torn, he noticed dully, torn and smeared with oil. And his suitcase with the rest of his clothes was gone.

He would go to the police, go and tell them that his suitcase was gone. He knew the word for suitcase because the young thief had shouted it. Amak. El amak. And suddenly he realised something that knocked the breath out of him as suddenly as a punch to the stomach. Every word in English, every word that he knew, had a corresponding word in this strange foreign language. Everything you could think of – hand, love, table, hot – was conveyed to these natives by another word, a word not English.

Debbie had known that, and that was why she was good at languages. He hadn't. He had expected everyone he met to drop this ridiculous charade and start speaking like normal people.

He stood up gingerly, breathing shallowly to make the pain in his stomach go away. After a while he began walking again, following the maze of the city in deeper. At last he found a small park and sat on a bench to rest.

A native came up to him almost immediately. "Cards?" the native said. "Look." He opened his embroidered bag.

Charles sighed. He was too tired to walk away. "I don't want any cards," he said. "I don't have any money."

"Of course not," the native said. "Look. They are beautiful, no?" He spread the brightly coloured cards on the grass. Charles saw a baseball player, a fortune teller, a student, some designs he didn't recognise. "Look," the native said again and turned over the next card. "The tourist.'"

Charles had to laugh, looking at the card of the man carrying suitcases. These people had been visited by tourists for so long that the tourist had become an archetype, a part of everyone's reality like kings and jokers. He looked closer at the card. Those suitcases were familiar. And the tourist – He jerked back as though shocked. It was him.

He stood quickly and began to run, ignoring the pain in his stomach. The native did not follow.

He noticed the card sellers on every corner after that. They called to him even if he crossed the street to avoid them. "Tiraz, tiraz!" they called after him. He knew what it meant now. Tourist.

As the sun set he became ravenously hungry. He walked around a beggar woman squatting in the street and saw, too late, a card seller waiting on the corner. The card seller held out something to him, some kind of pastry, and Charles took it, too hungry to refuse.

The pastry was filled with meat and very good. As though that were the signal the other card sellers he passed began to give him things – a skin of wine, a piece of fish wrapped in paper. One of them handed him money, far more money than a deck of cards would cost. It was growing dark. He took a room for the night with the money.

A card seller was waiting for him at the corner the next day. "All right," Charles said to him. Some of the belligerence had been knocked out of him. "I give up. What the hell's going on around here?"

"Look," the card seller said. He took his cards out of the embroidered bag. "It is in here." He squatted on the sidewalk, oblivious to the dirt, the people walking by, the fumes from the street. The street, Charles noticed as he sat next to him, seemed to be paved with bottle caps.

The card seller spread the cards in front of him. "Look," he said. "It is foretold. The cards are our oracle, our newspaper, our entertainment. All depends on how you read them." Charles wondered where the man had learned to speak English, but he didn't want to interrupt. "See," the man said as he turned over a card. "Here you are. The tourist. It was foretold that you would come to the city."

"And then what?" Charles asked. "How do I get back?"

"We have to ask the cards," the man said. Idly he turned over another card, the ruins of Marmaz. "Maybe we wait for the next printing."

"Next – " Charles said. "You mean the cards don't stay the same?"

"No," the man said. "Do your newspapers stay the same?"

"But – Who prints them?"

The man shrugged. "We do not know." He turned over another card, a young blonde woman.

"Debbie!" Charles said, startled.

"Yes," the man said. "The woman you came with. We had to convince her to go, so that you would fulfil the prophecy and come to the city. And then we took your pieces of paper, the ones that are so important to the tiraz. That is a stupid way to travel, if I may say so. In the city the only papers that are important to us are the cards, and if a man loses his cards he can easily get more."

"You – you took my passport?" Charles said. He did not feel

as angry as he would like. "My passport and my plane tickets? Where are they?"

"Ah," the man said. "For that you must ask the cards." He took out another set of cards from his bag and gave them to Charles. Before Charles could answer he stood up and walked away.

By midday Charles had found the small park again. He sat down and spread out the cards, wondering if there was anything to what the card seller had said. Debbie did not appear in his deck. Was his an earlier printing, then, or a later one?

An American couple came up to him as he sat puzzling over the cards. "There are those cards again," the woman said. "I just can't get over how quaint they are. How much are you charging for yours?" she asked Charles. "The man down the street said he'd give them to us for ten."

"Eight," Charles said without hesitation, gathering them up.

The woman looked at her husband. "All right," he said. He took a five and three ones from his wallet and gave them to Charles.

"Thank you, sor," Charles said.

The man grunted. "I thought he spoke English very well," the woman said as they walked away. "Didn't you?"

A card seller gave him three more decks of cards and an embroidered bag later that day. By evening he had sold two of the decks. A few nights later, he joined the sellers of cards as they waited in the small park for the new printing of the cards. Somewhere a bell tolled midnight. A woman with beautiful long dark hair and an embroidered shawl came out of the night and silently took out the decks of cards from her bag. Her silver bracelets flashed in the moonlight. She gave Charles twelve decks. The men around him were already tearing the boxes open and spreading the cards, reading the past, or the present, or the future.

After about three years Charles got tired of selling the cards. His teeth had turned red from chewing the nut everyone chewed and he had learned to smoke the cigarettes wrapped in leaves. The other men had always told him that someone who spoke English as well as he did should be a tour guide, and finally he decided that they were right. Now he takes groups of tourists through the ruins of Marmaz, telling them about the god of the sun and the goddess of the moon and whatever else he chooses to make up that day. He has never found out what country he lives in.

Yeyuka

GREG EGAN

On my last day in Sydney, as a kind of farewell, I spent the morning on Bondi Beach. I swam for an hour, then lay on the sand and stared at the sky. I dozed off for a while, and when I woke there were half a dozen booths set up amid the sun bathers, dispensing the latest fashion: solar tattoos. On a touch-screen the size of a full-length mirror, you could choose a design and then customise it, or create one from scratch with software assistance. Computer-controlled jets sprayed the undeveloped pigments onto your skin, then an hour of UV exposure rendered all the colours visible.

As the morning wore on, I saw giant yellow butterflies perched between shoulder blades, torsos wrapped in green-and-violet dragons, whole bodies wreathed in chains of red hibiscus. Watching these images materialise around me, I couldn't help thinking of them as banners of victory. Throughout my childhood, there'd been nothing more terrifying than the threat of melanoma – and by the turn of the millennium, nothing more hip than neck-to-knee lycra. Twenty years later, these elaborate decorations were designed to encourage, to boast of, irradiation. To proclaim, not that the sun itself had been tamed, but that our bodies had. To declare that cancer had been defeated.

I touched the ring on my left index finger, and felt a reassuring pulse through the metal. Blood flowed constantly around the hollow core of the device, diverted from a vein in my finger. The ring's inner surface was covered with billions of tiny sensors, spring-loaded funnel-shaped structures like microscopic Venus fly-traps, each just a few hundred atoms wide. Every sizable molecule in my bloodstream that collided with one of these traps was seized and shrink-wrapped, long enough and tightly enough to determine its shape and its chemical identity before it was released.

So the ring knew exactly what was in my blood. It also knew what belonged, and what didn't. Under its relentless scrutiny, the biochemical signature of a viral or bacterial infection, or even a microscopic tumour far downstream, could never escape detection for long – and once a diagnosis was made, treatment was almost instantaneous. Planted alongside the sensors were programmable catalysts, versatile molecules that could be reshaped under computer control. The ring could manufacture a wide range of drugs from raw materials circulating in the blood, just by choosing the right sequence of shapes for these catalysts – trapping the necessary ingredients together in nooks and crannies moulded to fit like plaster casts around their combined outlines.

With medication delivered within minutes or seconds, infections were wiped out before they could take hold, tiny clusters of cancer cells destroyed before they could grow or spread. Linked by satellite to a vast array of medical databases, and as much additional computing power as it required, the ring gave me a kind of electronic immune system, fast enough and smart enough to overcome any adversary.

Not everyone on the beach that morning would have had their own personal HealthGuard, but a weekly session on a shared family unit, or even a monthly check-up at their local GP, would have been enough to reduce their risk of cancer dramatically. And though melanoma was the least of my worries – fair-skinned, I was covered in sunscreen as usual; fatal or not, getting burnt was painful – with the ring standing guard against ten thousand other possibilities, I'd come to think of it as a vital part of my body. The day I'd installed it, my life expectancy had risen by fifteen years – and no doubt my bank's risk-assessment software had assumed a similar extension to my working life, since I'd be paying off the loan I'd needed to buy the thing well into my sixties.

I tugged gently at the plain metal band, until I felt a sharp warning from the needle-thin tubes that ran deep into the flesh. This model wasn't designed to be slipped on and off in an instant like the shared units, but it would only take a five-minute surgical procedure under local anaesthetic to remove it. In Uganda, a single HealthGuard machine served 40 million people – or rather, the lucky few who could get access to it. Flying in wearing my own personal version seemed almost as crass as arriving with a giant solar tattoo. Where I was headed, cancer had very definitely not been defeated.

Then again, nor had malaria, typhoid, yellow fever, schistosomiasis. I could have the ring immunise me against all of these and more, before removing it . . . but the malaria parasite was notoriously variable, so constant surveillance would provide far more reliable protection. I'd be no use to anyone lying in a hospital bed for half my stay. Besides, the average villager or shanty-town dweller probably wouldn't even recognise the thing, let alone resent it. I was being hypersensitive.

I gathered up my things and headed for the cycle rack. Looking back across the sand, I felt the kind of stab of regret that came upon waking from a dream of impossible good fortune and serenity, and for a moment I wanted nothing more than to close my eyes and rejoin it.

○

Lisa saw me off at the airport.

I said, "It's only three months. It'll fly past." I was reassuring myself, not her.

"It's not too late to change your mind." She smiled calmly; no pressure, it was entirely my decision. In her eyes, I was clearly suffering from some kind of disease – a very late surge of adolescent idealism, or a very early mid-life crisis – but she'd adopted a scrupulously non-judgmental bedside manner. It drove me mad.

"And miss my last chance ever to perform cancer surgery?"

That was a slight exaggeration; a few cases would keep slipping through the HealthGuard net for years. Most of my usual work was trauma, though, which was going through changes of its own. Computerised safeguards had made traffic accidents rare, and I suspected that within a decade no one would get the chance to stick their hand in a conveyor belt again. If the steady stream of gunshot and knife wounds ever dried up, I'd have to retrain for nose jobs and reconstructing rugby players. "I should have gone into obstetrics, like you."

Lisa shook her head. "In the next twenty years, they'll crack all the molecular signals, within and between mother and foetus. There'll be no premature births, no Caesareans, no complications. The HealthGuard will smooth my job away, too." She added, deadpan, "Face it, Martin, we're all doomed to obsolescence."

"Maybe. But if we are . . . it'll happen sooner in some places than others."

"And when the time comes, you might just head off to some place where you're still needed?"

She was mocking me, but I took the question seriously. "Ask me that when I get back. Three months without mod cons and I might be cured for life."

My flight was called. We kissed goodbye. I suddenly realised that I had no idea why I was doing this. The health of distant strangers? Who was I kidding? Maybe I'd been trying to fool myself into believing that I really was that selfless – hoping all the while that Lisa would talk me out of it, offering some face-saving excuse for me to stay. I should have known she'd call my bluff instead.

I said plainly, "I'm going to miss you. Badly."

"I should hope so." She took my hand, scowling, finally accepting the decision. "You're an idiot, you know. Be careful."

"I will." I kissed her again, then slipped away.

○

I was met at Entebbe airport by Magdalena Iganga, one of the oncologists on a small team that had been put together by

Médecins Sans Frontières to help overburdened Ugandan doctors tackle the growing number of Yeyuka cases. Iganga was Tanzanian, but she'd worked throughout eastern Africa, and as she drove her battered ethanol-powered car the thirty kilometres into Kampala, she recounted some of her brushes with the World Health Organization in Nairobi.

"I tried to persuade them to set up an epidemiological database for Yeyuka. Good idea, they said. Just put a detailed proposal to the cancer epidemiology expert committee. So I did. And the committee said, we like your proposal, but oh dear, Yeyuka is a contagious disease, so you'll have to submit this to the contagious diseases expert committee instead. Whose latest annual sitting I'd just missed by a week." Iganga sighed stoically. "Some colleagues and I ended up doing it ourselves, on an old 386 and a borrowed phone line."

"Three eight what?"

She shook her head. "Palaeocomputing jargon, never mind."

Though we were dead on the equator and it was almost noon, the temperature must have been 30 at most; Kampala was high above sea level. A humid breeze blew off Lake Victoria, and low clouds rolled by above us, gathering threateningly then dissipating, again and again. I'd been promised that I'd come for the dry season; at worst there'd be occasional thunderstorms.

On our left, between patches of marshland, small clusters of shacks began to appear. As we drew closer to the city, we passed through layers of shanty towns, the older and more organised verging on a kind of bedraggled suburbia, others looking more like out-and-out refugee camps. The tumours caused by the Yeyuka virus tended to spread fast but grow slowly, often partially disabling people for years before killing them, and when they could no longer manage heavy rural labour, they usually headed for the nearest city in the hope of finding work. Southern Uganda had barely recovered from HIV when Yeyuka cases began to appear, around 2013; in fact, some virologists believed that Yeyuka had arisen from a less virulent ancestor after gaining a foothold within the immune-suppressed population. And though

Yeyuka wasn't as contagious as cholera or tuberculosis, crowded conditions, poor sanitation and chronic malnourishment set up the shanty towns to bear the brunt of the epidemic.

As we drove north between two hills, the centre of Kampala appeared ahead of us, draped across a hill of its own. Compared to Nairobi, which I'd flown over a few hours before, Kampala looked uncluttered. The streets and low buildings were laid out in a widely spaced plan, neatly organised but lacking any rigid geometry of grid lines or concentric circles. There was plenty of traffic around us, both cycles and cars, but it flowed smoothly enough, and for all the honking and shouting going on the drivers seemed remarkably good humoured.

Iganga took a detour to the east, skirting the central hill. There were lushly green sports grounds and golf courses on our right, colonial-era public buildings and high-fenced foreign embassies on our left. There were no high-rise slums in sight, but there were makeshift shelters and even vegetable gardens on some stretches of parkland, traces of the shanty towns spreading inwards.

In my jet-lagged state, it was amazing to find that this abstract place that I'd been imagining for months had solid ground, actual buildings, real people. Most of my second-hand glimpses of Uganda had come from news clips set in war zones and disaster areas; from Sydney, it had been almost impossible to conceive of the country as anything more than a frantically edited video sequence full of soldiers, refugees and fly-blown corpses. In fact, rebel activity was confined to a shrinking zone in the country's far north, most of the last wave of Zairean refugees had gone home a year ago, and while Yeyuka was a serious problem, people weren't exactly dropping dead in the streets.

Makerere University was in the north of the city; Iganga and I were both staying at the guest house there. A student showed me to my room, which was plain but spotlessly clean; I was almost afraid to sit on the bed and rumple the sheets. After washing and unpacking, I met up with Iganga again and we walked across the campus to Mulago Hospital, which was affiliated with the university medical school. There was a soccer team practising across the road as we went in, a reassuringly mundane sight.

Iganga introduced me to nurses and porters left and right; everyone was busy but friendly, and I struggled to memorise the barrage of names. The wards were all crowded, with patients spilling into the corridors, a few in beds but most on mattresses or blankets. The building itself was dilapidated, and some of the equipment must have been thirty years old, but there was nothing squalid about the conditions; all the linen was clean, and the floor looked and smelt like you could do surgery on it.

In the Yeyuka ward, Iganga showed me the six patients I'd be operating on the next day. The hospital did have a CAT scanner, but it had been broken for the past six months, waiting for money for replacement parts, so flat X-rays with cheap contrast agents like barium were the most I could hope for. For some tumours, the only guide to location and extent was plain old palpation. Iganga guided my hands, and kept me from applying too much pressure; she'd had a great deal more experience at this than I had, and an over-zealous beginner could do a lot of damage. The world of three-dimensional images spinning on my workstation while the software advised on the choice of incision had receded into fantasy. Stubbornly, though, I did the job myself; gently mapping the tumours by touch, picturing them in my head, marking the X-rays or making sketches.

I explained to each patient where I'd be cutting, what I'd remove, and what the likely effects would be. Where necessary, Iganga translated for me – either into Swahili, or what she described as her 'broken Luganda'. The news was always only half good, but most people seemed to take it with a kind of weary optimism. Surgery was rarely a cure for Yeyuka, usually just offering a few years' respite, but it was currently the only option. Radiation and chemotherapy were useless, and the hospital's sole HealthGuard machine couldn't generate custom-made molecular cures for even a lucky few; seven years into the epidemic, Yeyuka wasn't yet well enough understood for anyone to have written the necessary software.

By the time I was finished it was dark outside. Iganga asked, "Do you want to look in on Ann's last operation?" Ann Collins was the Irish volunteer I was replacing.

"Definitely." I'd watched a few operations performed here, on video back in Sydney, but no VR scenarios had been available for proper 'hands on' rehearsals, and Collins would only be around to supervise me for a few more days. It was a painful irony: foreign surgeons were always going to be inexperienced, but no one else had so much time on their hands. Ugandan medical students had to pay a small fortune in fees – the World Bank had put an end to the new government's brief flirtation with state-subsidised training – and it looked like there'd be a shortage of qualified specialists for at least another decade.

We donned masks and gowns. The operating theatre was like everything else, clean but outdated. Iganga introduced me to Collins, the anaesthetist Eriya Okwera, and the trainee surgeon Balaki Masika.

The patient, a middle-aged man, was covered in orange Betadine-soaked surgical drapes, arranged around a long abdominal incision. I stood beside Collins and watched, entranced. Growing within the muscular wall of the small intestine was a grey mass the size of my fist, distending the peritoneum, the organ's translucent 'skin', almost to bursting point. It would certainly have been blocking the passage of food; the patient must have been on liquids for months.

The tumour was very loose, almost like a giant discoloured blood clot; the hardest thing would be to avoid dislodging any cancerous cells in the process of removing it, sending them back into circulation to seed another tumour. Before making a single cut in the intestinal wall, Collins used a laser to cauterise all the blood vessels around the growth, and she didn't lay a finger on the tumour itself at any time. Once it was free, she lifted it away with clamps attached to the surrounding tissue, as fastidiously as if she was removing a leaky bag full of some fatal poison. Maybe other tumours were already growing unseen in other parts of the body, but doing the best possible job, here and now, might still add three or four years to this man's life.

Masika began stitching the severed ends of the intestine together. Collins led me aside and showed me the patient's X-rays on a light-box. "This is the site of origin." There was a cavity clearly visible in the right lung, about half the size of the tumour she'd just removed. Ordinary cancers grew in a single location first, and then a few mutant cells in the primary tumour escaped to seed growths in the rest of the body. With Yeyuka, there were no 'primary tumours'; the virus itself uprooted the cells it infected, breaking down the normal molecular adhesives that kept them in place, until the infected organ seemed to be melting away. That was the origin of the name: yeyuka, to melt. Once set loose into the bloodstream, many of the cells died of natural causes, but a few ended up lodged in small capillaries – physically trapped, despite their lack of stickiness – where they could remain undisturbed long enough to grow into sizable tumours.

After the operation, I was invited out to a welcoming dinner in a restaurant down in the city. The place specialised in Italian food, which was apparently hugely popular, at least in Kampala. Iganga, Collins and Okwera, old colleagues by now, unwound noisily; Okwera, a solid man in his forties, grew mildly but volubly intoxicated and told medical horror stories from his time in the army. Masika, the trainee surgeon, was very softly spoken and reserved. I was something of a zombie from jet lag myself, and didn't contribute much to the conversation, but the warm reception put me at ease.

I still felt like an impostor, here only because I hadn't had the courage to back out, but no one was going to interrogate me about my motives. No one cared. It wouldn't make the slightest difference whether I'd volunteered out of genuine compassion, or just a kind of moral insecurity brought on by fears of obsolescence. Either way, I'd brought a pair of hands and enough general surgical experience to be useful. If you'd ever had to be a saint to heal someone, medicine would have been doomed from the start.

○

I was nervous as I cut into my first Yeyuka patient, but by the end of the operation, with a growth the size of an orange successfully removed from the right lung, I felt much more confident. Later the same day, I was introduced to some of the hospital's permanent surgical staff – a reminder that even when Collins left, I'd hardly be working in isolation. I fell asleep on the second night exhausted, but reassured. I could do this, it wasn't beyond me. I hadn't set myself an impossible task.

I drank too much at the farewell dinner for Collins, but the HealthGuard magicked the effects away. My first day solo was anticlimactic; everything went smoothly, and Okwera, with no high-tech hangover cure, was unusually subdued, while Masika was as quietly attentive as ever.

Six days a week, the world shrank to my room, the campus, the ward, the operating theatre. I ate in the guest house, and usually fell asleep an hour or two after the evening meal; with the sun diving straight below the horizon, by eight o'clock it felt like midnight. I tried to call Lisa every night, though I often finished in the theatre too late to catch her before she left for work, and I hated leaving messages, or talking to her while she was driving.

Okwera and his wife invited me to lunch the first Sunday, Masika and his girlfriend the next. Both couples were genuinely hospitable, but I felt like I was intruding on their one day together. The third Sunday, I met up with Iganga in a restaurant, then we wandered through the city on an impromptu tour.

There were some beautiful buildings in Kampala, many of them clearly war-scarred but lovingly repaired. I tried to relax and take in the sights, but I kept thinking of the routine – six operations, six days a week – stretching out ahead of me until the end of my stay. When I mentioned this to Iganga, she laughed. "All right. You want something more than assembly-line work? I'll line up a trip to Mubende for you. They have patients there who are too sick to be moved. Multiple tumours, all nearly terminal."

"Okay." Me and my big mouth; I knew I hadn't been seeing the worst cases, but I hadn't given much thought to where they all were.

We were standing outside the Sikh temple, beside a plaque describing Idi Amin's expulsion of Uganda's Asian community in 1972. Kampala was dotted with memorials to atrocities – and though Amin's reign had ended more than forty years ago, it had been a long path back to normality. It seemed unjust beyond belief that even now, in an era of relative political stability, so many lives were being ruined by Yeyuka. No more refugees marching across the countryside, no more forced expulsions – but cells cast adrift could bring just as much suffering.

I asked Iganga, "So why did you go into medicine?"

"Family expectations. It was either that or the law. Medicine seemed less arbitrary; nothing in the body can be overturned by an appeal to the High Court. What about you?"

I said, "I wanted to be in on the revolution. The one that was going to banish all disease."

"Ah, that one."

"I picked the wrong job, of course. I should have been a molecular biologist."

"Or a software engineer."

"Yeah. If I'd seen the HealthGuard coming fifteen years ago, I might have been right at the heart of the changes. And I'd have never looked back. Let alone sideways."

Iganga nodded sympathetically, quite unfazed by the notion that molecular technology might capture the attention so thoroughly that little things like Yeyuka epidemics would vanish from sight altogether. "I can imagine. Seven years ago, I was all set to make my fortune in one of the private clinics in Dar es Salaam. Rich businessmen with prostate cancer, that kind of thing. I was lucky in a way; before that market vanished completely, the Yeyuka fanatics were nagging me, bullying me, making little deals." She laughed. "I've lost count of the number of times I was promised I'd be co-author of a ground-breaking paper in *Nature Oncology* if I just helped out at some field clinic in the middle of nowhere. I was dragged into this, kicking and screaming, just when all my old dreams were going up in smoke."

"But now Yeyuka feels like your true vocation?"

She rolled her eyes. "Spare me. My ambition now is to retire to a highly paid consulting position in Nairobi or Geneva."

"I'm not sure I believe you."

"You should." She shrugged. "Sure, what I'm doing now is a hundred times more useful than any desk job, but that doesn't make it any easier. You know as well as I do that the warm inner glow doesn't last for a thousand patients; if you fought for every one of them as if they were your own family or friends, you'd go insane . . . so they become a series of clinical problems, which just happen to be wrapped in human flesh. And it's a struggle to keep working on the same problems, over and over, even if you're convinced that it's the most worthwhile job in the world."

"So why are you in Kampala right now, instead of Nairobi or Geneva?"

Iganga smiled. "Don't worry, I'm working on it. I don't have a date on my ticket out of here, like you do, but when the chance comes, believe me, I'll grab it just as fast as I can."

○

It wasn't until my sixth week, and my two-hundred-and-fourth operation, that I finally screwed up.

The patient was a teenaged girl with multiple infestations of colon cells in her liver. A substantial portion of the organ's left lobe would have to be removed, but her prognosis seemed relatively good; the right lobe appeared to be completely clean, and it was not beyond hope that the liver, directly downstream from the colon, had filtered all the infected cells from the blood before they could reach any other part of the body.

Trying to clamp the left branch of the portal vein, I slipped, and the clamp closed tightly on a swollen cyst at the base of the liver, full of grey-white colon cells. It didn't burst open, but it might have been better if it had; I couldn't literally see where the contents was squirted, but I could imagine the route very clearly: back as far as the Y-junction of the vein, where the blood flow would carry cancerous cells into the previously unaffected right lobe.

I swore for ten seconds, enraged by my own helplessness. I had none of the emergency tools I was used to: there was no drug I could inject to kill off the spilt cells while they were still more vulnerable than an established tumour, no vaccine on hand to stimulate the immune system into attacking them.

Okwera said, "Tell the parents you found evidence of leakage, so she'll need to have regular follow-up examinations."

I glanced at Masika, but he was silent.

"I can't do that."

"You don't want to cause trouble."

"It was an accident!"

"Don't tell her, and don't tell her family." Okwera regarded me sternly, as if I was contemplating something both dangerous and self-indulgent. "It won't help anyone if you dive into the shit for this. Not her, not you. Not the hospital. Not the volunteer programme."

The girl's mother spoke English. I told her there were signs that the cancer might have spread. She wept, and thanked me for my good work.

Masika didn't say a word about the incident, but by the end of the day I could hardly bear to look at him. When Okwera departed, leaving the two of us alone in the locker room, I said, "In three or four years there'll be a vaccine. Or even HealthGuard software. It won't be like this forever."

He shrugged, embarrassed. "Sure."

"I'll raise funds for the research when I get home. Champagne dinners with slides of photogenic patients, if that's what it takes." I knew I was making a fool of myself, but I couldn't shut up. "This isn't the nineteenth century. We're not helpless any more. Anything can be cured, once you understand it."

Masika eyed me dubiously, as if he was trying to decide whether or not to tell me to save my platitudes for the champagne dinners. Then he said, "We do understand Yeyuka. We have HealthGuard software written for it, ready and waiting to go. But we can't run it on the machine here. So we don't need funds for research. What we need is another machine."

I was speechless for several seconds, trying to make sense of this extraordinary claim. "The hospital's machine is broken – ?"

Masika shook his head. "The software is unlicensed. If we used it on the hospital's machine, our agreement with HealthGuard would be void. We'd lose the use of the machine entirely."

I could hardly believe that the necessary research had been completed without a single publication, but I couldn't believe Masika would lie about it either. "How long can it take HealthGuard to approve the software? When was it submitted to them?"

Masika was beginning to look like he wished he'd kept his mouth shut, but there was no going back now. He admitted warily, "It hasn't been submitted to them. It can't be – that's the whole problem. We need a bootleg machine, a decommissioned model with the satellite link disabled, so we can run the Yeyuka software without their knowledge."

"Why? Why can't they find out about it?"

He hesitated. "I don't know if I can tell you that."

"Is it illegal? Stolen?" But if it was stolen, why hadn't the rightful owners licensed the damned thing, so people could use it?

Masika replied icily, "Stolen *back*. The only part you could call 'stolen' was stolen back." He looked away for a moment, actually struggling for control. Then he said, "Are you sure you want to know the whole story?"

"Yes."

"Then I'll have to make a phone call."

○

Masika took me to what looked like a boarding house, student accommodation in one of the suburbs close to the campus. He walked briskly, giving me no time to ask questions, or even orient myself in the darkness. I had a feeling he would have liked to have blindfolded me, but it would hardly have made a difference; by the time we arrived I couldn't have said where we were to the nearest kilometre.

A young woman, maybe nineteen or twenty, opened the door. Masika didn't introduce us, but I assumed she was the person he'd phoned from the hospital, since she was clearly expecting us. She led us to a ground-floor room; someone was playing music upstairs, but there was no one else in sight.

In the room, there was a desk with an old-style keyboard and computer monitor, and an extraordinary device standing on the floor beside it: a rack of electronics the size of a chest of drawers, full of exposed circuit boards, all cooled by a fan half a metre wide.

"What is that?"

The woman grinned. "We modestly call it the Makerere super-computer. Five hundred and twelve processors, working in parallel. Total cost, fifty thousand shillings."

That was about fifty dollars. "How – ?"

"Recycling. Twenty or thirty years ago, the computer industry ran an elaborate scam: software companies wrote deliberately inefficient programs, to make people buy newer, faster computers all the time – then they made sure that the faster computers needed brand-new software to work at all. People threw out perfectly good machines every three or four years, and though some ended up as landfill, millions were saved. There's been a world-wide market in discarded processors for years, and the slowest now cost about as much as buttons. But all it takes to get some real power out of them is a little ingenuity."

I stared at the wonderful contraption. "And you wrote the Yeyuka software on this?"

"Absolutely." She smiled proudly. "First, the software characterises any damaged surface adhesion molecules it finds – there are always a few floating freely in the bloodstream, and their exact shape depends on the strain of Yeyuka, and the particular cells that have been infected. Then drugs are tailor-made to lock on to those damaged adhesion molecules, and kill the infected cells by rupturing their membranes." As she spoke, she typed on the keyboard, summoning up animations to illustrate each stage of the process. "If we can get this onto a real machine . . . we'll be able to cure three people a day."

Cure. Not just cut them open to delay the inevitable.

"But where did all the raw data come from? The RNA sequencing, the X-ray diffraction studies . . . ?"

The woman's smile vanished. "An insider at HealthGuard found it in the company archives, and sent it to us over the net."

"I don't understand. When did HealthGuard do Yeyuka studies? Why haven't they published them? Why haven't they written software themselves?"

She glanced uncertainly at Masika. He said, "HealthGuard's parent company collected blood from five thousand people in Southern Uganda in 2013. Supposedly to follow up on the effectiveness of their HIV vaccine. What they actually wanted, though, was a large sample of metastasising cells so they could perfect the biggest selling point of the HealthGuard: cancer protection. Yeyuka offered them the cheapest, simplest way to get the data they needed."

I'd been half expecting something like this since Masika's comments back in the hospital, but I was still shaken. To collect the data dishonestly was bad enough, but to bury information that was halfway to a cure – just to save paying for what they'd taken – was unspeakable.

I said, "Sue the bastards! Get everyone who had samples taken together for a class action: royalties plus punitive damages. You'll raise hundreds of millions of dollars. Then you can buy as many machines as you want."

The woman laughed bitterly. "We have no proof. The files were sent anonymously, there's no way to authenticate their origin. And can you imagine how much HealthGuard would spend on their defence? We can't afford to waste the next twenty years in a legal battle, just for the satisfaction of shouting the truth from the rooftops. The only way we can be sure of making use of this software is to get a bootleg machine, and do everything in silence."

I stared at the screen, at the cure being played out in simulation that should have been happening three times a day in Mulago hospital. She was right, though. However hard it was to stomach, taking on HealthGuard directly would be futile.

Walking back across the campus with Masika, I kept thinking of the girl with the liver infestation, and the possibility of undoing the moment of clumsiness that would otherwise almost certainly kill her. I said, "Maybe I can get hold of a bootleg machine in Shanghai. If I knew where to ask, where to look." They'd certainly be expensive, but they'd have to be much cheaper than a commissioned model, running without the usual software and support.

My hand moved almost unconsciously to check the metal pulse on my index finger. I held the ring up in the starlight. "I'd give you this, if it was mine to give. But that's thirty years away." Masika didn't reply, too polite to suggest that if I'd owned the ring outright, I wouldn't even have raised the possibility.

We reached the University Hall; I could find my way back to the guest house now. But I couldn't leave it at that; I couldn't face another six weeks of surgery unless I knew that something was going to come of the night's revelations. I said, "Look, I don't have connections to any black market, I don't have a clue how to go about getting a machine. But if you can find out what I have to do, and it's within my power . . . I'll do it."

Masika smiled, and nodded thanks, but I could tell that he didn't believe me. I wondered how many other people had made promises like this, then vanished back into the world-without-disease while the Yeyuka wards kept overflowing.

As he turned to go, I put a hand on his shoulder to stop him. "I mean it. Whatever it takes, I'll do it."

He met my eyes in the dark, trying to judge something deeper than this easy protestation of sincerity. I felt a sudden flicker of shame; I'd completely forgotten that I was an impostor, that I'd never really meant to come here, that two months ago a few words from Lisa would have seen me throw away my ticket, gratefully.

Masika said quietly, "Then I'm sorry that I doubted you. And I'll take you at your word."

○

Mubende was a district capital, half a day's drive west of Kampala. Iganga delayed our promised trip to the Yeyuka clinic there until my last fortnight, and once I arrived I could understand why. It was everything I'd feared: starved of funds, under-staffed and over-crowded. Patients' relatives were required to provide and wash the bedclothes, and half of them also seemed to be bringing in painkillers and other drugs bought at the local markets – some genuine, some ripoffs full of nothing but glucose or magnesium sulphate.

Most of the patients had four or five separate tumours. I treated two people a day, with operations lasting six to eight hours. In ten days, seven people died in front of me; dozens more died in the wards, waiting for surgery.

Or waiting for something better.

I shared a crowded room at the back of the clinic with Masika and Okwera, but even on the rare occasions when I caught Masika alone, he seemed reluctant to discuss the details of getting hold of a bootleg HealthGuard. He said, "Right now, the less you know the better. When the time comes, I'll fill you in."

The ordeal of the patients was overwhelming, but I felt more for the clinic's sole doctor and two nurses; for them, it never ended. The morning we packed our equipment into the truck and headed back for Kampala, I felt like a deserter from some stupid, pointless war: guilty about the colleagues I was leaving behind, but almost euphoric with relief to be out of it myself. I knew I couldn't have stayed on here – or even in Kampala – month after month, year after year. However much I wished that I could have been that strong, I understood now that I wasn't.

O

There was a brief, loud stuttering sound, then the truck squealed to a halt. The four of us were all in the back, guarding the equipment against potholes, with the tarpaulin above us blocking everything but a narrow rear view. I glanced at the others; someone outside shouted in Luganda at Akena Ibingira, the driver, and he started shouting back.

Okwera said, "Bandits."

I felt my heart racing. "You're kidding?"

There was another burst of gunfire. I heard Ibingira jump out of the cab, still muttering angrily.

Everyone was looking at Okwera for advice. He said, "Just cooperate, give them what they want." I tried to read his face; he seemed grim but not desperate – he expected unpleasantness, but not a massacre. Iganga was sitting on the bench beside me; I reached for her hand almost without thinking. We were both trembling. She squeezed my fingers for a moment, then pulled free.

Two tall, smiling men in dirty brown camouflage appeared at the back of the truck, gesturing with automatic weapons for us to climb out. Okwera went first, but Masika, who'd been sitting beside him, hung back. Iganga was nearer to the exit than me, but I tried to get past her; I had some half-baked idea that this would somehow lessen her risk of being taken off and raped. When one of the bandits blocked my way and waved her forward, I thought this fear had been confirmed.

Masika grabbed my arm, and when I tried to break free, he tightened his grip and pulled me back into the truck. I turned on him angrily, but before I could say a word he whispered, "She'll be all right. Just tell me: do you want them to take the ring?"

"*What?*"

He glanced nervously towards the exit, but the bandits had moved Okwera and Iganga out of sight. "I've paid them to do this. It's the only way. But say the word now and I'll give them the signal, and they won't touch the ring."

I stared at him, waves of numbness sweeping over my skin as I realised exactly what he was saying.

"You could have taken it off under anaesthetic."

He shook his head impatiently. "It's sending data back to HealthGuard all the time: cortisol, adrenaline, endorphins, prostaglandins. They'll have a record of your stress levels, fear, pain . . . if we took it off under anaesthetic, they'd *know* you'd given it away freely. This way, it'll look like a random theft. And your insurance company will give you a new one."

His logic was impeccable; I had no reply. I might have started protesting about insurance fraud, but that was all in the future, a separate matter entirely. The choice, here and now, was whether or not I let him have the ring by the only method that wouldn't raise suspicion.

One of the bandits was back, looking impatient. Masika asked plainly, "Do I call it off? I need an answer." I turned to him, on the verge of ranting that he'd wilfully misunderstood me, abused my generous offer to help him, and put all our lives in danger.

It would have been so much bullshit, though. He hadn't misunderstood me. All he'd done was taken me at my word.

I said, "Don't call it off."

The bandits lined us up beside the truck, and had us empty our pockets into a sack. Then they started taking watches and jewellery. Okwera couldn't get his wedding ring off, but stood motionless and scowling while one of the bandits applied more force. I wondered if I'd need a prosthesis, if I'd still be able to do surgery, but as the bandit approached me I felt a strange rush of confidence.

I held out my hand and looked up into the sky. I knew that anything could be healed, once it was understood.

The Difficulties Involved in Photographing Nix Olympica

BRIAN W. ALDISS

It was unprecedented for anyone stationed on Mars to refuse home leave. Ozzy Brooks refused. He secretly wanted to photograph Olympus Mons.

For his whole two-year tour of duty, Sgt Brooks had saved money and hoarded material. Had made friends with the transport section. Had ingratiated himself with the officer in charge of rations. Had gone out of his way to be nice to practically everyone in Atmosphere Control. Had wooed the guys in the geological section. Had made himself indispensable in Engineering.

Almost everyone in Fort Arcadia knew and, within their lights, liked little Sgt Brooks.

Brooks was small, dark-skinned, lightly built, neat-boned – ideal fodder for Mars. He had nondescript sandy hair which grew like lichen over his skull, with eyes to match. He had what are often referred to as ageless looks, and the rather blank stare that goes with those looks.

Behind that blank and inoffensive gaze lay ambition. Brooks was an intellectual. Brooks never drank. He rarely watched the TV screenings from Earth. Instead, he could be seen reading old books. He went to bed early. He never complained or scratched his armpits. And he seemed to know everything. It was amazing that the other troops stationed in Fort Arcadia liked him nevertheless: but Brooks had another qualification.

Ozzy Brooks was Fort Arcadia's Martian *t'ai chi* master. He taught two classes of *mar t'ai chi*, as he himself called it: an elementary class from eight to ten in the morning and an advanced class from eight to eleven in the evening. Even men for whom *mar t'ai chi* was not compulsory joined Brooks's classes, for they agreed that Brooks was a brilliant teacher; all felt better when each session was finished. Brooks's teaching was an antidote to the monotony of Mars.

After dismissing one of his morning classes, Brooks slipped out of his costume, put on denims, and strolled across the dome to Engineering, to work on the larger format camera he was building.

"What do you need a camera for on Mars?" Sgt Al Shapiro asked.

"I want to photograph Martian women if any turn up," Brooks said.

Shapiro laughed, with contempt in the sound.

Brooks's secret in life was that he did not hate anything. He hated no man. He did not hate the Army, he did not hate Mars. All the rest of the men, his friends, spent long hours trying to decide whether they hated the Army or Mars most. Sometimes Mars won, sometimes the Army.

"It's the boredom. The monotony," they said. Referring to both or either.

Brooks was never bored. In consequence, he did not find life monotonous. He did not dislike Army discipline, since he had always strictly disciplined himself. Certainly he missed women; but he consoled himself by saying that instead he had this unique opportunity to know the Red Planet.

He loved Mars. Mars was the ideal place on which to do *t'ai chi*. Despite his ordinary name, Brooks was an exotic. While his grandmother, a refugee from Vietnam, had had the fortune to marry a seventh-generation American, his great-grandparents were Chinese from Szechwan Province. A *t'ai chi* tradition had been passed down in the family from generation to generation. Ozzy Brooks hugged this knowledge to himself: Mars, with its lighter gravity, was the perfect planet on which to develop his art.

Some wise Chinese ancestor, many generations ago, had invented the postures of the White Crane *with Mars in mind.*

Under Brooks's American-ness ran a strong delight in his oriental heritage. He believed that it was a Chinese who had discovered the perfect way to live on another planet, in harmony with its elements, using those elements to become more perfect in oneself. Mars – he had realised this almost as soon as he had disembarked from the military spaceship – was the most Chinese of planets, even down to the *sang-de-boeuf* tint of its soil, the colour of ancient Chinese gateways and porcelains.

In Brooks's mind, Mars became an extension of China, the China of long ago, crammed with warriors, maidens as fair as white willows, and tombs loaded high with carvings and treasure. Beyond the dome of Arcadia, he thought he saw Cathay.

It was some while before he realised he had a friend in Sgt Al Shapiro.

He was working in the engineering laboratories, inserting the shutter mechanism in the 8x10 camera now rapidly nearing completion, when Shapiro strolled up. Shapiro was small, light on his feet, and darker in complexion than Brooks. He smiled at Brooks through a hank of black hair which hung across his face.

"What are you going to use that camera for, Ozzy?" he asked, as before.

"I take pictures, of course, what else?"

"You're not going to be able to take it back to Earth in your kit. It's too heavy."

"What a nuisance," said Brooks, blandly.

Shapiro paused, then said, "You should photograph Mars with it."

The remark took Brooks aback. He had intended to do nothing else. To hear someone else state his intention was to feel himself somehow robbed, as if a precious stone had been stolen.

He looked open-mouthed at Shapiro.

Mistaking his surprise, Shapiro lowered his voice and said, "Most guys see nothing in Mars, nothing at all. Except the officers. Do you notice when we're out doing manoeuvres, Colonel

Wolfe always says, 'Mars is fine fighting country'? That's how a professional soldier sees it, I guess. What do the men say about it? 'The dustbowl' – that's what they call Mars, the squaddies. They can't see it except as a torn-off chunk of America's Badlands. They've got no imagination."

"How do you see Mars, Al?" Brooks asked, very calm and in control again.

Shapiro gave his flitting smile.

"How do I see it? Why, when I take a look out there, I see it as a fantastic piece of natural engineering. Uncluttered by trees and all the vegetation that hides Earth. Mars is honest, a great series of cantilevers and buttresses and platforms. God's naked handiwork. I'm the only guy I know who'd like to get out there among it all."

"Some of the men like to go out for the pigeon shoots," Brooks said.

There were Mars jeeps which toured nearby gulleys firing off clay pigeons in all directions. These shoots formed one of the few outdoor recreations available. But no one ever ventured more than a mile from the fort.

Shapiro shrugged. "Kid stuff . . . I'd just like to figure on doing something memorable with my time on Mars. I've only got a month before they ship me back to Chicago."

Brooks put out his hand.

"That's the way I think too. I wish to do something memorable."

And so they came to draw up plans to photograph Olympus Mons from the ground.

○

Al Shapiro was as resourceful as Ozzy Brooks in getting what he wanted. He actually enjoyed the Army, and knew how to exploit all the weaknesses of that organisation. They indented for a week's base leave, they set about bribing Captain Jeschke in Transport to secure the unauthorised loan of a Mars jeep, they bartered services in return for supplies.

"I should be a general – I could run Mars single-handed!" Shapiro said, laughing.

And all the while, he went ahead with his work in Engineering, and Brooks taught *mar t'ai chi*, instructing his squads how to love Mars as the ally of all their muscular exertions – thus, in his quiet way, subverting the Army's purpose, which was to make the men hate the planet and anything on it which moved and was not capitalist.

Occasionally, manoeuvres were undertaken in conjunction with the EEC dome in Eridania. The men had to fire missiles on the arctic ranges, or crawl around, cursing, in the red dust. Brooks saw then that his subversion had not had much effect. Everyone wanted to go back to Earth. They had no vision. He longed to give them one.

"Before we leave here, we must make a model of Nix Olympica, and study it from all angles, so that we decide the ideal position to which to drive." Brooks nodded sagely as he spoke and looked sideways at Shapiro.

"Cartography," said Shapiro. "Lou Wright owes me a favour. Let's try Cartography."

They obtained more than maps and photographs. As the most prominent physical feature on Mars, the extinct volcano had warranted a plastic model, constructed by a bygone officer in the Army Geological survey. Brooks inspected it with interest before rejecting it.

"It's too small. We can make a much better one between us," he said.

What he felt was that this Army model of Olympus was contaminated by its source; it had no poetry. Whoever had ordered it had probably been concerned with how the sides of the crater could be scaled, or how the caldera itself might provide a base for ground-to-space missiles.

Brooks moulded his model of the gigantic volcano in plastic, colouring it with acrylics. Shapiro occasionally came over to admire his work.

"You see, the formation is about the size of the state of

Missouri. It rises to all of fifteen miles high," Brooks said. "The best idea is to approach it from the east. The lighting will be best from the east."

"What's your lens?"

"I'm taking a selection. The point about an 8x10 camera is that it will give terrific definition – though it feeds on sheet film, and I'll need a tripod to keep it steady."

"I can make you a tripod."

They surveyed the model of Olympus critically when it was finished. Brooks shook his head.

"It's a good model," Shapiro said. "Photograph it here against a black background and we can save ourselves a trip."

Although Brooks rarely laughed, he laughed now. Laughed and said nothing.

He was serenely happy drawing up his own map, entering the sparse names of features in fine calligraphic style, precision-drawing contour lines. The most dangerous aspect of the trip was its distance. They were contemplating a drive of almost seven hundred and ninety miles, with no filling stations on the way, and then the journey back. They would be unlikely to see anyone the whole trip, except possibly a patrol moving between the Arcadia base and the hemisphere of the planet held by the enemy.

No possible danger could deter Brooks. His mind was filled with his delight in having found a friend and in the prospects ahead. Ever since Mariner 9 had executed its fly-over back in 1971, Olympus Mons, the largest volcano in the solar system, had frequently been photographed, by both satellites and rockets. But never from the ground. Never as *he* would photograph it, with all the skill of an Ansel Adams.

He could visualise the prints now. They would be majestic, expressing both the violence and the deadness of the Martian landscape; he would create a serenity out of the conflicting tensions. He would create such an image that it would remain definitive: through the elusive art of photography, he would create a monument not only to the sublimity of the universe, but also to the greatness and the insignificance of mankind in the scheme of things.

With such exalted thoughts in his mind, Brooks had no room for fear.

The two men left Arcadia early one morning. Clad in suits, they slipped through one of the personnel locks in the main dome and made their way over to the transport hangar. There a stretched Mars jeep was waiting, loaded with fuel and supplies. As it rolled into the dim dawn light, the half-tracked vehicle resembled a cumbrous beetle.

There was little room to move in the cab. When they slept, their hammocks would be strung overhead. The ironically named Fort Arcadia was situated close to 50° North, in the veined recesses of the Arcadia Planitia. It was summer in the northern hemisphere of Mars, and they had a straightforward drive southwards to the giant volcano, according to the maps.

They reckoned on travelling for fourteen hours a day, and averaging something close to twenty-seven miles per hour, the best they could hope for over trackless terrain. They nodded with pleasure as the shabby collection of prefabricated buildings disappeared behind them, and they were alone with Mars. Shapiro was driving.

A chill, shrunken sun had pierced through the mists of the eastern horizon, where layers of salmon pink dissolved into the sky. The shadow of their vehicles spread across a terrain which resembled Earth's Gobi Desert. Dust lay in sculptured terraces, punctuated here and there by rocks of pumice. In the far distance to the right, a series of flat-topped escarpments suggested a kind of order completely lacking nearer at hand; they made their way through a geological rubbish dump.

This formless landscape was familiar to them from their military exercises. They had crawled through it, dressed in camouflaging sand-robes. Nothing moved but dusts and rusts; the rest – unlike Earth's restless territories – had endured without change for billions of years. It had no more life to offer than the Geological Survey map of the route pinned to the dash.

There was no cratering here, as in the southern hemisphere, to lend interest. Their one concern was to steer south, avoiding rocks and dust drifts. After the first hour of travel, with Al Shapiro at the wheel, Brooks began to want to talk. Shapiro, however, had gone silent. As the sun climbed in the pinkish sky, he became more silent. He offered the information that his family came from the Cicero area of Chicago, and then gave up entirely. Brooks, tired of trying to make conversation, resorted to whistling.

The sun arced overhead. The two sergeants took the wheel by turns, driving till the sun sloped to the west, to sink behind a low dust cloud. They had covered three hundred and seventy miles, and were pleased with their good progress. With nightfall, Shapiro found his voice again and was more cheerful; they ate a companionable supper from their rations before climbing into their hammocks and sleeping.

Once in the night, Brooks woke and peered out of the window. The stars and the Milky Way were there in glory, remote yet curiously intimate, as if they shone only for him, like a hope at the back of his mind. He was caught between the tensions of awe and enjoyment, like a troglodyte before its god, unable to tear his gaze away from the glitter until an hour had passed. He climbed back into his hammock, smiling into the fuggy darkness, and slept.

O

Next dawn revealed no sign of the dust storm glimpsed at sunset – to Brooks's secret relief. Joy came to him. He sang. Shapiro looked doleful.

"Are you okay?" Brooks asked.

"I'm fine, sure."

"Anything worrying you? You wanted to get out among it all, and here we are."

"I'm fine."

"The Tharsis Bulge should be in view in an hour or two. Tomorrow we'll be within sight of Nix Olympica."

"Its name's Olympus," Shapiro said, sourly.

"I like to call it by the old name, Al. Nix Olympica . . . That was the name bestowed on it before anyone had ever set foot on the planet, or even left Earth. Nix Olympica is the old name, the name of mystery, of remoteness. I like it best. I'm going to photograph Nix Olympica and give a new image to Earth, before they come and build a missile site in the crater. Let's hope the atmosphere stays clear of dust."

Shapiro shrugged and brushed his hair from his eyes. He said nothing.

They were rolling by six-thirty. By eight, the terrain was changing. Petrified lavas created a series of steps over the ancient sand-rocks. Their gravimeter began to show fluctuations in the gravity field.

Brooks pointed ahead.

"There's the Tharsis Bulge," he said. "From here it stretches to south of the equator."

"I can see it," Shapiro said, without responding to Brooks's excitement.

They began to steer south-east until the low wizened lips of Alba Patera lay distinctly to their left. The view ahead became increasingly formidable.

The Tharsis Bulge distorted half a hemisphere. Earth held no feature as majestic. At its north-western bastion stood the grim sentinel shape of Olympus, its cone rising sheer fifteen and a half miles above the surrounding plain. As yet, they were too distant to see more than a pimpled shoulder of the Bulge rising above the ancient lands like a great bruise. Black clouds of dust rolled above the bruise. From the clouds, lightning showered, flickered like burning magnesium wire, died, flickered elsewhere. High above both Bulge and dust clouds, wispy white clouds formed a halo in the dark sky.

They climbed. The engine throbbed. The hours passed, the landscape took on power. It was as though the ancient rock breathed upwards. Despite the jeep, Brooks could feel the strength of the great igneous upthrust through the soles of his feet – the 'Bubbling Well', as *t'ai chi* had it.

He breathed air deep into his *hora* centre. But Shapiro sank back in his seat.

"You are suffering agoraphobia, Al," Brooks said. "Don't worry. Now we have something marvellous to distract your mind."

Brooks's intention was to drive some way up into the Bulge until Nix Olympica lay to the west; from there, he estimated he could photograph the formation at its most dramatic, with falling ground behind it.

The terrain which had been merely rutted now became much more difficult to drive. Long parallel fractures, remarkably uniform in spacing and orientation, ran downhill in their path. There was no way of avoiding the fracturing; as the map indicated, the faults extended for at least a hundred miles on either side of their course. Each fracture had straight, almost vertical, cliffs and reasonably flat bottoms. They found a point where a landslide had destroyed a cliff. By working their tracks on alternate sides, they contrived to slip down a small landslide to the bottom of the fracture, after which it was simple to drive along it. It was the width of an eight-lane highway.

Cliffs boxed them in on either side. The sky above was leaden, relieved by a strip of white cloud low ahead. It was just a matter of proceeding straight. No canyon on Earth was ever like this one.

Brooks pointed into the shadowed side of the fracture at the foot of the cliff. A trace of white lay across small boulders.

"It's a mixture of frost and snow, by the look of it," he said.

The sight delighted him. At least there was one natural process still functioning on the dead surface of the planet.

"How're we going to get out of this fault?" Shapiro asked.

"We're in a crack at least two and a half billion years old," Brooks said, more or less to himself. Even Cathay was not that old.

"And the satellites can't pick us up while we're down here," Shapiro said.

But Brooks would have nothing of misgivings. They would emerge somehow. He had never enjoyed himself so much.

"Just imagine it – once a great torrent rushed along here, Al. We're on an old river bed."

"No, this wasn't formed by water," Shapiro said expertly. "It's the result of stresses in the Martian lithosphere. You'll be looking out for fish-bones next."

Although Brooks was silenced by this rejoinder, he spent the next hour alert for signs of departed life. What a triumph to see a fossil in the fracture walls! Once he cried out and stopped the jeep, to peer more closely at the cliff; there was nothing to be seen but a pattern of splintering in the rock.

"Nothing living has ever lived here – not ever," Shapiro said, and began to shiver.

It was impossible to say anything sympathetic, but Brooks understood how Shapiro felt. These unknown spaces chilled Shapiro as much as they excited Brooks; it was what came of being born in a crowded Chicago slum. Besides, he understood intellectually how absurd it was to be experiencing such intense pleasure in such a forbidding place. The mountains of Western Szechwan Province, from which his Chinese ancestors had come, might be almost as unwelcoming as this.

It turned out that Brooks's light-heartedness was not misplaced. The fracture cut into another at an oblique angle. Vast ramps, as smooth as if designed by mortal architect, led up to the general level of the Bulge. The jeep climbed with ease, and they emerged onto the rainless elevations of the Tharsis Bulge. They were 1.3 miles above the datum, Mars's equivalent of sea level. The read-out also showed a free-air gravity anomaly of 229 mgals. The wall of yellowish black dust had disappeared. Visibility was good in the thin atmosphere. The sun shone as if encased in lucite. There was a glazed aspect, too, to the great smooth features of the inclined plain about them, where strange bumps and undulations suggested bones under the basaltic skin.

"Wonderful!" Brooks said. He began to tease himself. "All we need now is for a devil to emerge and dance before us. A devil with a red and white face."

"For god's sake . . ." Shapiro protested. "Take your photographs and let's get home."

But Brooks wanted to climb out and dance. He was sick of

being cooped in the cab of the vehicle, sick of the perpetual noise of the engine and air-purifier. It would be a time for the *t'ai chi* solo dance, even with the space suit on. He would celebrate Mars as no one else had done.

He controlled himself. A few more hours' driving and they would see Nix Olympica itself. The sun was already descending. They had to make as much distance as they could before dark.

With nightfall, an electrical storm swept down from the heights. They stopped the jeep beside a corroded boulder. Flicking light surrounded them. Shapiro spent an hour checking through all the equipment, climbing restlessly about, and muttering to himself.

"One failure and we're dead," he said, catching Brooks's eye. "No one could get to us in time if anything went wrong. We embarked on this caper far too thoughtlessly. We should have planned it like a military operation."

"We shall see Nix Olympica tomorrow. Don't worry. Besides, imagine – wouldn't this spot really make a dramatic tomb?"

○

Shapiro was apologetic next morning. He did not realise that the desolate spaces of Mars would have such a bad effect on him. He knew he was acting foolishly. It was his determination to take a grip on himself. He was looking forward to seeing Olympus, and would be fine, he felt sure, on the way home. There was just – well, the realisation that their lives balanced on a knife-edge.

Clapping him affectionately on the shoulder, Brooks said, "Life is always lived on a knife-edge. Don't worry."

By ten that morning, when the sun was shining through its blue glaze, they caught sight of a dark crust beyond the curve of the horizon. It was the volcano.

Both men cheered.

The volcano grew throughout the day, arising from behind the humps of the Bulge. Hour by hour, they gained a clearer impression of its size. It was a vast tomb of igneous rock which would have dominated any continent on Earth. It would have stretched from Shapiro's Chicago to Buffalo, obliterating Lake Erie. It would have stretched from Switzerland to London, obliterating Paris and most of Belgium. It would have stretched from Lhasa in Tibet to Calcutta, obliterating Mount Everest like a molehill on its way.

Above its shoulders, where the sky was indigo, little demons of lightning danced, corkscrewing their way down into its scarred crust.

It could not be imagined or described. Only photographed.

Brooks brought his films from the refrigerator. He had three SLR cameras beside his home-made 'tank'. He went to work with cameras, lenses and filters when they were still over four hundred miles from the giant caldera of Olympus. In the thin air, it appeared deceptively close.

Talking excitedly as he worked, Brooks tried to explain what he felt to Shapiro, who drove with his gaze on the ridged ground ahead.

"Back in the eighteenth century, painters discriminated between the beautiful, the picturesque, and the sublime. You'd need to dream up another category for most of Mars, particularly the dull bits round Arcadia. You wouldn't find much that would square with definitions of 'beautiful' or 'picturesque', but here we have the sublime and then some . . . This monster has all the elements of awfulness and grandeur which the sublime requires. I wonder what the great painters would have made of Nix Olympica . . ."

The sun climbed to zenith, and then began to slope away down the western sky.

"Turn direct south, Al. Speed it up, if you can. I want to catch the sunset behind Nix. It should be wonderful."

Shapiro managed a laugh. "I'm doing my best, Ozzy. Don't want to shake the buggy to pieces."

Brooks began loading low-grain fast film into his cameras.

They were travelling over ground composed of flow after flow of lava, one wave upon another, slags, powders and ejecta cast upon the previous outpourings in grotesque patterns, as if the almost indestructible material had been bent on destroying itself, to the depth of hundreds of fathoms.

Whatever ferment had taken place over eons of time, those eons were themselves now eons past; since then, only silence covered the forbidding highlands – silence without motion, without so much as a wisp of steam from a solitary fumarole.

"Stop here!" Brooks exclaimed suddenly. "Where's that tripod? Oh, god . . . I must get on top of the jeep and film from there."

Grunting, Shapiro did as he was told. Brooks screwed his helmet on, draped his cameras and telescopic lenses over one shoulder, and climbed to the ground. He stood for a while, staring at the ground sloping towards the distant formation, and the sky, in which thin cloud curled like feather some five miles overhead. He took several shots at various shutter speeds almost without thought.

Looking back on his modest life, without distinction of any kind, he could hardly believe his luck. Night was descending on Mars, and he was here to photograph it. Even if Earth soon blew itself up, still he was here, and could record the moment.

His luck was crowned as he started to photograph from the top of the vehicle, using the 8x10 tank, steadying it with the tripod.

Phobos, the innermost moon, appeared to rise from the west – its orbital period being less than Mars's rotation period.

It glittered above the barricades of Nix Olympica. An ice cloud tailed like a pennant above the great volcano. The setting sun emerged from under a band of mist, spilling its light like broken egg along the horizon. The volcano was black in silhouette against the sky. The tank's shutter clicked, as moment by moment the light enriched itself.

Totally engrossed, Brooks slotted a polarising filter over the lens. Click. Wonderful.

The universe closed down like an oyster on the strip of brightness. The sun seemed to flare and was gone, leaving Nix Olympica to prop up its sky. Brooks opened up his aperture and kept shooting. He knew he would never witness anything like this again. Tomorrow night, they would be on their way home, racing the sinking gauge on the oxygen cylinders. Then it would be up to him to try and recreate this moment in his darkroom, where the hard work would be done.

Next morning, both sergeants were stirring before dawn.

"I've got to capture the first ray of light to touch those crater walls," Brooks said. "Let's try to get fifty miles nearer."

"How about something to eat first, Ozzy?"

"We can eat for the rest of our lives. You drive, okay?"

Shapiro drove while Brooks fussed over his equipment. He threw the vehicle recklessly forward, caught by Brooks's excitement.

He laughed.

"This'll be something to tell people about."

"No mistake there," Brooks said. "Maybe I'll publish an album of the best shots. Hey, Al, maybe we should climb the crater while we're here!"

"Forget it. Fifteen miles up in a space suit, with no climbing gear! I'm not mad even if you are."

They were racing across the bulbous incline. A worn stump of rock loomed ahead.

"Stop and I'll climb that," Brooks said.

When they got to it, the rock proved to be a small cone, a hundred yards across and several feet high. Unmoved by Shapiro's protests, Brooks unclamped the portable ladder from the jeep and climbed to the top. The crater was plugged with ancient magma and covered with dust. He got the tripod and the cameras in place just as the sun rose from behind a shoulder of Tharsis.

Click. This time, the fortress of Olympus was bright against a dark sky. For a moment, the outline of Tharsis was printed in shadow on its eastern flank. Click. Then like an iceberg of untold mass, it was floating on a sea of shadow. Click. The shadow withdrew across the plain towards the men. Mists rose. Click. For no more than five minutes, the great mesa was softened by evaporating carbon dioxide fumes. Click.

"Wonderful, wonderful!" said Brooks. He found that Shapiro had followed him up the ladder. Rapture was on both their faces.

They hugged each other and laughed. They took shots of each other standing by the volcanic cone.

They forgot to eat and, throughout the morning, drove as fast as they could towards the volcano. It was a magnet, bathed in light.

At midday, they stopped to drink ham and green pea soup.

They were still over one hundred and fifty miles from Olympus. It spread grandly before them: its great shield, its summit caldera – not a vent as in Earth's familiar stratovolcanoes but a relapse of the summit region – its flanking escarpments, its pattern of frozen lava runs, which from this distance resembled tresses of hair. From above, as Brooks knew, Nix Olympica resembled the nipple of a Martian Juno.

They gazed out at this brilliant formation as they slurped down their soup. It occupied one hundred and twelve degrees of their vision, although it was still so distant.

Shapiro turned from the sight and checked their instruments.

"We're doing okay, but getting near the safety margin on both fuel and oxygen. Are you almost ready to turn homewards, Ozzy?"

Brooks hesitated, then spoke in a nonchalant manner. "I'm almost ready. There's just one thing left to do. We've got some fine photographs in the bag, and by the time I bring the negatives up, there just could be a masterpiece or two among them. The only problem is the question of scale. Since there's no means of comparison in any of the pictures, you can't get an idea of the magnitude of Nix."

They looked at each other. Shapiro said. "You want me to leave you here and then drive the jeep nearer, so that you can have it in the foreground?"

"I don't want the truck in. Besides, I need to be mobile myself. I want you in it, Al – the human figure. I want to put you forward in the landscape. Then I move around taking shots."

Shapiro became rigid.

"I won't do that, Ozzy."

"Why not?"

"I won't do it."

"Tell me why."

"Because I just won't."

"Look, Al, we'll never be out of sight of each other. We'll be in radio contact. You'll be able to see the jeep all the while. All you have to do is stand where I put you. It'll take an hour, no more."

"No, I said. I'm not standing out in that landscape alone. That's flat, okay?"

They glowered at each other.

"You go out there. I'll take the damned pictures."

"I'm not afraid to go out there. Come on, Al, we've come all this way. There's nothing to be scared of, for Christ's sake. One hour, that's all I ask."

Shapiro dropped his gaze, clenching his fists together.

"You can't make me do it."

"I'm not making you. What's so difficult? You just do it."

"Suppose something happens?"

"Nothing has happened here for century after century. Not a thing."

Shapiro expelled a sigh. His face showed the tension inside him. His skin gleamed in the flat light.

"Okay. I'll do it, I guess."

"Okay." Brooks hesitated then said, "I appreciate it, Al. The medics haven't yet got round to naming a fear of wide open alien spaces, but they will. I know it must take some fighting."

"I'll conquer it. Just don't talk about it," said Al, his teeth chattering, as Brooks helped him secure the helmet of his suit.

"Sometimes there's need for talk. Remember, the same demons and spirits haunt the wide open spaces of Mars as those of Earth. No difference really, since all apparitions are in the mind. If we import demons, then we can conquer them, because they must obey our laws."

"I'll try and bear that in mind," said Shapiro, forcing his teeth to stop chattering. "Now let me out before I think better of it."

○

All the while Brooks drove back and forth about that portion of the Bulge, taking his historic shots of Nix Olympica, he was aware of what the distant white figure was undergoing as it stood alone in the grotesque landscape. He proceeded without haste, but he worked as fast as possible, concentrating now on his wide-angle lenses.

The end result of the men's endeavour was the series of photographs which became historic records of mankind's expansion through the solar system. They rank as works of art. As for Brooks, despite a period of fame, he eventually died in penury. General Shapiro ended up as Officer Commanding, Mars Base; his memoirs, in four volumes, contain an account of his first reconnaissance of Olympus – which differs considerably from the facts as set down here.

Seven American Nights

GENE WOLFE

ESTEEMED AND LEARNED MADAME:

As I last wrote you, it appears to me likely that your son Nadan
(may Allah preserve him!) has left the old capital and travelled –
of his own will or another's – north into the region about the Bay
of Delaware. My conjecture is now confirmed by the discovery in
those regions of the notebook I enclose. It is not of American
manufacture, as you see; and though it holds only the records of
a single week, several suggestive items therein provide us new
reason to hope.

I have photocopied the contents to guide me in my investiga-
tions; but I am alert to the probability that you, Madame, with
your superior knowledge of the young man we seek, may discover implications I have overlooked. Should that be the case, I
urge you to write me at once.

Though I hesitate to mention it in connection with so encour-
aging a finding, your most recently due remission has not yet
arrived. I assume that this tardiness results from the procrastina-
tion of the mails, which is here truly abominable. I must warn
you, however, that I shall be forced to discontinue the search
unless funds sufficient for my expenses are forthcoming before
the advent of winter.

With inexpressible respect,
HASSAN KERBELAI

Here I am at last! After twelve mortal days aboard the *Princess Fatimah* – twelve days of cold and ennui – twelve days of bad food and throbbing engines – the joy of being on land again is like the delight a condemned man must feel when a letter from the shah snatches him from beneath the very blade of death. America! America! Dull days are no more! They say that everyone who comes here either loves or hates you, America – by Allah I love you now!

Having begun this record at last, I find I do not know where to begin. I had been reading travel diaries before I left home; and so when I saw you, O Book, lying so square and thick in your stall in the bazaar – why should I not have adventures too, and write a book like Osman Aga's? Few come to this sad country at the world's edge after all, and most who do land farther up the coast.

And that gives me the clue I was looking for – how to begin. America began for me as coloured water. When I went out on deck yesterday morning, the ocean had changed from green to yellow. I had never heard of such a thing before, neither in my reading, nor in my talks with Uncle Mirza, who was here thirty years ago. I am afraid I behaved like the greatest fool imaginable, running about the ship babbling, and looking over the side every few minutes to make certain the rich mustard colour was still there and would not vanish the way things do in dreams when we try to point them out to someone else. The steward told me he knew. Golam Gassem the grain merchant (whom I had tried to avoid meeting for the entire trip until that moment) said, "Yes, yes," and turned away in a fashion that showed he had been avoiding me too, and that it was going to take more of a miracle than yellow water to change his feelings.

One of the few native Americans in first class came out just then: Mister – as the style is here – Tallman, husband of the lovely Madam Tallman, who really deserves such a tall man as myself. (Whether her husband chose that name in self-derision, or in the hope that it would erase others' memory of his infirmity; or whether it was his father's, and is merely one of the countless ironies of fate, I do not know. There was something wrong with his back.) As if I had not made enough spectacle of myself already, I took this Mr Tallman by the sleeve and told him to look over the side, explaining that the sea had turned yellow. I am afraid Mr Tallman turned white himself instead, and turned something else too – his back – looking as though he would have struck me if he dared. It was comic enough, I suppose – I heard some of the other passengers chuckling about it afterward – but I don't believe I have seen such hatred in a human face before. Just then the captain came strolling up, and I – considerably deflated but not flattened yet, and thinking that he had not over-heard Mr Tallman and me – mentioned for the final time that day that the water had turned yellow. "I know," the captain said. "It's his country" (here he jerked his head in the direction of the piti-ful Mr Tallman), "bleeding to death."

○

Here it is evening again, and I see that I stopped writing last night before I had so much as described my first sight of the coast. Well, so be it. At home it is midnight, or nearly, and the life of the cafés is at its height. How I wish that I were there now, with you, Yasmin, not webbed among these red- and purple-clad strangers, who mob their own streets like an invading army, and duck into their houses like rats into their holes. But you, Yasmin, or Mother, or whoever may read this, will want to know of my day – only you are sometimes to think of me as I am now, bent over an old, scarred table in a decayed room with two beds, listening to the hastening feet in the streets outside.

I slept late this morning; I suppose I was more tired from the voyage than I realised. By the time I woke, the whole of the city was alive around me, with vendors crying fish and fruits under my shuttered window, and the great wooden wains the Americans call *trucks* rumbling over the broken concrete on their wide iron wheels, bringing up goods from the ships in the Potomac anchorage. One sees very odd teams here, Yasmin. When I went to get my breakfast (one must go outside to reach the lobby and dining room in these American hotels, which I would think would be very inconvenient in bad weather) I saw one of these *trucks* with two oxen, a horse and a mule in the traces, which would have made you laugh. The drivers crack their whips all the time.

The first impression one gets of America is that it is not as poor as one has been told. It is only later that it becomes apparent how much has been handed down from the previous century. The streets here are paved, but they are old and broken. There are fine, though decayed, buildings everywhere (this hotel is one – the Inn of Holidays, it is called), more modern in appearance than the ones we see at home, where for so long traditional architecture was enforced by law. We are on Maine Street, and when I had finished my breakfast (it was very good, and very cheap by our standards, though I am told it is impossible to get anything out of season here) I asked the manager where I should go to see the sights of the city. He is a short and phenomenally ugly man, something of a hunchback as so many of them are. "There are no tours," he said. "Not any more."

I told him that I simply wanted to wander about by myself, and perhaps sketch a bit.

"You can do that. North for the buildings, south for the theatre, west for the park. Do you plan to go to the park, Mr Jaffarzadeh?"

"I haven't decided yet."

"You should hire at least two securities if you go to the park – I can recommend an agency."

"I have my pistol."

"You'll need more than that, sir."

Naturally, I decided then and there that I would go to the park, and alone. But I have determined not to spend this, the sole, small coin of adventure this land has provided me so far, before I discover what else it may offer to enrich my existence.

Accordingly, I set off for the north when I left the hotel. I have not, thus far, seen this city, or any American city, by night. What they might be like if these people thronged the streets then, as we do, I cannot imagine. Even by clearest day, there is the impression of carnival, of some mad circus whose performance began a hundred or more years ago and has not ended yet.

At first it seemed that only every fourth or fifth person suffered some trace of the genetic damage that destroyed the old America, but as I grew more accustomed to the streets, and thus less quick to dismiss as Americans and no more the unhappy old woman who wanted me to buy flowers and the boy who dashed shrieking between the wheels of a *truck*, and began instead to look at them as human beings – in other words, just as I would look at some chance-met person on one of our own streets – I saw that there was hardly a soul not marked in some way. These deformities, though they are individually hideous, in combination with the bright, ragged clothing so common here, give the meanest assemblage the character of a pageant. I sauntered along, hardly out of earshot of one group of street musicians before encountering another, and in a few strides passed a man so tall that he was taller seated on a low step than I standing; a bearded dwarf with a withered arm; and a woman whose face had been divided by some devil into halves, one large-eyed and idiotically despairing, the other squinting and sneering.

○

There can be no question about it – Yasmin must not read this. I have been sitting here for an hour at least, staring at the flame of the candle. Sitting and listening to something that from time to time beats against the steel shutters that close the window of this room. The truth is that I am paralysed by a fear that entered me – I do not know from whence – yesterday, and has been growing ever since.

Everyone knows that these Americans were once the most skilled creators of consciousness-altering substances the world has ever seen. The same knowledge that permitted them to forge the chemicals that destroyed them, so that they might have bread that never staled, innumerable poisons for vermin, and a host of unnatural materials for every purpose, also contrived synthetic alkaloids that produced endless feverish imaginings.

Surely some, at least, of these skills remain. Or if they do not, then some of the substances themselves, preserved for eighty or a hundred years in hidden cabinets, and no doubt growing more dangerous as the world forgets them. I think that someone on the ship may have administered some such drug to me.

○

That is out at last! I felt so much better at having written it – it took a great deal of effort – that I took several turns about this room. Now that I have written it down, I do not believe it at all.

Still, last night I dreamed of that bread, of which I first read in the little schoolroom of Uncle Mirza's country house. It was no complex, towering 'literary' dream such as I have sometimes had, and embroidered, and boasted of afterward over coffee. Just the vision of a loaf of soft white bread lying on a plate in the centre of a small table: bread that retained the fragrance of the oven (surely one of the most delicious in the world) though it was smeared with grey mould. Why would the Americans wish such a thing? Yet all the historians agree that they did, just as they wished their own corpses to appear living forever.

It is only this country, with its colourful, fetid streets, deformed people, and harsh, alien language, that makes me feel as drugged and dreaming as I do. Praise Allah that I can speak Farsi to you, O Book. Will you believe that I have taken out every article of clothing I have, just to read the makers' labels? Will *I* believe it, for that matter, when I read this at home?

○

The public buildings to the north – once the great centre, as I understand it, of political activity – offer a severe contrast to the streets of the still-occupied areas. In the latter, the old buildings are in the last stages of decay, or have been repaired by makeshift and inappropriate means; but they seethe with the life of those who depend upon such commercial activity as the port yet provides, and with those who depend on them, and so on. The monumental buildings, because they were constructed of the most imperishable materials, appear almost whole, though there are a few fallen columns and sagging porticos, and in several places small trees (mostly the sad *carpinus caroliniana*, I believe) have rooted in the crevices of walls. Still, if it is true, as has been written, that Time's beard is grey not with the passage of years but with the dust of ruined cities, it is here that he trails it. These imposing shells are no more than that. They were built, it would seem, to be cooled and ventilated by machinery. Many are windowless, their interiors now no more than sunless caves, reeking of decay; into these I did not venture. Others had had fixed windows that once were mere walls of glass; and a few of these remained, so that I was able to sketch their construction. Most, however, are destroyed. Time's beard has swept away their very shards.

Though these old buildings (with one or two exceptions) are deserted, I encountered several beggars. They seemed to be Americans whose deformities preclude their doing useful work, and one cannot help but feel sorry for them, though their appearance is often as distasteful as their importunities. They offered to show me the former residence of their Padshah, and as an excuse to give them a few coins I accompanied them, making them first pledge to leave me when I had seen it.

The structure they pointed out to me was situated at the end of a long avenue lined with impressive buildings; so I suppose they must have been correct in thinking it once important. Hardly more than the foundation, some rubble and one ruined wing remain now, and it cannot have been originally of an enduring construction. No doubt it was actually a summer palace or something of that kind. The beggars have now forgotten its very name, and call it merely 'the white house'.

When they had guided me to this relic, I pretended that I wanted to make drawings, and they left as they had promised. In five or ten minutes, however, one particularly enterprising fellow returned. He had no lower jaw, so that I had quite a bit of difficulty in understanding him at first; but after we had shouted back and forth a good deal – I telling him to depart and threatening to kill him on the spot, and he protesting – I realised that he was forced to make the sound of *d* for *b*, *n* for *m*, and *t* for *p*; and after that we got along better.

I will not attempt to render his speech phonetically, but he said that since I had been so generous, he wished to show me a great secret – something foreigners like myself did not even realise existed.

"Clean water," I suggested.

"No, no. A great, great secret, Captain. You think all this is dead." He waved a misshapen hand at the desolated structures that surrounded us.

"Indeed I do."

"One still lives. You would like to see it? I will guide. Don't worry about the others – they're afraid of me. I will drive them away."

"If you are leading me into some kind of ambush, I warn you, you will be the first to suffer."

He looked at me very seriously for a moment, and a man seemed to stare from the eyes in that ruined face, so that I felt a twinge of real sympathy. "See there? The big building to the south, on Pennsylvania? Captain, my father's father's father was chief of a department" ("detartnent") "there. I would not betray you."

From what I have read of this country's policies in the days of his father's father's father, that was little enough reassurance, but I followed him.

We went diagonally across several blocks, passing through two ruined buildings. There were human bones in both, and remembering his boast, I asked him if they had belonged to the workers there.

"No, no." He tapped his chest again – a habitual gesture, I suppose – and scooping up a skull from the floor held it beside his own head so that I could see that it exhibited cranial deformities much like his own. "We sleep here, to be shut behind strong walls from the things that come at night. We die here, mostly in winter-time. No one buries us."

"You should bury each other," I said.

He tossed down the skull, which shattered on the terrazzo floor, waking a thousand dismal echoes. "No shovel, and few are strong. But come with me."

At first sight the building to which he led me looked more decayed than many of the ruins. One of its spires had fallen, and the bricks lay in the street. Yet when I looked again, I saw that there must be something in what he said. The broken windows had been closed with ironwork at least as well made as the shutters that protect my room here; and the door, though old and weathered, was tightly shut, and looked strong.

"This is the Museum," my guide told me. "The only part left, almost, of the Silent City that still lives in the old way. Would you like to see inside?"

I told him that I doubted that we would be able to enter.

"Wonderful machines." He pulled at my sleeve. "You *see* in, Captain. Come."

We followed the building's walls around several corners, and at last entered a sort of alcove at the rear. Here there was a grill set in the weed-grown ground, and the beggar gestured toward it proudly. I made him stand some distance off, then knelt as he had indicated to look through the grill.

There was a window of unshattered glass beyond the grill. It was very soiled now, but I could see through into the basement of the building, and there, just as the beggar had said, stood an orderly array of complex mechanisms.

I stared for some time, trying to gain some notion of their purpose; and at length an old American appeared among them, peering at one and then another, and whisking the shining bars and gears with a rag.

The beggar had crept closer as I watched. He pointed at the old man, and said, "Still come from north and south to study here. Some day we are great again." Then I thought of my own lovely country, whose eclipse – though without genetic damage – lasted twenty-three hundred years. And I gave him money, and told him that, yes, I was certain America would be great again some day, and left him, and returned here.

I have opened the shutters so that I can look across the city to
the obelisk and catch the light of the dying sun. Its fields and valleys of fire do not seem more alien to me, or more threatening,
than this strange, despondent land. Yet I know that we are all one
– the beggar, the old man moving among the machines of a dead
age, those machines themselves, the sun, and I. A century ago,
when this was a thriving city, the philosophers used to speculate
on the reason that each neutron and proton and electron exhibited
the same mass as all the others of its kind. Now we know that
there is only one particle of each variety, moving backward and
forward in time, an electron when it travels as we do, a positron
when its temporal displacement is retrograde, the same few particles appearing billions of billions of times to make up a single
object, and the same few particles forming all the objects, so that
we are all the sketches, as it were, of the same set of pastels.

○

I have gone out to eat. There is a good restaurant not far from the
hotel, better even than the dining room here. When I came back
the manager told me that there is to be a play tonight at the theatre, and assured me that because it is so close to his hotel (in
truth, he is very proud of this theatre, and no doubt its proximity
to his hotel is the only circumstance that permits the hotel to
remain open) I will be in no danger if I go without an escort. To
tell the truth, I am a little ashamed that I did not hire a boat today
to take me across the channel to the park; so now I will attend the
play, and dare the night streets.

Here I am again, returned to this too-large, too-bare, uncar-
peted room, which is already beginning to seem a second home,
with no adventures to retail from the dangerous benighted streets.
The truth is that the theatre is hardly more than a hundred paces
to the south. I kept my hand on the butt of my pistol and walked
along with a great many other people (mostly Americans) who
were also going to the theatre, and felt something of a fool.

The building is as old as those in the Silent City, I should think;

but it has been kept in some repair. There was more of a feeling of gaiety (though to me it was largely an alien gaiety) among the audience than we have at home, and less of the atmosphere of what I may call the sacredness of Art. By that I knew that the drama really is sacred here, as the colourful clothes of the populace make clear in any case. An exaggerated and solemn respect always indicates a loss of faith.

Having recently come from my dinner, I ignored the stands in the lobby at which the Americans – who seem to eat constantly when they can afford it – were selecting various cold meats and pastries, and took my place in the theatre proper. I was hardly in my seat before a pipe-puffing old gentleman, an American, desired me to move in order that he might reach his own. I stood up gladly, of course and greeted him as 'Grandfather', as our own politeness (if not theirs) demands. But while he was settling himself and I was still standing beside him, I caught a glimpse of his face from the exact angle at which I had seen it this afternoon, and recognised him as the old man I had watched through the grill.

Here was a difficult situation. I wanted very much to draw him into conversation, but I could not well confess that I had been spying on him. I puzzled over the question until the lights were extinguished and the play began.

It was Vidal's *Visit to a Small Planet*, one of the classics of the old American theatre, a play I have often read about but never (until now) seen performed. I would have liked it much better if it had been done with the costumes and settings of its proper period; unhappily, the director had chosen to 'modernise' the entire affair, just as we sometimes present *Rustam Beg* as if Rustam had been a hero of the war just past. General Powers was a contemporary American soldier with the mannerisms of a cowardly bandit, Spelding a publisher of libellous broadsheets, and so on. The only characters that gave me much pleasure were the limping spaceman, Kreton, and the ingenue, Ellen Spelding, played as and by a radiantly beautiful American blonde.

All through the first act my mind had been returning (particularly during Spelding's speeches) to the problem of the old man

77

beside me. By the time the curtain fell, I had decided that the best way to start a conversation might be to offer to fetch him a kebab – or whatever he might want – from the lobby, since his thread-bare appearance suggested that he might be ready enough to be treated, and the weakness of his legs would provide an admirable excuse. I tried the gambit as soon as the flambeaux were relit, and it worked as well as I could have wished. When I returned with a paper tray of sandwiches and bitter drinks, he remarked to me quite spontaneously that he had noticed me flexing my right hand during the performance.

"Yes," I said, "I had been writing a good deal before I came here."

That set him off, and he began to discourse, frequently with a great deal more detail than I could comprehend, on the topic of writing machines. At last I halted the flow with some question that must have revealed that I knew less of the subject than he had supposed. "Have you ever," he asked me, "carved a letter in a potato, and moistened it with a stamp pad, and used it to imprint paper?"

"As a child, yes. We use a turnip, but no doubt the principle is the same."

"Exactly; and the principle is that of extended abstraction. I ask you – on the lowest level, what is communication?"

"Talking, I suppose."

His shrill laugh rose above the hubbub of the audience. "Not at all! Smell" (here he gripped my arm), "smell is the essence of communication. Look at that word *essence* itself. When you smell another human being, you take chemicals from his body into your own, analyse them, and from the analysis you accurately deduce his emotional state. You do it so constantly and so automatically that you are largely unconscious of it, and say simply, 'He seemed frightened,' or 'He was angry.' You see?"

I nodded, interested in spite of myself.

"When you speak, you are telling another how you would smell if you smelled as you should and if he could smell you properly from where he stands. It is almost certain that speech was not developed until the glaciations that terminated the Pliocene stimulated mankind to develop fire, and the frequent inhalation of wood smoke had dulled the olfactory organs."

"I see."

"No, you hear – unless you are by chance reading my lips, which in this din would be a useful accomplishment." He took an enormous bite of his sandwich, spilling pink meat that had surely come from no natural animal. "When you write, you are telling the other how you would speak if he could hear you, and when you print with your turnip, you are telling him how you would write. You will notice that we have already reached the third level of abstraction."

I nodded again.

"It used to be believed that only a limited number K of levels of abstraction were possible before the original matter disappeared altogether – some very interesting mathematical work was done about seventy years ago in an attempt to derive a generalised expression for K for various systems. Now we know that the number can be infinite if the array represents an open curve, and that closed curves are also possible."

"I don't understand."

"You are young and handsome – very fine looking, with your wide shoulders and black moustache; let us suppose a young woman loves you. If you and I and she were crouched now on the limb of a tree, you would scent her desire. Today, perhaps she tells you of that desire. But it is also possible, is it not, that she may write you of her desire?"

Remembering Yasmin's letters, I assented.

"But suppose those letters are perfumed – a musky, sweet perfume. You understand? A closed curve – the perfume is not the odour of her body, but an artificial simulation of it. It may not be what she feels, but it is what she tells you she feels. Your real love is for a whale, a male deer and a bed of roses." He was about to say more, but the curtain went up for the second act.

I found that act both more enjoyable, and more painful, than the first. The opening scene, in which Kreton (soon joined by

Ellen) reads the mind of the family cat, was exceptionally effective. The concealed orchestra furnished music to indicate cat thoughts; I wish I knew the identity of the composer, but my playbill does not provide the information. The bedroom wall became a shadow screen, where we saw silhouettes of cats catching birds, and then, when Ellen tickled the real cat's belly, making love. As I have said, Kreton and Ellen were the play's best characters. The juxtaposition of Ellen's willowy beauty and high-spirited naiveté, and Kreton's clear desire for her illuminated perfectly the Paphian difficulties that would confront a powerful telepath, were such persons to exist.

On the other hand, Kreton's summoning of the presidents, which closes the act, was as objectionable as it could possibly have been made. The foreign ruler conjured up by error was played as a Turk, and as broadly as possible. I confess to feeling some prejudice against that bloodthirsty race myself, but what was done was indefensible. When the president of the World Council appeared, he was portrayed as an American.

By the end of that scene I was in no very good mood. I think that I have not yet shaken off the fatigues of the crossing; and they, combined with a fairly strenuous day spent prowling around the ruins of the Silent City, had left me now in that state in which the smallest irritation takes on the dimensions of a mortal insult. The old curator beside me discerned my irascibility, but mistook the reason for it, and began to apologise for the state of the American stage, saying that all the performers of talent emigrated as soon as they gained recognition, and returned only when they had failed on the eastern shore of the Atlantic.

"No, no," I said. "Kreton and the girl are very fine, and the rest of the cast is at least adequate."

He seemed not to have heard me. "They pick them up wherever they can – they choose them for their faces. When they have appeared in three plays, they call themselves actors. At the Smithsonian – I am employed there, perhaps I've already mentioned it – we have tapes of real theatre: Laurence Olivier, Orson Welles, Katharine Cornell. Spelding is a barber, or at least he was.

He used to put his chair under the old Kennedy statue and shave the passers-by. Ellen is a trollop, and Powers a drayman. That lame fellow Kreton used to snare sailors for a singing house on Portland Street."

His disparagement of his own national culture embarrassed me, though it put me in a better mood. (I have noticed that the two often go together – perhaps I am secretly humiliated to find that people of no great importance can affect my interior state with a few words or some mean service.) I took my leave of him and went to the confectioner's stand in the lobby. The Americans have a very pretty custom of duplicating the speckled eggs of wild birds in marzipan, and I bought a box of these – not only because I wanted to try them myself, but because I felt certain they would prove a treat for the old man, who must seldom have enough money to afford luxuries of that kind. I was quite correct – he ate them eagerly. But when I sampled one, I found its odour (as though I were eating artificial violets) so unpleasant that I did not take another.

"We were speaking of writing," the old man said. "The closed curve and the open curve. I did not have time to make the point that both could be achieved mechanically; but the monograph I am now developing turns upon that very question, and it happens that I have examples with me. First the closed curve. In the days when our president was among the world's ten most powerful men – the reality of the Paul Laurent you see on the stage there – each president received hundreds of requests every day for his signature. To have granted them would have taken hours of his time. To have refused them would have raised a brigade of enemies."

"What did they do?"

"They called upon the resources of science. That science devised the machine that wrote this."

From within his clean, worn coat he drew a folded sheet of paper. I opened it and saw that it was covered with the text of what appeared to be a public address, written in a childish scrawl. Mentally attempting to review the list of the American presidents

81

I had seen in some digest of world history long ago, I asked whose hand it was.

"The machine's. Whose hand is being imitated here is one of the things I am attempting to discover."

In the dim light of the theatre it was almost impossible to make out the faded script, but I caught the word *Sardinia*. "Surely, by correlating the contents to historical events it should be possible to date it quite accurately."

The old man shook his head. "The text itself was composed by another machine to achieve some national psychological effect. It is not probable that it bears any real relationship to the issues of its day. But now look here." He drew out a second sheet, and unfolded it for me. So far as I could see, it was completely blank. I was still staring at it when the curtain went up.

As Kreton moved his toy aircraft across the stage, the old man took a final egg and turned away to watch the play. There was still half a carton left, and I, thinking that he might want more later, and afraid that they might be spilled from my lap and lost underfoot, closed the box and slipped it into the side pocket of my jacket.

The special effects for the landing of the second spaceship were well done; but there was something else in the third act that gave me as much pleasure as the cat scene in the second. The final curtain hinges on the device our poets call the *Peri's asphodel*, a trick so shopworn now that it is acceptable only if it can be presented in some new light. The one used here was to have John – Ellen's lover – find Kreton's handkerchief and, remarking that it seemed perfumed, bury his nose in it. For an instant, the shadow wall used at the beginning of the second act was illuminated again to graphically (or I should say pornographically) present Ellen's desire, conveying to the audience that John had, for that moment, shared the telepathic abilities of Kreton, whom all of them had now entirely forgotten.

The device was extremely effective, and left me feeling that I had by no means wasted my evening. I joined the general applause as the cast appeared to take their bows; then, as I was turning to leave, I noticed that the old man appeared very ill. I asked if he were all right, and he confessed ruefully that he had eaten too much, and thanked me again for my kindness – which must at that time have taken a great deal of resolution.

I helped him out of the theatre, and when I saw that he had no transportation but his feet, told him I would take him home. He thanked me again, and informed me that he had a room at the museum.

Thus the half-block walk from the theatre to my hotel was transformed into a journey of three or four kilometres, taken by moonlight, much of it through rubble-strewn avenues of the deserted parts of the city.

During the day I had hardly glanced at the stark skeleton of the old highway. Tonight, when we walked beneath its ruined overpasses, they seemed inexpressibly ancient and sinister. It occurred to me then that there may be a time-flaw, such as astronomers report from space, somewhere in the Atlantic. How is it that this western shore is more antiquated in the remains of a civilisation not yet a century dead than we are in the shadow of Darius? May it not be that every ship that plows that sea moves through ten thousand years?

O

For the past hour – I find I cannot sleep – I have been debating whether to make this entry. But what good is a travel journal, if one does not enter everything? I will revise it on the trip home, and present a cleansed copy for my mother and Yasmin to read.

It appears that the scholars at the museum have no income but that derived from the sale of treasures gleaned from the past; and I bought a vial of what is supposed to be the greatest creation of the old hallucinatory chemists from the woman who helped me get the old man into bed. It is – it was – about half the height of my smallest finger. Very probably it was alcohol and nothing more, though I paid a substantial price.

I was sorry I had bought it before I left, and still more sorry when I arrived here; but at the time it seemed that this would be my only opportunity, and I could think of nothing but to seize the adventure. After I have swallowed the drug I will be able to speak with authority about these things for the remainder of my life.

Here is what I have done. I have soaked the porous sugar of one of the eggs with the fluid. The moisture will soon dry up. The drug – if there is a drug – will remain. Then I will rattle the eggs together in an empty drawer, and each day, beginning tomorrow night, I will eat one egg.

○

I am writing today before I go down to breakfast, partly because I suspect that the hotel does not serve so early. Today I intend to visit the park on the other side of the channel. If it is as dangerous as they say, it is very likely I will not return to make any entry tonight. If I do return – well, I will plan for that when I am here again.

After I had blown out my candle last night I could not sleep, though I was tired to the bone. Perhaps it was only the excitement of the long walk back from the museum; but I could not free my mind from the image of Ellen. My wandering thoughts associated her with the eggs, and I imagined myself Kreton, sitting up in bed with the cat on my lap. In my daydream (I was not asleep) Ellen brought me my breakfast on a tray, and the breakfast consisted of the six candy eggs.

When my mind had exhausted itself with this kind of imagery, I decided to have the manager procure a girl for me so that I could rid myself of the accumulated tensions of the voyage. After about an hour during which I sat up reading, he arrived with three; and when he had given me a glimpse of them through the half-open door, he slipped inside and shut it behind him, leaving them standing in the corridor. I told him I had only asked for one.

"I know, Mr Jaffarzadeh, I know. But I thought you might like to have a choice."

None of them – from the glimpse I had had – resembled Ellen;

but I thanked him for his thoughtfulness and suggested that he bring them in.

"I wanted to tell you first, sir, that you must allow me to set the price with them – I can get them for much less than you, sir, because they know they cannot deceive me, and they must depend on me to bring them to my guests in the future." He named a sum that was in fact quite trivial.

"That will be fine," I said. "Bring them in."

He bowed and smiled, making his pinched and miserly face as pleasant as possible and reminding me very much of a picture I had once seen of an imp summoned before the Court of Suleiman. "But first, sir, I wished to inform you that if you would like all three – together – you may have them for the price of two. And should you desire only two of the three, you may have them for one and one half the price of one. All are very lovely, and I thought you might want to consider it."

"Very well, I have considered it. Show them in."

"I will light another candle," he said, bustling about the room. "There is no charge, sir, for candles at the rate you're paying. I can put the girls on your bill as well. They'll be down as room service – you understand, I'm sure."

When the second candle was burning and he had positioned it to his liking on the nightstand between the two beds, he opened the door and waved in the girls, saying, "I'll go now. Take what you like and send out the others." (I feel certain this was a stratagem – he felt I would have difficulty in getting any to leave, and so would have to pay for all three.)

Yasmin must never see this – that is decided. It is not just that this entire incident would disturb her greatly, but because of what happened next. I was sitting on the bed nearest the door, hoping to decide quickly which of the three most resembled the girl who had played Ellen. The first was too short, with a wan, pinched face. The second was tall and blonde, but plump. The third, who seemed to stumble as she entered, exactly resembled Yasmin.

For a few seconds I actually believed it was she. Science has so accustomed us to devising and accepting theories to account for the facts we observe, however fantastic, that our minds must begin their manufacture before we are aware of it. Yasmin had grown lonely for me. She had booked passage a few days after my own departure, or perhaps had flown, daring the notorious American landing facilities. Arriving here, she had made inquiries at the consulate, and was approaching my door as the manager lit his candle, and not knowing what was taking place had entered with prostitutes he had engaged.

It was all moonshine, of course. I jumped to my feet and held up the candle, and saw that the third girl, though she had Yasmin's large, dark eyes and rounded little chin, was not she. For all her night-black hair and delicate features, she was indisputably an American; and as she came toward me (encouraged, no doubt, because she had attracted my attention) I saw that like Kreton in the play she had a club foot.

○

As you see, I returned alive from the park after all. Tonight before I retire I will eat an egg; but first I will briefly set down my experiences.

The park lies on the opposite side of the Washington Channel, between the city and the river. It can be reached by land only at the north end. Not choosing to walk so far and return, I hired a little boat with a tattered red sail to carry me to the southern tip, which is called Hains Point. Here there was a fountain, I am told, in the old times; but nothing remains of it now.

We had clear, sunny spring weather, and made our way over exhilarating swells of wave with nothing of the deadly wallowing that oppressed me so much aboard the *Princess Fatimah*. I sat in the bow and watched the rolling greenery of the park on one side of the channel and the ruins of the old fort on the other, while an elderly man handled the tiller, and his thin, sun-browned granddaughter, aged about eleven, worked the sail.

When we rounded the point, the old man told me that for very little more he would take me across to Arlington to see the remains of what is supposed to be the largest building of the country's antiquity. I refused, determined to save that experience for another time, and we landed where a part of the ancient concrete coping remained intact.

The tracks of old roads run up either shore; but I decided to avoid them, and made my way up the centre, keeping to the highest ground in so far as I could. Once, no doubt, the whole area was devoted to pleasure. Very little remains, however, of the pavilions and statuary that must have dotted the ground. There are little, worn-away hills that may once have been rockeries but are now covered with soil, and many stagnant pools. In a score of places I saw the burrows of the famous giant American rats, though I never saw the animals themselves. To judge from the holes, their size has not been exaggerated – there were several I could have entered with ease.

The wild dogs, against which I had been warned by both the hotel manager and the old boatman, began to follow me after I had walked about a kilometre north. They are short-haired, and typically blotched with black and brown flecked with white. I would say their average weight was about twenty-five kilos. With their erect ears and alert, intelligent faces they did not seem particularly dangerous; but I soon noticed that whichever way I turned, the ones in back of me edged nearer. I sat on a stone with my back to a pool and made several quick sketches of them, then decided to try my pistol. They did not seem to know what it was, so I was able to centre the red aiming laser very nicely on one big fellow's chest before I pressed the stud for a high energy pulse.

For a long time afterward, I heard the melancholy howling of these dogs behind me. Perhaps they were mourning their fallen leader. Twice I came across rusting machines that may have been used to take invalids through the gardens in such fair weather as I myself experienced today. Uncle Mirza says I am a good colourist, but I despair of ever matching the green-haunted blacks with which the declining sun painted the park.

I met no one until I had almost reached the piers of the abandoned railway bridge. Then four or five Americans who pretended to beg surrounded me. The dogs, who as I understand it live mostly upon the refuse cast up by the river, were honest in their intentions and cleaner in their persons. If these people had been like the pitiful creatures I had met in the Silent City, I would have thrown them a few coins; but they were more or less able-bodied men and women who could have worked, and chose instead to rob. I told them that I had been forced to kill a fellow Countryman of theirs (not mentioning that he was a dog) who had assaulted me; and asked where I could report the matter to the police. At that they backed off, and permitted me to walk around the northern end of the channel in peace, though not without a thousand savage looks. I returned here without further incident, tired and very well satisfied with my day.

○

I have eaten one of the eggs! I confess I found it difficult to take the first taste; but marshalling my resolution was like pushing at a wall of glass – all at once the resistance snapped, and I picked the thing up and swallowed it in a few bites. It was piercingly sweet, but there was no other flavour. Now we will see. This is more frightening than the park by far.

○

Nothing seemed to be happening, so I went out to dinner. It was twilight, and the carnival spirit of the streets was more marked than ever – coloured lights above all the shops, and music from the rooftops where the wealthier natives have private gardens. I have been eating mostly at the hotel, but was told of a 'good' American-style restaurant not too far south on Maine Street.

It was just as described – people sitting on padded benches in alcoves. The table tops are of a substance like fine-grained, greasy, artificial stone. They looked very old. I had the Number One Dinner – buff-coloured fish soup with the pasty American bread on the side, followed by a sandwich of ground meat and raw vegetables doused with a tomato sauce and served on a soft, oily roll. To tell the truth, I did not much enjoy the meal; but it seems a sort of duty to sample more of the American food than I have thus far.

I am very tempted to end the account of my day here, and in fact I laid down this pen when I had written *thus far*, and made myself ready for bed. Still, what good is a dishonest record? I will let no one see this – just keep it to read over after I get home.

Returning to the hotel from the restaurant, I passed the theatre. The thought of seeing Ellen again was irresistible; I bought a ticket and went inside. It was not until I was in my seat that I realised that the bill had changed.

The new play was *Mary Rose*. I saw it done by an English company several years ago, with great authenticity, and it struck me that (like Mary herself) it had far outlived its time. The American production was as inauthentic as the other had been correct. For that reason, it retained – or I should have said it had acquired – a good deal of interest.

Americans are superstitious about the interior of their country, not its coasts, so Mary Rose's island had been shifted to one of the huge central lakes. The highlander, Cameron, had accordingly become a Canadian, played by General Powers' former aide. The Speldings had become the Morelands, and the Morelands had become Americans. Kreton was Harry, the knife-throwing wounded soldier; and my Ellen had become Mary Rose.

The role suited her so well that I imagined the play had been selected as a vehicle for her. Her height emphasised the character's unnatural immaturity, and her slenderness, and the vulnerability of her pale complexion, would have told us, I think, if the play had not, that she had been victimised unaware. More important than any of these things was a wild and innocent affinity for the supernatural, which she projected to perfection. It was that quality alone (as I now understood) that had made us believe on the preceding night that Kreton's spaceship might land in the Speldings' rose garden – he would have been drawn to Ellen, though he had never seen her. Now it made Mary

Rose's disappearances and reappearances plausible and even likely; it was as likely that unseen spirits lusted for Mary Rose as that Lieutenant Blake (previously John Randolf) loved her.

Indeed it was more likely. And I had no sooner realised that, than the whole mystery of *Mary Rose* – which had seemed at once inexplicable and banal when I had seen it well played in Teheran – lay clear before me. We of the audience were the envious and greedy spirits. If the Morelands could not see that one wall of their comfortable drawing room was but a sea of dark faces, if Cameron had never noticed that we were the backdrop of his island, the fault was theirs. By rights then, Mary Rose should have been drawn to us when she vanished. At the end of the second act I began to look for her, and in the beginning of the third I found her, standing silent and unobserved behind the last row of seats. I was only four rows from the stage, but I slipped out of my place as unobtrusively as I could, and crept up the aisle toward her.

I was too late. Before I had gone halfway, it was nearly time for her entrance at the end of the scene. I watched the rest of the play from the back of the theatre, but she never returned.

Same night. I am having a good deal of trouble sleeping, though while I was on the ship I slept nine hours a night, and was off as soon as my head touched the pillow.

The truth is that while I lay in bed tonight I recalled the old curator's remark that the actresses were all prostitutes. If it is true and not simply an expression of hatred for younger people whose bodies are still attractive, then I have been a fool to moan over the thought of Mary Rose and Ellen when I might have had the girl herself.

Her name is Ardis Dahl – I just looked it up in the playbill. I am going to the manager's office to consult the city directory there.

○

Writing before breakfast. Found the manager's office locked last night. It was after two. I put my shoulder against the door and got it opened easily enough. (There was no metal socket for the bolt such as we have at home – just a hole mortised in the frame.) The directory listed several Dahls in the city, but since it was nearly eight years out of date it did not inspire a great deal of confidence. I reflected, however, that in a backwater like this people were not likely to move about so much as we do at home, and that if it were not still of some utility, the manager would not be likely to retain it; so I selected the one that appeared from its address to be nearest the theatre, and set out.

The streets were completely deserted. I remember thinking that I was now doing what I had previously been so afraid to do, having been frightened of the city by reading. How ridiculous to suppose that robbers would be afoot now, when no one else was. What would they do, stand for hours at the empty corners?

The moon was full and high in the southern sky, showering the street with the lambent white fluid of its light. If it had not been for the sharp, unclean odour so characteristic of American residential areas, I might have thought myself walking through an illustration from some old book of wonder tales, or an actor in a children's pantomime, so bewitched by the scenery that he has forgotten the audience.

(In writing that – which to tell the truth I did not think of at the time, but only now, as I sat here at my table – I realised that that is in fact what must happen to the American girl I have been in the habit of calling Ellen but must now learn to call Ardis. She could never perform as she does if it were not that in some part of her mind her stage became her reality.)

The shadows about my feet were a century old, tracing faithfully the courses they had determined long before New Tabriz came to jewel the lunar face with its sapphire. Webbed with thoughts of her – my Ellen, my Mary Rose, my Ardis! – and with the magic of that pale light that commands all the tides, I was elevated to a degree I cannot well describe.

Then I was seized by the thought that everything I felt might be no more than the effect of the drug.

At once, like someone who falls from a tower and clutches at the very wisps of air, I tried to return myself to reality. I bit the interior of my checks until the blood filled my mouth, and struck the unfeeling wall of the nearest building with my fist. In a moment the pain sobered me. For a quarter hour or more I stood at the curbside, spitting into the gutter and trying to clean and bandage my knuckles with strips torn from my handkerchief. A thousand times I thought what a sight I would be if I did in fact succeed in seeing Ellen, and I comforted myself with the thought that if she were indeed a prostitute it would not matter to her – I could offer her a few additional rials and all would be well.

Yet that thought was not really much comfort. Even when a woman sells her body, a man flatters himself that she would not do so quite so readily were he not who he is. At the very moment I drooled blood into the street, I was congratulating myself on the strong, square face so many have admired; and wondering how I should apologise if in kissing her I smeared her mouth with red.

Perhaps it was some faint sound that brought me to myself; perhaps it was only the consciousness of being watched. I drew my pistol and turned this way and that, but saw nothing.

Yet the feeling endured. I began to walk again; and if there was any sense of unreality remaining, it was no longer the unearthly exultation I had felt earlier. After a few steps I stopped and listened. A dry sound of rattling and scraping had followed me. It too stopped now.

I was nearing the address I had taken from the directory. I confess my mind was filled with fancies in which I was rescued by Ellen herself, who in the end should be more frightened than I, but who would risk her lovely person to save mine. Yet I knew these *were* but fancies, and the thing pursuing me was not, though it crossed my mind more than once that it might be some *druj* made to seem visible and palpable to me.

Another block, and I had reached the address. It was a house no different from those on either side – built of the rubble of buildings that were older still, three-storeyed, heavy-doored, and almost without windows. There was a bookshop on the ground floor (to judge by an old sign) with living quarters above it. I crossed the street to see it better, and stood, wrapped again in my dreams, staring at the single thread of yellow light that showed between the shutters of a gable window.

As I watched that light, the feeling of being watched myself grew upon me. Time passed, slipping through the waist of the universe's great hourglass like the eroded soil of this continent slipping down her rivers to the seas. At last my fear and desire – desire for Ellen, fear of whatever it was that glared at me with invisible eyes – drove me to the door of the house. I hammered the wood with the butt of my pistol, though I knew how unlikely it was that any American would answer a knock at such a time of night, and when I had knocked several times, I heard slow steps from within.

The door creaked open until it was caught by a chain. I saw a grey-haired man, fully dressed, holding an old-fashioned, long-barrelled gun. Behind him a woman lifted a stub of smoking candle to let him see; and though she was clearly much older than Ellen, and was marked, moreover, by the deformities so prevalent here, there was a certain nobility in her features and a certain beauty as well, so that I was reminded of the fallen statue that is said to have stood on an island farther north, and which I have seen pictured.

I told the man that I was a traveller – true enough! – and that I had just arrived by boat from Arlington and had no place to stay, and so had walked into the city until I had noticed the light of his window. I would pay, I said, a silver rial if they would only give me a bed for the night and breakfast in the morning, and I showed them the coin. My plan was to become a guest in the house so that I might discover whether Ellen was indeed one of the inhabitants; if she were, it would have been an easy matter to prolong my stay.

The woman tried to whisper in her husband's ear, but save for a look of nervous irritation he ignored her. "I don't dare let a stranger in." From his voice, I might have been a lion, and his gun a trainer's chair. "Not with no one here but my wife and myself."

"I see," I told him. "I quite understand your position."

"You might try the house on the corner," he said, shutting the

93

door, "but don't tell them Dahl sent you." I heard the heavy bar dropped into place at the final word.

I turned away – and then by the mercy of Allah who is indeed compassionate happened to glance back one last time at the thread of yellow between the shutters of that high window. A flicker of scarlet higher still caught my attention, perhaps only because the light of the setting moon now bathed the rooftop from a new angle. I think the creature I glimpsed there had been waiting to leap upon me from behind, but when our eyes met it launched itself toward me. I had barely time to lift my pistol before it struck me and slammed me to the broken pavement of the street.

For a brief period I think I lost consciousness. If my shot had not killed the thing as it fell, I would not be sitting here writing this journal this morning. After half a minute or so I came to myself enough to thrust its weight away, stand up, and rub my bruises. No one had come to my aid; but neither had anyone rushed from the surrounding houses to kill and rob me. I was as alone with the creature that lay dead at my feet as I had been when I only stood watching the window in the house from which it had sprung.

After I found my pistol and assured myself that it was still in working order, I dragged the thing to a spot of moonlight. When I glimpsed it on the roof, it had seemed a feral dog, like the one I had shot in the park. When it lay dead before me, I had thought it a human being. In the moonlight I saw it was neither, or perhaps both. There was a blunt muzzle; and the height of the skull above the eyes, which anthropologists say is the surest badge of humanity and speech, had been stunted until it was not greater than I have seen in a macaque. Yet the arms and shoulders and pelvis – even a few filthy rags of clothing – all bespoke mankind. It was a female, with small, flattened breasts still apparent on either side of the burn channel.

At least ten years ago I read about such things in Osman Aga's *Mystery Beyond the Sun's Setting*; but it was very different to stand shivering on a deserted street corner of the old capital and examine the thing in the flesh. By Osman Aga's account (which no one, I think, but a few old women has ever believed) these creatures were in truth human beings – or at least the descendants of human beings. In the last century, when the famine gripped their country and the irreversible damage done to the chromosomal structures of the people had already become apparent, some few turned to the eating of human flesh. No doubt the corpses of the famine supplied their food at first; and no doubt those who ate of them congratulated themselves that by so doing they had escaped the effects of the enzymes that were then still used to bring slaughter animals to maturity in a matter of months. What they failed to realise was that the bodies of the human beings they ate had accumulated far more of these unnatural substances than were ever found in the flesh of the short-lived cattle. From them, according to *Mystery Beyond the Sun's Setting*, rose such creatures as the thing I had killed.

But Osman Aga has never been believed. So far as I know, he is a mere popular writer, with a reputation for glorifying Caspian resorts in recompense for free lodging, and for indulging in absurd expeditions to breed more books and publicise the ones he has already written – crossing the desert on a camel and the Alps on an elephant – and no one else has ever, to my knowledge, reported such things from this continent. The ruined cities filled with rats and rabid bats, and the terrible whirling dust storms of the interior, have been enough for other travel writers. Now I am sorry I did not contrive a way to cut off the thing's head; I feel sure its skull would have been of interest to science.

○

As soon as I had written the preceding paragraph, I realised that there might still be a chance to do what I had failed to do last night. I went to the kitchen, and for a small bribe was able to secure a large, sharp knife, which I concealed beneath my jacket.

It was still early as I ran down the street, and for a few minutes I had high hopes that the thing's body might still be lying where

I had left it; but my efforts were all for nothing. It was gone, and there was no sign of its presence – no blood, no scar from my beam on the house. I poked into alleys and waste cans. Nothing. At last I came back to the hotel for breakfast, and I have now (it is mid-morning) returned to my room to make my plans for the day.

Very well. I failed to meet Ellen last night – I shall not fail today. I am going to buy another ticket for the play, and tonight I will not take my seat, but wait behind the last row where I saw her standing. If she comes to watch at the end of the second act as she did last night, I will be there to compliment her on her performance and present her with some gift. If she does not come, I will make my way backstage – from what I have seen of these Americans, a quarter rial should get me anywhere, but I am willing to loosen a few teeth if I must.

O

What absurd creatures we are! I have just reread what I wrote this morning, and I might as well have been writing of the philosophic speculations of the Congress of Birds or the affairs of the demons in Domdaniel, or any other subject on which neither I nor anyone else knows or can know a thing. O Book, you have heard what I supposed would occur, now let me tell you what actually took place.

I set out as I had planned to procure a gift for Ellen. On the advice of the hotel manager, I followed Maine Street north until I reached the wide avenue that passes close by the obelisk. Around the base of this still imposing monument is held a perpetual fair in which the merchants use the stone blocks fallen from the upper part of the structure as tables. What remains of the shaft is still, I should say, upwards of one hundred metres high; but it is said to have formerly stood three or four times that height. Much of the fallen material has been carted away to build private homes.

There seems to be no logic to the prices in this country, save for the general rule that foodstuffs are cheap and imported machinery – cameras and the like – costly. Textiles are expensive, which no doubt explains why so many of the people wear ragged clothes that they mend and dye in an effort to make them look new. Certain kinds of jewellery are quite reasonable; others sell for much larger prices than they would in Teheran. Rings of silver or white gold set, usually, with a single modest diamond, may be had in great numbers for such low prices that I was tempted into buying a few to take home as an investment. Yet I saw bracelets that would have sold at home for no more than half a rial, for which the seller asked ten times that much. There were many interesting antiques, all of which are alleged to have been dug from the ruined cities of the interior at the cost of someone's life. When I had talked to five or six vendors of such items, I was able to believe that I knew how the country was depopulated.

After a good deal of this pleasant, wordy shopping, during which I spent very little, I selected a bracelet made of old coins – many of them silver – as my gift to Ellen. I reasoned that women always like jewellery, and that such a showy piece might be of service to an actress in playing some part or other, and that the coins must have a good deal of intrinsic value. Whether she will like it or not – if she ever receives it – I do not know; it is still in the pocket of my jacket.

When the shadow of the obelisk had grown long, I returned here to the hotel and had a good dinner of lamb and rice, and retired to groom myself for the evening. The five remaining candy eggs stood staring at me from the top of my dresser. I remembered my resolve, and took one. Quite suddenly I was struck by the conviction that the demon I believed I had killed the night before had been no more than a phantom engendered by the action of the drug.

What if I had been firing my pistol at mere empty air? That seemed a terrible thought – indeed it seems so to me still. A worse one is that the drug really may have rendered visible – as some say those ancient preparations were intended to – a real but spiritual being. If such things in fact walk what we take to be unoccupied rooms and rooftops, and the empty streets of night, it would explain many sudden deaths and diseases, and perhaps the sudden changes for the worse we sometimes see in others and others in us, and even the birth of evil men. This morning I called the thing a *druj*; it may be true.

Yet if the drug had been in the egg I ate last night, then the egg I held was harmless. Concentrating on that thought, I forced myself to eat it all, then stretched myself upon the bed to wait.

Very briefly I slept and dreamed. Ellen was bending over me, caressing me with a soft, long-fingered hand. It was only for an instant, but sufficient to make me hope that dreams are prophecies.

If the drug was in the egg I consumed, that dream was its only result. I got up and washed, and changed my clothes, sprinkling my fresh shirt liberally with our Pamir rosewater, which I have observed the Americans hold in high regard. Making certain my ticket and pistol were both in place, I left for the theatre.

The play was still *Mary Rose*. I intentionally entered late (after Harry and Mrs Otery had been talking for several minutes), then lingered at the back of the last row as though I were too polite to disturb the audience by taking my seat. Mrs Otery made her exit; Harry pulled his knife from the wood of the packing case and threw it again, and when the mists of the past had marched across the stage, Harry was gone, and Moreland and the parson were chatting to the tune of Mrs Moreland's knitting needles. Mary Rose would be on stage soon. My hope that she would come out to watch the opening scene had come to nothing; I would have to wait until she vanished at the end of Act II before I could expect to see her.

I was looking for a vacant seat when I became conscious of someone standing near me. In the dim light I could tell little except that he was rather slender, and a few centimetres shorter than I.

Finding no seat, I moved back a step or two. The newcomer touched my arm and asked in a whisper if I could light his cigarette. I had already seen that it was customary to smoke in the theatres here, and I had fallen into the habit of carrying matches to light the candles in my room. The flare of the flame showed the narrow eyes and high cheekbones of Harry – or as I preferred to think of him, Kreton. Taken somewhat aback, I murmured some inane remark about the excellence of his performance.

"Did you like it? It is the least of all parts – I pull the curtain to open the show, then pull it again to tell everyone it's time to go home."

Several people in the audience were looking angrily at us, so we retreated to a point at the head of the aisle that was at least legally in the lobby, where I told him I had seen him in *Visit to a Small Planet* as well.

"Now *there* is a play. The character – as I am sure you saw – is good and bad at once. He is benign, he is mischievous, he is hellish."

"You carried it off wonderfully well, I thought."

"Thank you. This turkey here – do you know how many roles it has?"

"Well, there's yourself, Mrs Otery, Mr Amy – "

"No, no." He touched my arm to stop me. "I mean *roles*, parts that require real acting. There's one – the girl. She gets to skip about the stage as an eighteen-year-old whose brain atrophied at ten; and at least half what she does is wasted on the audience because they don't realise what's wrong with her until Act I is almost over."

"She's wonderful," I said. "I mean Mlle Dahl."

Kreton nodded and drew on his cigarette. "She is a very competent ingenue, though it would be better if she weren't quite so tall."

"Do you think there's any chance that she might come out here – as you did?"

"Ah," he said, and looked me up and down.

For a moment I could have sworn that the telepathic ability he was credited with in *Visit to a Small Planet* was no fiction; nevertheless, I repeated my question: "Is it probable or not?"

"There's no reason to get angry – no, it's not likely. Is that enough payment for your match?"

"She vanishes at the end of the second act, and doesn't come on stage again until near the close of the third."

Kreton smiled. "You've read the play?"

"I was here last night. She must be off for nearly forty minutes, including the intermission."

"That's right. But she won't be here. It's true she goes out front sometimes – as I did myself tonight – but I happen to know she has company backstage."

"Might I ask who?"

"You might. It's even possible I might answer. You're Moslem, I suppose – do you drink?"

"I'm not a *strict* Moslem; but no, I don't. I'll buy you a drink gladly enough, if you want one, and have coffee with you while you drink it."

We left by a side door and elbowed our way through the crowd in the street. A flight of narrow and dirty steps descending from the sidewalk led us to a cellar tavern that had all the atmosphere of a private club. There was a bar with a picture (now much dimmed by dirt and smoke) of the cast of a play I did not recognise behind it, three tables, and a few alcoves. Kreton and I slipped into one of these and ordered from a barman with a misshapen head. I suppose I must have stared at him, because Kreton said, "I sprained my ankle stepping out of a saucer, and now I am a convalescent soldier. Should we make up something for him too? Can't we just say the potter is angry sometimes?"

"The potter?" I asked.

" 'None answered this; but after Silence spake/A Vessel of a more ungainly Make:/They sneer at me for leaning all awry;/What! Did the Hand then of the Potter shake?' "

I shook my head. "I've never heard that; but you're right, he looks as though his head had been shaped in clay, then knocked in on one side while it was still wet."

"This is a republic of hideousness as you have no doubt already seen. Our national symbol is supposed to be an extinct eagle; it is in fact the nightmare."

"I find it a very beautiful country," I said. "Though I confess that many of your people are unsightly. Still there are the ruins, and you have such skies as we never see at home."

"Our chimneys have been filled with wind for a long time."

"That may be for the best. Blue skies are better than most of the things made in factories."

"And not all our people are unsightly," Kreton murmured.

"Oh no. Mlle Dahl – "

"I had myself in mind."

I saw that he was baiting me, but I said, "No, you aren't hideous – in fact, I would call you handsome in an exotic way. Unfortunately, my tastes run more toward Mlle Dahl."

"Call her Ardis – she won't mind."

The barman brought Kreton a glass of green liqueur, and me a cup of the weak, bitter American coffee.

"You were going to tell me who she is entertaining."

"Behind the scenes." Kreton smiled. "I just thought of that – I've used the phrase a thousand times, as I suppose everyone has. This time it happens to be literally correct, and its birth is suddenly made plain, like Oedipus's. No, I don't think I promised I would tell you that – though I suppose I said I might. Aren't there other things you would really rather know? The secret hidden beneath Mount Rushmore, or how you might meet her yourself?"

"I will give you twenty rials to introduce me to her, with some assurance that something will come of the introduction. No one need ever find out."

Kreton laughed. "Believe me, I would be more likely to boast of my profit than keep it secret – though I would probably have to divide my fee with the lady to fulfil the guarantee."

"You'll do it then?"

He shook his head, still laughing. "I only pretend to be corrupt; it goes with this face. Come backstage after the show tonight, and I'll see that you meet Ardis. You're very wealthy, I presume, and if you're not, we'll say you are anyway. What are you doing here?"

"Studying your art and architecture."

"Great reputation in your own country, no doubt?"

"I am a pupil of Akhon Mirza Ahmak; he has a great reputation, surely. He even came here, thirty years ago, to examine the miniatures in your National Gallery of Art."

"Pupil of Akhon Mirza Ahmak, pupil of Akhon Mirza Ahmak," Kreton muttered to himself. "That is very good – I must remember it. But now," – he glanced at the old clock behind the bar – "it's time we got back. I'll have to freshen my makeup before I go on in the last act. Would you prefer to wait in the theatre, or just come around to the stage door when the play's over? I'll give you a card that will get you in."

"I'll wait in the theatre," I said, feeling that would offer less chance for mishap; also because I wanted to see Ellen play the ghost again.

"Come along then – I have a key for that side door."

I rose to go with him, and he threw an arm about my shoulder that I felt it would be impolite to thrust away. I could feel his hand, as cold as a dead man's, through my clothing, and was reminded unpleasantly of the twisted hands of the beggar in the Silent City.

We were going up the narrow stairs when I felt a gentle touch inside my jacket. My first thought was that he had seen the outline of my pistol, and meant to take it and shoot me. I gripped his wrist and shouted something – I do not remember what. Bound together and struggling, we staggered up the steps and into the street.

In a few seconds we were the centre of a mob – some taking his side, some mine, most only urging us to fight, or asking each other what the disturbance was. My pocket sketchpad, which he must have thought held money, fell to the ground between us. Just then the American police arrived – not by air as the police would have come at home, but astride shaggy, hulking horses, and swinging whips. The crowd scattered at the first crackling arc from the lashes, and in a few seconds they had beaten Kreton to the ground. Even at the time I could not help thinking what a terrible thing it must be to be one of these people, whose police are so quick to prefer any prosperous-looking foreigner to one of their own citizens.

They asked me what had happened (my questioner even dismounted to show his respect for me), and I explained that Kreton had tried to rob me, but that I did not want him punished. The truth was that seeing him sprawled unconscious with a burn across his face had put an end to any resentment I might have felt toward him; out of pity, I would gladly have given him the few rials I carried. They told me that if he had attempted to rob me he must be charged, and that if I would not accuse him they would do so themselves.

I then said that Kreton was a friend; and that on reflection I felt certain that what he had attempted had been intended as a prank. (In maintaining this I was considerably handicapped by not knowing his real name, which I had read on the playbill but forgotten, so that I was forced to refer to him as 'this poor man'.)

At last the policeman said, "We can't leave him in the street, so we'll have to bring him in. How will it look if there's no complaint?"

Then I understood that they were afraid of what their superiors might say if it became known that they had beaten him unconscious when no charge was made against him; and when I became aware that if I would not press charges, the charges they would bring themselves would be far more serious – assault or attempted murder – I agreed to do what they wished, and signed a form alleging the theft of my sketchbook.

When they had gone at last, carrying the unfortunate Kreton across a saddlebow, I tried to re-enter the theatre. The side door through which we had left was locked, and though I would gladly have paid the price of another ticket, the box office was closed. Seeing that there was nothing further to be done, I returned here, telling myself that my introduction to Ellen, if it ever came, would have to wait for another day.

Very truly it is written that we walk by paths that are always turning. In recording these several pages I have managed to restrain my enthusiasm, though when I described my waiting at the back of the theatre for Ardis, and again when I recounted how Kreton had promised to introduce me to her, I was forced for minutes at a time to lay down my pen and walk about the room singing and whistling, and – to reveal everything – jumping over the beds! But now I can conceal no longer. I have seen her! I have touched her hand; I am to see her again tomorrow; and there is every hope that she will become my mistress!

I had undressed and laid myself on the bed (thinking to bring this journal up to date in the morning) and had even fallen into the first doze of sleep, when there was a knock at the door. I slipped into my robe and pressed the release.

It was the only time in my life that for even an instant I thought I might be dreaming – actually asleep – when in truth I was up and awake.

How feeble it is to write that she is more beautiful in person than she appears on the stage. It is true, and yet it is a supreme irrelevance. I have seen more beautiful women – indeed Yasmin is, I suppose, by the formal standards of art, more lovely. It is not Ardis' beauty that draws me to her – the hair like gold, the translucent skin that then still showed traces of the bluish makeup she had worn as a ghost, the flashing eyes like the clear, clean skies of America. It is something deeper than that; something that would remain if all that were somehow taken away. No doubt she has habits that would disgust me in someone else, and the vanity that is said to be so common in her profession, and yet I would do anything to possess her.

Enough of this. What is it but empty boasting, now that I am on the point of winning her?

She stood in my doorway. I have been trying to think how I can express what I felt then. It was as though some tall flower, a lily perhaps, had left the garden and come to tap at my door, a thing that had never happened before in all the history of the world, and would never happen again.

"You are Nadan Jaffarzadeh?"

I admitted that I was, and shamefacedly, twenty seconds too late, moved out of her way.

She entered, but instead of taking the chair I indicated, turned to face me; her blue eyes seemed as large as the coloured eggs on the dresser, and they were filled with a melting hope. "You are the man, then, that Bobby O'Keene tried to rob tonight."

I nodded.

"I know you – I mean, I know your face. This is insane. You came to *Visit* on the last night and brought your father, and then to *Mary Rose* on the first night, and sat in the third or fourth row. I thought you were an American, and when the police told me your name I imagined some greasy fat man with gestures. Why on earth would Bobby want to steal from *you*?"

"Perhaps he needed the money."

She threw back her head and laughed. I had heard her laugh in *Mary Rose* when Simon was asking her father for her hand; but that had held a note of childishness that (however well suited to the part) detracted from its beauty. This laugh was the merriment of houris sliding down a rainbow. "I'm sure he did. He always needs money. You're sure, though, that he meant to rob you? You couldn't have . . ."

She saw my expression and let the question trail away. The truth is that I was disappointed that I could not oblige her, and at last I said, "If you want me to be mistaken, Ardis, then I was mistaken. He only bumped against me on the steps, perhaps, and tried to catch my sketchbook when it fell."

She smiled, and her face was the sun smiling upon roses. "You would say that for me? And you know my name?"

"From the programme. I came to the theatre to see you – and that was not my father, who it grieves me to say is long dead, but only an old man, an American, whom I had met that day."

"You brought him sandwiches at the first intermission – I was watching you through the peephole in the curtain. You must be a very thoughtful person."

"Do you watch everyone in the audience so carefully?"

She blushed at that, and for a moment could not meet my eyes.

"But you will forgive Bobby, and tell the police that you want them to let him go? You must love the theatre, Mr Jef– Jaff– "

"You've forgotten my name already. It is Jaffarzadeh, a very commonplace name in my country."

"I hadn't forgotten it – only how to pronounce it. You see, when I came here I had learned it without knowing who you were, and so I had no trouble with it. Now you're a real person to me and I can't say it as an actress should." She seemed to notice the chair behind her for the first time, and sat down.

I sat opposite her. "I'm afraid I know very little about the the-atre."

"We are trying to keep it alive here, Mr Jaffar, and – "

"Jaffarzadeh. Call me Nadan – then you won't have so many syllables to trip over."

She took my hand in hers, and I knew quite well that the ges-ture was as studied as a salaam and that she felt she was playing me like a fish; but I was beside myself with delight. To be played by *her!* To have *her* eager to cultivate my affection! And the fish will pull her in yet – wait and see!

"I will," she said. "Nadan. And though you may know little of the theatre, you feel as I do – as we do – or you would not come. It has been such a long struggle; all the history of the stage is a struggle, the gasping of a beautiful child born at the point of death. The moralists, censorship and oppression, technology, and now poverty have all tried to destroy her. Only we, the actors and audiences, have kept her alive. We have been doing well here in Washington, Nadan."

"Very well indeed," I said. "Both the productions I have seen have been excellent."

"But only for the past two seasons. When I joined the company it had nearly fallen apart. We revived it – Bobby and Paul and I. We could do it because we cared, and because we were able to find a few naturally talented people who can take direction. Bobby is the best of us – he can walk away with any part that calls for a touch of the sinister . . ."

She seemed to run out of breath. I said, "I don't think there will be any trouble about getting him free."

"Thank God. We're getting the theatre on its feet again now. We're attracting new people, and we've built up a following – people who come to see every production. There's even some money ahead at last. But *Mary Rose* is supposed to run another two weeks, and after that we're doing *Faust*, with Bobby as Mephistopheles. We've simply no one who can take his place, no one who can come close to him."

"I'm sure the police will release him if I ask them to."

"They *must*. We have to have him tomorrow night. Bill – someone you don't know – tried to go on for him in the third act tonight. It was just ghastly. In Iran you're very polite; that's what I've heard."

"We enjoy thinking so."

"We're not. We never were; and as . . ."

Her voice trailed away, but a wave of one slender arm evoked everything – the cracked plaster walls became as air, and the decayed city, the ruined continent, entered the room with us. "I understand," I said.

"They – we – were betrayed. In our souls we have never been sure by whom. When we feel cheated we are ready to kill; and maybe we feel cheated all the time."

She slumped in her chair, and I realised, as I should have long before, how exhausted she was. She had given a performance that had ended in disaster, then had been forced to plead with the police for my name and address, and at last had come here from the station house, very probably on foot. I asked when I could obtain O'Keene's release.

"We can go tomorrow morning, if you'll do it."

"You wish to come too?"

She nodded, smoothed her skirt, and stood. "I'll have to know. I'll come for you about nine, if that's all right."

"If you'll wait outside for me to dress, I'll take you home."

"That's not necessary."

"It will only take a moment," I said.

The blue eyes held something pleading again. "You're going to come in with me – that's what you're thinking, I know. You have two beds here – bigger, cleaner beds than the one I have in my little apartment; if I were to ask you to push them together, would you still take me home afterward?"

It was as though I were dreaming indeed – a dream in which everything I wanted – the cosmos purified – delivered itself to me. I said, "You won't have to leave at all – you can spend the night with me. Then we can breakfast together before we go to release your friend."

She laughed again, lifting that exquisite head. "There are a hundred things at home I need. Do you think I'd have breakfast with you without my cosmetics, and in these dirty clothes?"

"Then I will take you home – yes, though you lived in Kazvin. Or on Mount Kaf."

She smiled. "Get dressed, then. I'll wait outside, and I'll show you my apartment; perhaps you won't want to come back here afterward."

She went out, her wooden-soled American shoes clicking on the bare floor, and I threw on trousers, shirt and jacket, and jammed my feet into my boots. When I opened the door, she was gone. I rushed to the barred window at the end of the corridor, and was in time to see her disappear down a side street. A last swirl of her skirt in a gust of night wind, and she had vanished into the velvet dark.

For a long time I stood there looking out over the ruinous buildings. I was not angry – I do not think I could be angry with her. I was, though here it is hard to tell the truth, in some way glad. Not because I feared the embrace of love – I have no doubt of my ability to suffice any woman who can be sated by man – but because an easy exchange of my cooperation for her person would have failed to satisfy my need for romance, for adventure of a certain type, in which danger and love are twined like coupling serpents. Ardis, my Ellen, will provide that, surely, as neither Yasmin nor the pitiful wanton who was her double could. I sense that the world is opening for me only now; that I am being born; that that corridor was the birth canal, and that Ardis in leaving me was drawing me out toward her.

When I returned to my own door, I noticed a bit of paper on the floor before it. I transcribe it exactly here, though I cannot transmit its scent of lilacs.

You are a most attractive man and I want very much to stretch the truth and tell you you can have me freely when Bobby is free but I won't sell myself etc. Really I *will* sell myself for Bobby but I have other fish to fry tonight. I'll see you in the morning and if you can get Bobby out or even try hard you'll have (real) love from the vanishing

Mary Rose

○

Morning. Woke early and ate here at the hotel as usual, finishing about eight. Writing this journal will give me something to do while I wait for Ardis. Had an American breakfast today, the first time I have risked one. Flakes of pastry dough toasted crisp and drenched with cream, and with it strudel and the usual American coffee. Most natives have spiced pork in one form or another, which I cannot bring myself to try; but several of the people around me were having egg dishes and oven-warmed bread, which I will sample tomorrow.

I had a very unpleasant dream last night; I have been trying to put it out of my mind ever since I woke. It was dark, and I was under an open sky with Ardis, walking over ground much rougher than anything I saw in the park on the farther side of the channel. One of the hideous creatures I shot the night before last was pursuing us – or rather, lurking about us, for it appeared first to the left of us, then to the right, silhouetted against the night sky. Each time we saw it, Ardis grasped my arm and urged me to shoot, but the little indicator light on my pistol was glowing red to show that there was not enough charge left for a shot. All very silly, of course, but I am going to buy a fresh powerpack as soon as I have the opportunity.

○

It is late afternoon – after six – but we have not had dinner yet. I am just out of the tub, and sit here naked, with today's candy egg

109

laid (pinker even than I) beside this book on my table. Ardis and I had a sorry, weary time of it, and I have come back here to make myself presentable. At seven we will meet for dinner; the curtain goes up at eight, so it can't be a long one, but I am going backstage to watch the play from the wings, where I will be able to talk to her when she isn't performing.

I just took a bite of the egg – no unusual taste, nothing but an unpleasant sweetness. The more I reflect on it, the more inclined I am to believe that the drug was in the first I ate. No doubt the monster I saw had been lurking in my brain since I read *Mysteries*, and the drug freed it. True, there were bloodstains on my clothes (the Peri's asphodel!) but they could as easily have come from my cheek, which is still sore. I have had my experience, and all I have left is my candy. I am almost tempted to throw out the rest. Another bite.

Still twenty minutes before I must dress and go for Ardis – she showed me where she lives, only a few doors from the theatre. To work then.

Ardis was a trifle late this morning, but came as she had promised. I asked where we were to go to free Kreton, and when she told me – a still-living building at the eastern end of the Silent City – I hired one of the rickety American caleches to drive us there. Like most of them, it was drawn by a starved horse; but we made good time.

The American police are organised on a peculiar system. The national secret police (officially, the Federated Enquiry Divisions) are in a tutorial position to all the others, having power to review their decisions, promote, demote and discipline, and as the ultimate reward, enrol personnel from the other organisations. In addition they maintain a uniformed force of their own. Thus when an American has been arrested by uniformed police, his friends can seldom learn whether he has been taken by the local police, by the FED uniformed national force, or by members of the FED secret police posing as either of the foregoing.

Since I had known nothing of these distinctions previously, I had no way of guessing which of the three had O'Keene; but the local police to whom Ardis had spoken the night before had given her to understand that he had been taken by them. She explained all this to me as we rattled along, then added that we were now going to the FED Building to secure his release. I must have looked as confused as I felt at this, because she added, "Part of it is a station for the Washington Police Department – they rent the space from the FED."

My own impression (when we arrived) was that they did no such thing – that the entire apparatus was no more real than one of the scenes in Ardis's theatre, and that all the men and women to whom we spoke were in fact agents of the secret police, wielding ten times the authority they pretended to possess, and going through a solemn ritual of deception. As Ardis and I moved from office to office, explaining our simple errand, I came to think that she felt as I did, and that she had refrained from expressing these feelings to me in the cab not only because of the danger, the fear that I might betray her or the driver be a spy, but because she was ashamed of her nation, and eager to make it appear to me, a foreigner, that her government was less devious and meretricious than is actually the case.

If this is so – and in that windowless warren of stone I was certain it was – then the very explanation she proffered in the cab (which I have given in its proper place) differentiating clearly between local police, uniformed FED police and secret police was no more than a children's fable, concealing an actuality less forthright and more convoluted.

Our questioners were courteous to me, much less so to Ardis, and (so it seemed to me) obsessed by the idea that something more lay behind the simple incident we described over and over again – so much so in fact that I came to believe it myself. I have neither time nor patience enough to describe all these interviews, but I will attempt to give a sample of one.

We went into a small, windowless office crowded between two others that appeared empty. A middle-aged American woman was seated behind a metal desk. She appeared normal and reasonably attractive until she spoke; then her scarred gums showed that she had once had two or three times the proper number of teeth – forty or fifty, I suppose, in each jaw – and that the dental surgeon who had extracted the supernumerary ones had not always, perhaps, selected those he suffered to remain as wisely as he might. She asked, "How is it outside? The weather? You see, I don't know, sitting in here all day."

Ardis said, "Very nice."

"Do you like it, *Hajji*? Have you had a pleasant stay in our great country?"

"I don't think it has rained since I've been here."

She seemed to take the remark as a covert accusation. "You came too late for the rains, I'm afraid. This is a very fertile area, however. Some of our oldest coins show heads of wheat. Have you seen them?" She pushed a small copper coin across the desk, and I pretended to examine it. There are one or two like it in the bracelet I bought for Ardis, and which I still have not presented to her. "I must apologise on behalf of the District for what happened to you," the woman continued. "We are making every effort to control crime. You have not been victimised before this?"

I shook my head, half suffocated in that airless office, and said I had not been.

"And now you are here." She shuffled the papers she held, then pretended to read from one of them. "You are here to secure the release of the thief who assaulted you. A very commendable act of magnanimity. May I ask why you brought this young woman with you? She does not seem to be mentioned in any of these reports."

I explained that Ardis was a coworker of O'Keene's, and that she had interceded for him.

"Then it is you, Ms Dahl, who are really interested in securing this prisoner's release. Are you related to him?"

And so on.

At the conclusion of each interview we were told either that the matter was completely out of the hands of the person to whom we had just spent half an hour or an hour talking, that it was necessary to obtain a clearance from someone else, or that an additional deposition had to be made. About two o'clock we were sent to the other side of the river – into what my guidebooks insist is an entirely different jurisdiction – to visit a penal facility. There we were forced to look for Kreton among five hundred or so miserable prisoners, all of whom stank and had lice. Not finding him, we returned to the FED Building past the half-overturned and yet still brooding figure called the Seated Man, and the ruins and beggars of the Silent City, for another round of interrogations. By five, when we were told to leave, we were both exhausted, though Ardis seemed surprisingly hopeful. When I left her at the door of her building a few minutes ago, I asked her what they would do tonight without Kreton.

"Without Harry, you mean." She smiled. "The best we can, I suppose, if we must. At least Paul will have someone ready to stand in for him tonight."

We shall see how well it goes.

○

I have picked up this pen and replaced it on the table ten times at least. It seems very likely that I should destroy this journal instead of continuing with it, were I wise; but I have discovered a hiding place for it which I think will be secure.

When I came back from Ardis's apartment tonight there were only two candy eggs remaining. I am certain – absolutely certain – that three were left when I went to meet Ardis. I am almost equally sure that after I had finished making the entry in this book, I put it, as I always do, at the left side of the drawer. It was on the right side.

It is possible that all this is merely the doing of the maid who cleans the room. She might easily have supposed that a single candy egg would not be missed, and have shifted this book while cleaning the drawer, or peeped inside out of curiosity.

I will assume the worst, however. An agent sent to investigate my room might be equipped to photograph these pages – but he might not, and it is not likely that he himself would have a reading knowledge of Farsi. Now I have gone through the book and eliminated all the passages relating to my reason for visiting this leprous country. Before I leave this room tomorrow I will arrange indicators – hairs and other objects whose positions I shall carefully record – that will tell me if the room has been searched again.

Now I may as well set down the events of the evening, which were truly extraordinary enough.

I met Ardis as we had planned, and she directed me to a small restaurant not far from her apartment. We had no sooner seated ourselves than two heavy-looking men entered. At no time could I see plainly the face of either, but it appeared to me that one was the American I had met aboard the *Princess Fatimah* and that the other was the grain dealer I had so assiduously avoided there, Golam Gassem. It is impossible, I think, for my divine Ardis ever to look less than beautiful; but she came as near to it then as the jaws of nature permit – the blood drained from her face, her mouth opened slightly, and for a moment she appeared to be a lovely corpse. I began to ask what the trouble was, but before I could utter a word she touched my lips to silence me, and then, having some-what regained her composure, said, "They have not seen us. I am leaving now. Follow me as though we were finished eating." She stood, feigned to pat her lips with a napkin (so that the lower half of her face was hidden) and walked out into the street.

I followed her, and found her laughing not three doors away from the entrance to the restaurant. The change in her could not have been more startling if she had been released from an enchantment. "It is so funny," he said. "Though it wasn't then. Come on, we'd better go; you can feed me after the show."

I asked her what those men were to her.

"Friends," she said, still laughing.

"If they are friends, why were you so anxious that they not see you? Were you afraid they would make us late?" I knew that such a trivial explanation could not be true, but I wanted to leave her a means of evading the question if she did not want to confide in me.

She shook her head. "No, no. I didn't want either to think I did not trust him. I'll tell you more later, if you want to involve your-self in our little charade."

"With all my heart."

She smiled at that – that sun-drenched smile for which I would gladly have entered a lion pit. In a few more steps we were at the rear entrance to the theatre, and there was no time to say more. She opened the door, and I heard Kreton arguing with a woman I later learned was the wardrobe mistress. "You are free," I said, and he turned to look at me.

"Yes. Thanks to you, I think. And I do thank you."

Ardis gazed on him as though he were a child saved from drowning. "Poor Bobby. Was it very bad?"

"It was frightening, that's all. I was afraid I'd never get out. Do you know Terry is gone?"

She shook her head, and said, "What do you mean?" but I was certain – and here I am not exaggerating or colouring the facts, though I confess I have occasionally done so elsewhere in this chronicle – that she had known it before he spoke.

"He simply isn't here. Paul is running around like a lunatic. I hear you missed me last night."

"God, yes," Ardis said, and darted off too swiftly for me to follow.

Kreton took my arm. I expected him to apologise for having tried to rob me; but he said, "You've met her, I see."

"She persuaded me to drop the charges against you."

"Whatever it was you offered me – twenty rials? I'm morally entitled to it, but I won't claim it. Come and see me when you're ready for something more wholesome – and meanwhile, how do you like her?"

"That is something for me to tell her," I said, "not you."

Ardis returned as I spoke, bringing with her a balding black man with a moustache. "Paul, this is Nadan. His English is very good – not so British as most of them. He'll do, don't you think?"

"He'll have to – you're sure he'll do it?"

"He'll love it," Ardis said positively, and disappeared again.

It seemed that 'Terry' was the actor who played Mary Rose's husband and lover, Simon; and I – who had never acted in so much as a school play – was to be pressed into the part. It was about half an hour before curtain time, so I had all of fifty minutes to learn my lines before my entrance at the end of the first act.

Paul, the director, warned me that if my name were used, the audience would be hostile; and since the character (in the version of the play they were presenting) was supposed to be an American, they would see errors where none existed. A moment later, while I was still in frantic rehearsal, I heard him saying, "The part of Simon Blake will be taken by Ned Jefferson."

The act of stepping onto the stage for the first time was really the worst part of the entire affair. Fortunately I had the advantage of playing a nervous young man come to ask for the hand of his sweetheart, so that my shaky laughter and stammer became 'acting'.

My second scene – with Mary Rose and Cameron on the magic island – ought by rights to have been much more difficult than the first. I had had only the intermission in which to study my lines, and the scene called for pessimistic apprehension rather than mere anxiety. But all the speeches were short, and Paul had been able by that time to get them lettered on large sheets of paper, which he and the stage manager held up in the wings. Several times I was forced to extemporise, but though I forgot the playwright's words, I never lost my sense of the *trend* of the play, and was always able to contrive something to which Ardis and Cameron could adapt their replies.

In comparison to the first and second acts, my brief appearance in the third was a holiday; yet I have seldom been so exhausted as I was tonight when the stage darkened for Ardis's final confrontation with Kreton, and Cameron and I, and the middle-aged people who had played the Morelands, were able to creep away.

We had to remain in costume until we had taken our bows, and it was nearly midnight before Ardis and I got something to eat at the same small, dirty bar outside which Kreton had tried to rob me. Over the steaming plates she asked me if I had enjoyed acting, and I had to nod.

"I thought you would. Under all that solidity you're a very dramatic person, I think."

I admitted it was true, and tried to explain why I feel that what I call *the romance of life* is the only thing worth seeking. She did not understand me, and so I passed it off as the result of having been brought up on the *Shah Namah*, of which I found she had never heard.

We went to her apartment. I was determined to take her by force if necessary – not because I would have enjoyed brutalising her, but because I felt she would inevitably think my love far less than it was if I permitted her to put me off a second time. She showed me about her quarters (two small rooms in great disorder), then, after we had lifted into place the heavy bar that is the sigil of every American dwelling, put her arms about me. Her breath was fragrant with the arrack I had bought for her a few minutes before. I feel sure now that for the rest of my life that scent will recall this evening to me.

When we parted, I began to unloose the laces that closed her blouse, and she at once pinched out the candle. I pleaded that she was thus depriving me of half the joy I might have had of her love; but she would not permit me to relight it, and our caresses and the embraces of our couplings were exchanged in perfect darkness. I was in ecstasy. To have seen her, I would have blinded myself; yet nothing could have increased my delight.

When we separated for the last time, both spent utterly, and she left to wash, I sought for matches. First in the drawer of the unsteady little table beside the bed, then among the disorder of my own clothes, which I had dropped to the floor and we had kicked about. I found some eventually, but could not find the candle – Ardis, I think, had hidden it. I struck a match; but she had covered herself with a robe. I said, "Am I never to see you?"

"You will see me tomorrow. You're going to take me boating, and we'll picnic by the water, under the cherry trees. Tomorrow night the theatre will be closed for Easter, and you can take me to a party. But now you are going home, and I am going to go to sleep." When I was dressed and standing in her doorway, I asked her if she loved me; but she stopped my mouth with a kiss.

I have already written about the rest – returning to find two eggs instead of three, and this book moved. I will not write of that again. But I have just – between this paragraph and the last – read over what I wrote earlier tonight, and it seems to me that one sentence should have had more weight than I gave it: when I said that in my role as Simon I never lost the *trend* of the play.

What the fabled secret buried by the old Americans beneath their carved mountain may be I do not know; but I believe that if it is some key to the world of human life, it must be some form of that. Every great man, I am sure, consciously or not, in those terms or others, has grasped that secret – save that in the play that is our life we can grapple that trend and draw it to left or right if we have the will.

So I am doing now. If the taking of the egg was not significant, yet I will make it so – indeed I already have, when I infused one egg with the drug. If the scheme in which Ardis is entangled – with Golam Gassem and Mr Tallman if it be they – is not some affair of statecraft and dark treasure, yet I will make it so before the end. If our love is not a great love, destined to live forever in the hearts of the young and the mouths of the poets, it will be so before the end.

○

Once again I am here; and in all truth I am beginning to wonder if I do not write this journal only to read it. No man was ever happier than I am now – so happy, indeed, that I was sorely tempted not to taste either of the two eggs that remain. What if the drug, in place of hallucination, self-knowledge and euphoria, brings permanent and despairing madness? Yet I have eaten it nonetheless, swallowing the whole sweet lump in a few bites. I would rather risk whatever may come than think myself a coward. With equanimity I await the effects.

The fact is that I am too happy for all the Faustian determination I penned last night. (How odd that *Faust* will be the company's next production. Kreton will be Mephistopheles of course – Ardis said as much, and it would be certain in any case. Ardis herself will be Margaret. But who will play the Doctor?) Yet now, when all the teeth-gritting, table-pounding determination is gone, I know that I will carry out the essentials of the *plan* more surely than ever – with the ease, in fact, of an accomplished violinist sawing out some simple tune while his mind roves elsewhere. I have been looking at the ruins of the Jeff (as they call it), and it has turned my mind again to the fate of the old Americans. How often they, who chose their leaders for superficial appearances of strength, wisdom and resolution, must have elected them only because they were as fatigued as I was last night.

I had meant to buy a hamper of delicacies, and call for Ardis about one, but she came for me at eleven with a little basket already packed. We walked north along the bank of the channel until we reached the ruins of the old tomb to which I have already referred, and the nearly circular artificial lake the Americans call the Basin. It is rimmed with flowering trees – old and gnarled, but very beautiful in their robes of white blossom. For some little American coin we were given command of a bright blue boat with a sail twice or three times the size of my handkerchief, in which to dare the halcyon waters of the lake.

When we were well away from the people on shore, Ardis asked me, rather suddenly, if I intended to spend all my time in America here in Washington.

I told her that my original plan had been to stay here no more than a week, then make my way up the coast to Philadelphia and the other ancient cities before I returned home; but that now that I had met her I would stay here forever if she wished it.

"Haven't you ever wanted to see the interior? This strip of beach we live on is kept half alive by the ocean and the trade that crosses it; but a hundred miles inland lies the wreck of our entire civilisation, waiting to be plundered."

"Then why doesn't someone plunder it?" I asked.

"They do. A year never passes without someone bringing some great prize out – but it is so large . . ." I could see her looking beyond the lake and the fragrant trees. "So large that whole cities are lost in it. There was an arch of gold at the entrance to St. Louis

119

– no one knows what became of it. Denver, the Mile High City, was nested in silver mines; no one can find them now."

"Many of the old maps must still be in existence."

Ardis nodded slowly, and I sensed that she wanted to say more than she had. For a few seconds there was no sound but the water lapping against the side of the boat.

"I remember having seen some in the museum in Teheran – not only our maps, but some of your own from a hundred years ago."

"The courses of the rivers have changed," she said. "And when they have not, no one can be sure of it."

"Many buildings must still be standing, as they are here, in the Silent City."

"That was built of stone – more solidly than anything else in the country. But yes, some, many, are still there."

"Then it would be possible to fly in, land somewhere, and pillage them."

"There are many dangers, and so much rubble to look through that anyone might search for a lifetime and only scratch the surface."

I saw that talking of all this only made her unhappy, and tried to change the subject. "Didn't you say that I could escort you to a party tonight? What will that be like?"

"Nadan, I have to trust someone. You've never met my father, but he lives close to the hotel where you are staying, and has a shop where he sells old books and maps." (So I had visited the right house – almost – after all!) "When he was younger, he wanted to go into the interior. He made three or four trips, but never got farther than the Appalachian foothills. Eventually he married my mother and didn't feel any longer that he could take the risks . . ."

"I understand."

"The things he had sought to guide him to the wealth of the past became his stock in trade. Even today, people who live farther inland bring him old papers; he buys them and resells them. Some of those people are only a step better than the ones who dig up the cemeteries for the wedding rings of the dead women."

I recalled the rings I had bought in the shadow of the broken obelisk, and shuddered, though I do not believe Ardis observed it.

"I said that some of them were hardly better than the grave robbers. The truth is that some are worse – there are people in the interior who are no longer people. Our bodies are poisoned – you know that, don't you? All of us Americans. They have adapted – that's what Father says – but they are no longer human. He made his peace with them long ago, and he trades with them still."

"You don't have to tell me this."

"Yes I do – I must. Would you go into the interior, if I went with you? The government will try to stop us if they learn of it, and to confiscate anything we find."

I assured her with every oath I could remember that with her beside me I would cross the continent on foot if need be.

"I told you about my father. I said that he sells the maps and records they bring him. What I did not tell you is that he reads them first. He has never given up, you see, in his heart."

"He has made a discovery?" I asked.

"He's made many – hundreds. Bobby and I have used them. You remember those men in the restaurant? Bobby went to each of them with a map and some of the old letters. He's persuaded them to help finance an expedition into the interior, and made each of them believe that we'll help him cheat the other – that keeps them from combining to cheat us, you see."

"And you want me to go with you?" I was beside myself with joy.

"We weren't going to go at all – Bobby was going to take the money, and go to Baghdad or Marrakesh, and take me with him. But, Nadan," here she leaned forward, I remember, and took my hands in hers, "there really is a secret. There are many, but one better – more likely to be true, more likely to yield truly immense wealth than all the others. I know you would share fairly with me. We'll divide everything, and I'll go back to Teheran with you."

I know that I have never been more happy in my life than I was then, in that silly boat. We sat together in the stern, nearly sinking

121

it, under the combined shade of the tiny sail and Ardis's big straw hat, and kissed and stroked one another until we would have been pilloried a dozen times in Iran.

At last, when I could bear no more unconsummated love, we ate the sandwiches Ardis had brought, and drank some warmish, fruit-flavoured beverage, and returned to shore.

When I took her home a few minutes ago, I very strongly urged her to let me come upstairs with her; I was on fire for her, sick to impale her upon my own flesh and pour myself into her as some mad god before the coming of the Prophet might have poured his golden blood into the sea. She would not permit it – I think because she feared that her apartment could not be darkened enough to suit her modesty. I am determined that I will yet see her.

○

I have bathed and shaved to be ready for the party, and as there is still time I will insert here a description of the procession we passed on the way back from the lake. As you see, I have not yet completely abandoned the thought of a book of travels.

A very old man – I suppose a priest – carried a cross on a long pole, using it as a staff, and almost as a crutch. A much younger one, fat and sweating, walked backward before him swinging a smoking censer. Two robed boys carrying large candles preceded them, and they were followed by more robed children, singing, who fought with nudges and pinches when they felt the fat man was not watching them.

Like everyone else, I have seen this kind of thing done much better in Rome; but I was more affected by what I saw here. When the old priest was born, the greatness of America must have been a thing of such recent memory that few can have realised it had passed forever; and the entire procession – from the flickering candles in clear sunshine, to the dead leader lifted up, to his inattentive, bickering followers behind – seemed to me to incarnate the philosophy and the dilemma of these people. So I felt, at least, until I saw that they watched it as uncomprehendingly as they might if they themselves were only travellers abroad, and I realised that its ritualised plea for life renewed was more foreign to them than to me.

○

It is very late – three, my watch says.

I resolved again not to write in this book. To burn it or tear it to pieces, or to give it to some beggar; but now I am writing once again because I cannot sleep. The room reeks of my vomit, though I have thrown open the shutters and let in the night.

How could I have loved that? (And yet a few moments ago, when I tried to sleep, visions of Ellen pursued me back to wakefulness.)

The party was a masque, and Ardis had obtained a costume for me – a fantastic gilded armour from the wardrobe of the theatre. She wore the robes of an Egyptian princess, and a domino. At midnight we lifted our masks and kissed, and in my heart I swore that tonight the mask of darkness would be lifted too.

When we left, I carried with me the bottle we had brought, still nearly half full; and before she pinched out the candle I persuaded her to pour out a final drink for us to share when the first frenzy of our desire was past. She – it – did as I asked, and set it on the little table near the bed. A long time afterward, when we lay gasping side by side, I found my pistol with one groping hand and fired the beam into the wide-bellied glass. Instantly it filled with blue fire from the burning alcohol. Ardis screamed, and sprang up.

○

I ask myself now how I could have loved; but then, how could I in one week have come so near to loving this corpse-country? Its eagle is dead – Ardis is the proper symbol of its rule.

One hope, one very small hope remains. It is possible that what I saw tonight was only an illusion, induced by the egg. I know now that the thing I killed before Ardis's father's house was real,

123

and between this paragraph and the last I have eaten the last egg. If hallucinations now begin, I will know that what I saw by the light of the blazing arrack was in truth a thing with which I have lain, and in one way or another will see to it that I never return to corrupt the clean wombs of the women of our enduring race. I might seek to claim the miniatures of our heritage after all, and allow the guards to kill me – but what if I were to succeed? I am not fit to touch them. Perhaps the best end for me would be to travel alone into this maggot-riddled continent; in that way I will die at fit hands.

○

Later. Kreton is walking in the hall outside my door, and the tread of his twisted black shoes jars the building like an earthquake. I heard the word *police* as though it were thunder. My dead Ardis, very small and bright, has stepped out of the candle-flame, and there is a hairy face coming through the window.

○

The old woman closed the notebook. The younger woman, who had been reading over her shoulder, moved to the other side of the small table and seated herself on a cushion, her feet politely positioned so that the soles could not be seen. "He is alive then," she said.

The older woman remained silent, her grey head bowed over the notebook, which she held in both hands.

"He is certainly imprisoned, or ill; otherwise he would have been in touch with us." The younger woman paused, smoothing the fabric of her chador *with her right hand, while the left toyed with the gem simulator she wore on a thin chain. "It is possible that he has already tried, but his letters have miscarried."*

"You think this is his writing?" the older woman asked, opening the notebook at random. When the younger did not answer she added, "Perhaps. Perhaps."

Tourist Trade

STEPHEN DEDMAN

She wore skintights and shades and a jacket open all the way down, and walked as though she owned the whole city. Maybe she did, at that; everything else on Earth was for sale, so why not Manhattanland? She was human, too, at least originally; a Zhir might have chosen that tiny body, but it wouldn't walk like *that*, and it certainly wouldn't stroll into a blind alley. She must have had those legs since she was thirteen. I wondered what they were worth.

Seven muggers followed her into the alley before I could cross the street. I heard the first scream and the sound of something breaking a few seconds later. By the time I was in a position to see the show, there was a knife-slash across the woman's jacket and the first mugger was on all fours, his mouth and chin and moustache wet with blood. It was easy to guess what had happened; he'd been a little faster than she'd expected, but she'd managed to grab his wrist and disarm him and throw him face-first into a wall before he'd done any real damage. The others were already backing away when she hook-kicked the first in the ribs; he rolled with it, and scampered out of range, leaving his carpet-knife as a souvenir. The Guild doesn't pay them to be heroes.

I whistled, piercingly, and the pack turned around and stared at me: a moment later, they'd melted into the darkness so well that even I couldn't see them. I walked into the alley cautiously, bowing when I was a safe three metres from the woman.

"Who the fuck are you?" she growled.

"Edgar Allan Poe, at your service, my lady – "

"Cut the crap."

" – but you can call me Eddy."

She looked at me for a moment. Her night eyes must have been better than mine: probably infra-red. Zhir stardrive kills anything larger than a single cell; anyone who wants to travel between worlds has to have a braintape played into an android body. This one was obviously a combat model.

"Shouldn't you have a blackbird on your shoulder or something? What are you doing here?"

"I live here," I replied. "I'm one of the attractions; the city pays me to walk around, pose for holos for the tourists, give directions, that sort of thing. What about you?"

She laughed. "I'm from out of town. New Geneva. And I didn't need any help."

"No, probably not."

"So why did you butt in?"

"I knew you were outnumbered." I glanced pointedly at the rip in her jacket. "A lot of tourists underestimate the risks. Where are you going now?"

She picked up the knife, and pocketed it. "Are you a cop, too?"

I laughed. "I've been called a lot of things, but never that. I just thought you might need a guide. I know this city as well as anyone, the scum and the dregs and everything in between; whatever it is you want, my lady, I can show it to you."

She looked as though she was considering it, but then she shrugged. "No thanks. I have a map, and my grandparents used to live here."

"Some things aren't on any map."

"It's a good map."

"Things move," I warned her. "Some of them have to hide from the Zhir. And some of them you won't get into without a guide, someone they know and trust . . ."

"No thanks," she repeated. I shrugged, stepped aside, and then followed her along 42nd at what I hoped was a discreet distance, but maybe I misjudged it; she turned on her heel and confronted me after fifty metres.

"What do *you* want?"

I could have told her that I liked short women, but I didn't want to be found dying in a gutter. "I'm taking the subway."

"Isn't that a bit anachronistic?"

I shrugged. "No more than you are. Besides, no one cares about history any more – this is Manhattanland; it's a theme park, not a museum – and I'm sort of off duty. Going to Central Park?"

"What makes you think that?"

"You're looking for muggers to beat up, where else would you go?"

"Is that illegal or something?"

I laughed again. "Not here. You're a tourist; for you, nothing is illegal. Only expensive."

"How much would it cost me if I killed you?"

I grinned. "I'm not cheap; like I said, I'm one of the attractions. Nor am I easy, unless you have a gun." She didn't even blink; of *course* she had a gun. Good. "Of course, the Zhir might have other ideas about what is and isn't legal, if they knew what you did while you were here . . ."

She ignored that. "And the muggers are there? In Central Park?"

"If you know where to look; Central Park's pretty big, but a guide – "

"I thought you were off duty."

"This I do for a commission."

She turned her back on me and quickened her pace; short as she was, she was fast, and I probably couldn't have caught her if she hadn't stopped to look at a display of knives in a window. "What do you want?" she demanded, wearily.

"I think you're going to get hurt."

"What business is that of yours?"

"I get a commission from the hospital and the ambulance, too."

She reached out and grabbed me by the lapels of my greatcoat, lifting me half a metre off the ground. "It's cheaper than letting them loot your body," I added, mildly. "There's a real market for parts like yours."

hat if you get hurt, too?"

ı'm a landmark; I have immunity. Sort of like Virgil in the *erno*."

She put me down, shaking her head. "I guess I can't stop you."

I smiled. "You're a good guesser."

She looked around. Times Square was empty apart from the hookers and hustlers and rubberneckers. "What if I just beat the crap out of that pimp?"

"Not a very private place for a murder, and convincing the city that it was self-defence would probably cost you an arm and a leg. The city keeps half, his family gets the rest . . . buying all these witnesses would cost you even more."

"What about the subway?"

"Sorry, no. You want to play Bernie Goetz, you have to book ahead."

She stared, probably wondering whether or not I was serious, then sauntered down the graffiti-scrawled stairs into the subway. She stopped when she reached the gates, stared at her credcard, and looked around helplessly. I coughed quietly, and when she turned and drew her gun, I threw her a subway token. She caught it between two fingers.

"There haven't been any clerks down here for years," I said. "I could tell you where you could buy some . . ."

She glared, and then shrugged. "Okay, you've made your point. How much commission?"

○

The carriage was empty but for a stony-faced Guardian Angel and a bag lady coughing up her lungs. Most of the graffiti read 'ZHIR OUT!' "Were your grandparents mugged?" I asked.

She was silent for nearly a minute, then she nodded.

"But the Zhir took them to New Geneva and they lived happily ever after?"

"No. My grandmother and my father went to Covenant; my grandfather was stabbed to death near here for a few dollars."

"When was this?"

"1990."

Seventy-five years ago . . . I revised my estimate of her age sharply upwards. Of course, androids don't age. "And you've come here to avenge them?"

She didn't bother answering, but of course she had. Zhir may not believe in revenge or feuding, but we're less like the Zhir than they realise: for one thing, Zhir children are almost exactly like their parents, psychologically as well as physically, because Zhir pass on most of their memories with other genetic material and they don't seem to understand that we don't do the same. This woman's grandmother must have been virtuous enough by Zhir standards, or she wouldn't have passed a psycho-scan and gotten off Earth, but that didn't mean the woman sitting next to me was a saint.

She stared at the bag lady. "Is the air that bad here?"

"You don't need to breathe, either, do you? Yeah, it's that bad; we're still using the same sort of tech that we were when the Zhir arrived."

"Why?"

"No one on Earth invents anything any more. Why should they? The Zhir invented it all millennia ago, and it's a lot faster and just a little bit cheaper to buy it from them, even if they do jack up their prices when they deal with perverts like us."

"It's not that bad."

"The hell it's not. They won't let us have anything we could use to get offworld or use as a weapon against them. They won't sell us stunners, even for our cops, because it's easier to bullet-proof an android than it is to stunproof one. Their energy technology is right out – "

"Conversion is dangerous."

"We're still burning coal and oil and radioactives, and we're nearly out of *those*; you wouldn't believe how much power it takes just to heat the sewers so the alligators don't die, and the sky's too thick for any solar panels we can build to work worth a damn. If the Zhir won't sell us total conversion – and believe me, we'll buy their fail-safes as well, if we can – they must have tech that's centuries out of date that we could use."

She considered that for a moment, then shrugged. "Unfortunately, there's not much left on Earth that you can trade with them – "

"Tell me about it. We let them take too much when they first arrived, before we realised that they were going to give us fuck-all in exchange. They've taken cloning cells of all our animals for their zoos, they've looted our museums of everything they think has any value and the stuff we wouldn't sell at their price, they copied. Tourist trade is nearly all we have left."

"And you try to rob us."

"And the Zhir didn't rob us?" She snorted. "Sure, we'll take what you have if we can, but no one forced you to come here."

"Why did those guys follow me into that alley?"

"They knew you wanted to party – you wouldn't have gone down there otherwise – but they probably weren't sure what *sort* of party. A lot of tourists still come here looking for rough trade and hope the Zhir don't read their braintapes on their way home – they don't, do they?"

"I don't think so."

"None of your friends ever came to Earth before? Never went to Pornoland or Gangworld or Vegas or anything else the Zhir would execute you for if they knew about it?" She didn't answer. "You're taking a hell of a chance if – "

"Everybody I know who's been to Earth came back okay," she said, quietly. "I know the Zhir can read braintapes, but I don't think they ever do. Maybe they think it's bad manners or something, or maybe they really believe that we're like them, that any-one whose ancestors passed a psycho-scan simply wouldn't do anything – well, that the Zhir wouldn't like."

"I hope you're right. Anyway, they probably guessed that you wanted to fight, but like I said, a lot of tourists overestimate their chances, especially if they depend on their stunners. Someone who was really fast on the draw might get two or three muggers before the others reached him; it was just their bad luck that you knew how to fight. And a stunner costs as much on the black market as a Porsche with a tank of gas; it's worth taking a few risks for. Besides, they're another attraction, in their way; it wouldn't be Manhattanland without muggers. They even belong to the Extra's Guild, and they're really hard on scabs. But don't get me wrong; they'd kill you if they could, and smile while they did. Here's our stop."

○

The platform was lit by one flickering fluorescent light; all the others had burnt out or been stolen and were rarely replaced. I noticed Crazy Joe standing in the darkness, on his way home from his daily vigil at Lennon's shrine, and tried to sneak past him, but he noticed the girl and turned on me. "Alan! Hail quisling well met!" he cackled. "You still sucking scum?"

I feel sorry for the old fool, sometimes; I'd try explaining things to him, but he can't keep his mouth shut long enough to listen. "We all got to live, Joe."

"Yeah? Why?"

"'cause it pisses off the Zhir, I guess."

He stared at us, and then laughed. "Sharp. Very sharp. Careful you don't cut yourself with that one; it might have two edges."

I shrugged, and hustled the girl towards the exit. "You're a traitor to your kind, Alan," Joe said, almost kindly.

"I got a wife and kids, Joe. What's your boyfriend do for money?"

"*Fucking traitor!*" He spat at my feet; fortunately, he was too devout a Lennonist (and too broke) to carry a gun, and too cowardly to come at me without one.

"Nevermore," I replied, softly, and the girl and I kept walking until we were on Park Avenue.

"Is that your real name?" she asked, softly. "Alan?"

"Yeah."

She nodded. "I'm Lisa."

"Hi."

"Do you really have a wife and kids?"

"Yeah. The eldest, Nikki, is on Avalon, and we're trying to save enough to get the others offworld. We'd love to join her, but of course, we never will . . . and she's never come back here. I just hope she's not ashamed of us."

"What does your wife do?"

"Simone? She teaches martial arts. Used to be a dancer, when she was younger. You'd probably like each other."

We crossed the street in silence. "How did you get to be Edgar Allan Poe?"

"I was too short for King Kong and too hairy for Ed Koch."

"I'm serious."

"Okay. I look enough like him to pass, I'm literate in English and French, I'd read some of his stories, I was about the right age, and I'm not allergic to cats. Besides, my family's been in show business for a long time, like Poe's; my grandfather used to work in Disneyland, the original one, back when humans used to go there to look at androids." I smiled, but she didn't smile back.

There were probably lights in Central Park, once, but not in my lifetime. It wasn't as dangerous as it looked, but it was bad enough that even the muggers travelled in groups. Lisa walked in without hesitation. "The way that guy was talking . . . is that how most New Yorkers feel about us, really?"

"Most Earthers," I replied, nodding. "They hate you even more than they hate the Zhir . . . though most of us would do exactly the same as you did, if we were given the chance. Someone's following us."

"Yes, I know. Three of them." I shut up. "You're obviously pretty smart; why are you still on Earth?"

"Well, when I was a teenager, I slept with anyone who said yes in a language I understood. And I said yes to a few others. Most of them were women, but not all; one of them is now Crazy Joe's boyfriend, which is the *real* reason Joe hates me." Zhir mate for life, and they regard any other form of behaviour as unnatural and evil. "If I showed up for a psycho-scan, the Zhir'd have me killed."

"And your wife . . . ?"

I shrugged. Zhir hate parent-child incest even more than they hate homosexuality. Unfortunately, because they have no concept of rape, they execute the children as well as the parents. "So, yeah, most of us hate you, but some of us realise we depend on you too. You're the only hope we – "

I heard leaves rustling, and suddenly some idiot dropped out of a tree and landed a few feet in front of Lisa. She kicked him under the chin while he was trying to stand; he measured his length in the mud, and stayed there. Two guys rushed her, one from the right, one from the left; she grabbed the first and threw him into the second. Before they were back on their feet, I felt the muzzle of a gun stroking the back of my neck. I cleared my throat. "Nevermore," I intoned.

The gun pulled back slightly as another mugger appeared – at least two metres tall, and built like a weight-lifter, but slower than the others. The gunman swore, softly. "She with you?"

"No," replied Lisa, as she closed with the giant. The gunman sighed, and fired a burst at her head. I ducked, in case there were any ricochets. The impact knocked her down; she fell expertly, and rolled; the giant raised a foot to stomp on her, and she kicked his other leg out from beneath him. The giant fell; Lisa was back on her feet an instant later, and the machine-pistol fired again. Unfortunately, he missed, and she ran at him. I didn't see what happened, but the giant did; he threw up, and then scrambled back into the bushes. The other two muggers simply vanished.

Lisa re-appeared from behind me a moment later. She looked totally clean; I guess her clothes were friction-free or something. She handed me the gun, but I shook my head and kept my hands by my sides.

"You could sell it; it must be worth something . . ."

"No, thanks. We'd better get out of here."

"Why?"

"The shots. No one else is going to show up here, unless it's the cops."

She shrugged, threw the machine-pistol into the bushes, and

headed back to Park Avenue. I followed, being careful not to step in anyone. "What're you tagging along for?" she asked, looking up and down the street for a cab. "Haven't I paid you enough?"

"What're you going to do now?"

"What?"

"If you still want to fight someone, I know a place where they have fights every night. Choice of weapons, all comers, last one to walk out claims the pot."

She kept her back to me, but I could almost hear her thinking. "Or, if you're tired, I can get you into a snuff movie, an S&M club, or a dog-fight . . ."

She snorted. "I don't get tired. This place . . ."

"Yes?"

A cab appeared, and she flagged it down. "Where is it?"

"You won't get in without me."

The taxi chugged to a halt a few metres away. Lisa looked at her watch, and then nodded. "Okay. Where do we go?"

O

The cabbie dropped us outside McGuirk's Suicide Hall, and I waited until he was gone before taking Lisa around the corner: I wouldn't want *everyone* to be able to find the place.

There were no signs outside, but the stairwell walls were lined with ancient photos and pin-ups of big-breasted porno stars and strippers, left over from the days when it had been a girlie bar. Lisa raised an eyebrow at the collection, obviously amused. The bouncer at the door was only half a head taller than me, but his chest measurement rivalled that of many of the silicon-stuffed strippers, and his pin-striped suit looked as though it should have electronic locks. He held out a hand the size of a baseball mitt, coughed, and intoned, in Italian, " 'Abandon hope, all ye who enter by me.' "

"She's with me, Mike."

"Not with that gun, she isn't," he said, switching to English.

I shrugged, and turned back to Lisa. "He wants your stunner."

Lisa hesitated. The gun was worth a fortune, but she obviously wanted in; it was almost palpable. She looked up at Mike, and smiled. "Can I give it to him?"

I hate it when they trust me. Mike looked at me, slightly puzzled, then shrugged. "Yeah, I guess so."

"Okay." She reached into her pocket, and pulled out the stunner. It was disguised as a pink plastic .25 automatic with a laser sight; it even had a forged Chanel logo. I pocketed it, and Mike stood aside, holding the massive door open and waving Lisa in. As soon as she stepped in front of me, I put the stunner to her head and squeezed the trigger.

She collapsed immediately, without any time to look surprised. I held the beam on her head long enough to completely wipe her memory – it takes less than a minute – and then Mike picked her up and carried her in.

The braintaper we'd built probably didn't look like a Zhir model – it more than half-filled the room, and most of the parts came from Laser Shack – but it worked. And unlike the Zhir, we didn't destroy the originals: I'd played my braintape into an android a year ago, and this would be Simone's third. One of them must have gotten to Avalon and Nikki by now . . . unless Lisa was wrong and the Zhir *were* reading the braintapes and destroying the ones they considered wrong or tainted. Or maybe our tapes just didn't survive Zhir stardrive. Until Nikki returned to Earth or sent us a message, we had no way of knowing what had happened, so we could only continue trying . . .

I looked at Lisa, then pocketed her gun and walked away. Sometimes I wish I could explain to some of them. It's not revenge for stranding us here, it's just survival. They *are* our only hope. And none of them are innocents; we lure them here with rape and murder and give them every chance to turn back, we're no worse than they are . . .

Are we?

In the Bowl

JOHN VARLEY

Never buy anything at a second-hand organbank. And while I'm
handing out good advice, don't outfit yourself for a trip to Venus
until you *get* to Venus.

I wish I had waited. But while shopping around at Coprates a
few weeks before my vacation, I happened on this little shop and
was talked into an infraeye at a very good price. What I should
have asked myself was, what was an infraeye doing on Mars in
the first place?

Think about it. No one wears them on Mars. If you want to see at
night, it's much cheaper to buy a snooperscope. That way you can
take the damn thing off when the sun comes up. So this eye must
have come back with a tourist from Venus. And there's no telling
how long it sat there in the vat until this sweet-talking old guy gave
me his line about how it belonged to a nice little old schoolteacher
who never . . . ah, well. You've probably heard it before.

If only the damn thing had gone on the blink before I left
Venusburg. You know Venusburg: town of steamy swamps and
sleazy hotels where you can get mugged as you walk down the
public streets, lose a fortune at the gaming tables, buy any pleasure in the known universe, hunt the prehistoric monsters that
wallow in the fetid marshes that are just a swamp-buggy ride out
of town. You do? Then you should know that after hours – when
they turn all the holos off and the place reverts to an ordinary
cluster of silvery domes sitting in darkness and eight-hundred-
degree temperature and pressure enough to give you a sinus

headache just *thinking* about it, when they shut off all the tourist razzle-dazzle – it's no trouble to find your way to one of the rental agencies around the spaceport and get medicanical work done. They'll accept Martian money. Your Solar Express Card is honoured. Just walk right in, no waiting.

However . . .

I had caught the daily blimp out of Venusburg just hours after I touched down, happy as a clam, my infraeye working beautifully. By the time I landed in Cui-Cui town, I was having my first inklings of trouble. Barely enough to notice; just the faintest hazing in the right-side peripheral vision. I shrugged it off. I had only three hours in Cui-Cui before the blimp left for Last Chance. I wanted to look around. I had no intention of wasting my few hours in a bodyshop getting my eye fixed. If it was still acting up at Last Chance, then I'd see about it.

Cui-Cui was more to my liking than Venusburg. There was not such a cast-of-thousands feeling there. On the streets of Venusburg the chances are about ten to one against meeting a real human being; everyone else is a holo put there to spice up the image and help the streets look not quite so *empty*. I quickly tired of zoot-suited pimps that I could see right through trying to sell me boys and girls of all ages. What's the *point*? Just try to touch one of those beautiful people.

In Cui-Cui the ratio was closer to fifty-fifty. And the theme was not decadent corruption but struggling frontier. The streets were very convincing mud, and the wooden storefronts were tastefully done. I didn't care for the eight-legged dragons with eyestalks that constantly lumbered through the place, but I understand they are a memorial to the fellow who named the town. That's all right, but I doubt if he would have liked to have one of the damn things walk through him like a twelve-ton tank made of pixie dust.

I barely had time to get my feet 'wet' in the 'puddles' before the blimp was ready to go again. And the eye trouble had cleared up. So I was off to Last Chance.

I should have taken a cue from the name of the town. And I had every opportunity to do so. While there, I made my last purchase of supplies for the bush. I was going out where there wasn't an air station on every corner, and so I decided I could use a tagalong.

Maybe you've never seen one. They're modern science's answer to the backpack. Or maybe to the mule train, though in operation they remind you of the safari bearers in old movies, trudging stolidly along behind the White Hunter with bales of supplies on their heads. The thing is a pair of metal legs exactly as long as your legs, with equipment on the top and an umbilical cord attaching the contraption to your lower spine. What it does is provide you with the capability of living on the surface for four weeks instead of the five days you get from your Venus-lung.

The medico who sold me mine had me lying right there on his table with my back laid open so he could install the tubes that carry air from the tanks in the tagalong into my Venus-lung. It was a golden opportunity to ask him to check the eye. He probably would have, because while he was hooking me up he inspected and tested my lung and charged me nothing. He wanted to know where I bought it, and I told him Mars. He clucked and said it seemed all right. He warned me to never let the level of oxygen in the lung get too low, to always charge it up before I left a pressure dome, even if I was only going out for a few minutes. I assured him that I knew all that and would be careful. So he connected the nerves into a metal socket in the small of my back and plugged the tagalong into it. He tested it several ways and said the job was done.

And I didn't ask him to look at the eye. I just wasn't thinking about the eye then. I'd not even gone out on the surface yet, so I'd no real occasion to see it in action. Oh, things looked a little different, even in visible light. There were different colours and very few shadows, and the image I got out of the infraeye was fuzzier than the one from the other eye. I could close one eye, then the other, and see a real difference. But I wasn't thinking about it.

So I boarded the blimp the next day for the weekly scheduled flight to Lodestone, a company mining town close to the Fahrenheit Desert. Though how they were able to distinguish a desert from anything else on Venus was still a mystery to me. I was enraged to find that, though the blimp left half-loaded, I had to pay two fares: one for me and one for my tagalong. I thought briefly of carrying the damn thing in my lap but gave it up after a ten-minute experiment in the depot. It was full of sharp edges and poking angles, and the trip was going to be a long one. So I paid. But the extra expense had knocked a large hole in my budget.

From Cui-Cui the steps got closer together and harder to reach. Cui-Cui is two thousand kilometres from Venusburg, and it's another thousand to Lodestone. After that the passenger service is spotty. I did find out how Venusians defined a desert, though. A desert is a place not yet inhabited by human beings. So long as I was able to board a scheduled blimp, I wasn't there yet.

The blimps played out on me in a little place called Prosperity, population seventy-five humans and one otter. I thought the otter was a holo playing in the pool in the town square. The place didn't look prosperous enough to afford a real pool like that with real water. But it was. It was a transient town catering to prospectors. I understand that a town like that can vanish overnight if the prospectors move on. The owners of the shops just pack up and haul the whole thing away. The ratio of the things you see in a frontier town to what really is there is something like a hundred to one.

I learned with considerable relief that the only blimps I could catch out of Prosperity were headed in the direction I had come from. There was nothing at all going the other way. I was happy to hear that and felt it was only a matter of chartering a ride into the desert. Then my eye faded out entirely.

I remember feeling annoyed; no, more than annoyed. I was really angry. But I was still viewing it as a nuisance rather than a disaster. It was going to be a matter of some lost time and some wasted money.

I quickly learned otherwise. I asked the ticket seller (this was in a saloon-drugstore-arcade; there was no depot in Prosperity) where I could find someone who'd sell and install an infraeye. He laughed at me.

"Not out here you won't, brother," he said. "Never have had

anything like that out here. Used to be a medico in Ellsworth, three stops back on the local blimp, but she moved back to Venusburg a year ago. Nearest thing now is in Last Chance."

I was stunned. I knew I was heading out for the deadlands, but it had never occurred to me that any place would be lacking in something so basic as a medico. Why, you might as well not sell food or air as not sell medicanical services. People might actually *die* out here. I wondered if the planetary government knew about this disgusting situation.

Whether they did or not, I realised that an incensed letter to them would do me no good. I was in a bind. Adding quickly in my head, I soon discovered that the cost of flying back to Last Chance and buying a new eye would leave me without enough money to return to Prosperity and still make it back to Venusburg. My entire vacation was about to be ruined just because I tried to cut some corners buying a used eye.

"What's the matter with the eye?" the man asked me.

"Huh? Oh, I don't know. I mean, it's just stopped working. I'm blind in it, that's what's wrong." I grasped at a straw, seeing the way he was studying my eye. "Say, you don't know anything about it, do you?"

He shook his head and smiled ruefully at me. "Naw. Just a little here and there. I was thinking if it was the muscles that was giving you trouble, bad tracking or something like that – "

"No. No vision at all."

"Too bad. Sounds like a shot nerve to me. I wouldn't try to fool around with that. I'm just a tinkerer." He clucked his tongue sympathetically. "You want that ticket back to Last Chance?"

I didn't know what I wanted just then. I had planned this trip for two years. I almost bought the ticket, then thought what the hell. I was here, and I should at least look around before deciding what to do. Maybe there was someone here who could help me. I turned back to ask the clerk if he knew anyone, but he answered before I got it out.

"I don't want to raise your hopes too much," he said, rubbing his chin with a broad hand. "Like I say, it's not for sure, but – "

"Yes, what is it?"

"Well, there's a kid lives around here who's pretty crazy about medico stuff. Always tinkering around, doing odd jobs for people, fixing herself up; you know the type. The trouble is she's pretty loose in her ways. You might end up worse when she's through with you than when you started."

"I don't see how," I said. "It's not working at all; what could she do to make it any worse?"

He shrugged. "It's your funeral. You can probably find her hanging around the square. If she's not there, check the bars. Her name's Ember. She's got a pet otter that's always with her. But you'll know her when you see her."

○

Finding Ember was no problem. I simply backtracked to the square and there she was, sitting on the stone rim of the fountain. She was trailing her toes in the water. Her otter was playing on a small waterslide, looking immensely pleased to have found the only open body of water within a thousand kilometres.

"Are you Ember?" I asked, sitting down beside her.

She looked up at me with that unsettling stare a Venusian can inflict on a foreigner. It comes of having one blue or brown eye and one that is all red, with no white. I looked that way myself, but I didn't have to look at it.

"What if I am?"

Her apparent age was about ten or eleven. Intuitively, I felt that it was probably very close to her actual age. Since she was supposed to be handy at medicanics, I could have been wrong. She had done some work on herself, but of course there was no way of telling how extensive it might have been. Mostly it seemed to be cosmetic. She had no hair on her head. She had replaced it with a peacock fan of feathers that kept falling into her eyes. Her scalp skin had been transplanted to her lower legs and forearms, and the hair there was long, blonde, and flowing. From the contours of her face I was sure that her skull was a mass of file marks and bone putty from where she'd fixed the understructure to reflect the face she wished to wear.

"I was told that you know a little medicanics. You see, this eye has – "

She snorted. "I don't know who would have told you *that*. I know a hell of a lot about medicine. I'm not just a backyard tinkerer. Come on, Malibu."

She started to get up, and the otter looked back and forth between us. I don't think he was ready to leave the pool.

"Wait a minute. I'm sorry if I hurt your feelings. Without knowing anything about you, I'll admit that you must know more about it than anyone else in town."

She sat back down, finally had to grin at me.

"So you're in a spot, right? It's me or no one. Let me guess: you're here on vacation, that's obvious. And either time or money is preventing you from going back to Last Chance for professional work." She looked me up and down. "I'd say it was money."

"You hit it. Will you help me?"

"That depends." She moved closer and squinted into my infraeye. She put her hands on my cheeks to hold my head steady. There was nowhere for me to took but her face. There were no scars visible on her; at least she was that good. Her upper canines were about five millimetres longer than the rest of her teeth.

"Hold still. Where'd you get this?"

"Mars."

"Thought so. It's a Gloom Piercer, made by Northern Bio. Cheap model; they peddle 'em mostly to tourists. Maybe ten, twelve years old."

"Is it the nerve? The guy I talked to – "

"Nope." She leaned back and resumed splashing her feet in the water. "Retina. The right side is detached, and it's flopped down over the fovea. Probably wasn't put on very tight in the first place. They don't make those things to last more than a year."

I sighed and slapped my knees with my palms. I stood up, held out my hand to her.

"Well, I guess that's that. Thanks for your help."

She was surprised. "Where you going?"

"Back to Last Chance, then to Mars to sue a certain organbank. There are laws for this sort of thing on Mars."

"Here, too. But why go back? I'll fix it for you."

○

We were in her workshop, which doubled as her bedroom and kitchen. It was just a simple dome without a single holo. It was refreshing after the ranch-style houses that seemed to be the rage in Prosperity. I don't wish to sound chauvinistic, and I realise that Venusians need some sort of visual stimulation, living as they do in a cloud-covered desert. Still, the emphasis on illusion there was never to my liking. Ember lived next door to a man who lived in a perfect replica of the palace at Versailles. She told me that when he shut his holo generator off his *real* possessions would have fit in a knapsack. Including the holo generator.

"What brings you to Venus?"

"Tourism."

She looked at me out of the corner of her eye as she swabbed my face with nerve deadener. I was stretched out on the floor, since there was no furniture in the room except a few work tables.

"All right. But we don't get many tourists this far out. If it's none of my business, just say so."

"It's none of your business."

She sat up. "Fine. Fix your own eye." She waited with a half-smile on her face. I eventually had to smile, too. She went back to work, selecting a spoon-shaped tool from a haphazard pile at her knees.

"I'm an amateur geologist. Rock hound, actually. I work in an office, and weekends I get out in the country and hike around. The rocks are an excuse to get me out there, I guess."

She popped the eye out of its socket and reached in with one finger to deftly unhook the metal connection along the optic nerve. She held the eyeball up to the light and peered into the lens.

"You can get up now. Pour some of this stuff into the socket and squint down on it." I did as she asked and followed her to the workbench.

She sat on a stool and examined the eye more closely. Then she stuck a syringe into it and drained out the aqueous humour, leaving the orb looking like a turtle egg that's dried in the sun. She sliced it open and started probing carefully. The long hairs on her forearms kept getting in the way. So she paused and tied them back with rubber bands.

"Rock hound," she mused. "You must be here to get a look at the blast jewels."

"Right. Like I said, I'm strictly a small-time geologist. But I read about them and saw one once in a jeweller's shop on Phobos. So I saved up and came to Venus to try and find one of my own."

"That should be no problem. Easiest gems to find in the known universe. Too bad. People out here were hoping they could get rich off them." She shrugged. "Not that there's not some money to be made off them. Just not the fortune everybody was hoping for. Funny; they're as rare as diamonds used to be, and to make it even better, they don't duplicate in the lab the way diamonds do. Oh, I guess they could make 'em, but it's way too much trouble." She was using a tiny device to staple the detached retina back onto the rear surface of the eye.

"Go on."

"Huh?"

"Why can't they make them in the lab?"

She laughed. "You *are* an amateur geologist. Like I said, they could, but it'd cost too much. They're a blend of a lot of different elements. A lot of aluminium, I think. That's what makes rubies red, right?"

"Yes."

"It's the other impurities that make them so pretty. And you have to make them in high pressure and heat, and they're so unstable that they usually blow before you've got the right mix. So it's cheaper to go out and pick 'em up."

"And the only place to pick them up is in the middle of the Fahrenheit Desert."

145

"Right." She seemed to be finished with her stapling. She straightened up to survey her work with a critical eye. She frowned, then sealed up the incision she had made and pumped the liquid back in. She mounted it in a calliper and aimed a laser at it, then shook her head when she read some figures on a read-out by the laser.

"It's working," she said. "But you really got a lemon. The iris is out of true. It's an ellipse, about point two four eccentric. It's going to get worse. See that brown discolouration on the left side? That's progressive decay in the muscle tissue, poisons accumulating in it. And you're a dead cinch for cataracts in about four months."

I couldn't see what she was talking about, but I pursed my lips as if I did.

"But will it last that long?"

She smirked at me. "Are you looking for a six-month warranty? Sorry, I'm not a member of the VMA. But if it isn't legally binding, I guess I'd feel safe in saying it ought to last that long. Maybe."

"You sure go out on a limb, don't you?"

"It's good practice. We future medicos must always be on the alert for malpractice suits. Lean over here and I'll put it in."

"What I was wondering," I said, as she hooked it up and eased it back into the socket, "is whether I'd be safe going out in the desert for four weeks with this eye."

"No," she said promptly, and I felt a great weight of disappointment. "Nor with any eye," she quickly added. "Not if you're going alone."

"I see. But you think the eye would hold up?"

"Oh, sure. But you wouldn't. That's why you're going to take me up on my astounding offer and let me be your guide through the desert."

I snorted. "You think so? Sorry, this is going to be a solo expedition. I planned it that way from the first. That's what I go out rock hunting for in the first place: to be alone." I dug my credit meter out of my pouch. "Now, how much do I owe you?"

She wasn't listening but was resting her chin on her palm and looking wistful.

"He goes out so he can be alone, did you hear that, Malibu?" The otter looked up at her from his place on the floor. "Now take me, for instance. Me, I know what being alone is all about. It's the crowds and big cities I crave. Right, old buddy?" The otter kept looking at her, obviously ready to agree to anything.

"I suppose so," I said. "Would a hundred be all right?" That was about half what a registered medico would have charged me, but like I said, I was running short.

"You're not going to let me be your guide? Final word?"

"No. Final. Listen, it's not you, it's just – "

"I know. You want to be alone. No charge. Come on, Malibu." She got up and headed for the door. Then she turned around.

"I'll be seeing you," she said, and winked at me.

○

It didn't take me too long to understand what the wink had been all about. I can see the obvious on the third or fourth go-around.

The fact was that Prosperity was considerably bemused to have a tourist in its midst. There wasn't a rental agency or hotel in the entire town. I had thought of that but hadn't figured it would be too hard to find someone willing to rent his private skycycle if the price was right. I'd been saving out a large chunk of cash for the purpose of meeting extortionate demands in that department. I felt sure the locals would be only too willing to soak a tourist.

But they weren't taking. Just about everyone had a skycycle, and absolutely everyone who had one was uninterested in renting it. They were a necessity to anyone who worked out of town, which everyone did, and they were hard to get. Freight schedules were as spotty as the passenger service. And every person who turned me down had a helpful suggestion to make. As I say, after the fourth or fifth such suggestion I found myself back in the town square. She was sitting just as she had been the first time, trailing her feet in the water. Malibu never seemed to tire of the waterslide.

"Yes," she said, without looking up. "It so happens that I *do* have a skycycle for rent."

I was exasperated, but I had to cover it up. She had me over the proverbial barrel.

"Do you always hang around here?" I asked. "People tell me to see you about a skycycle and tell me to look here, almost like you and this fountain are a hyphenated word. What else do you do?"

She fixed me with a haughty glare. "I repair eyes for dumb tourists. I also do body work for everyone in town at only twice what it would cost them in Last Chance. And I do it damn well, too, though those rubes'd be the last to admit it. No doubt Mr Lamara at the ticket station told you scandalous lies about my skills. They resent it because I'm taking advantage of the cost and time it would take them to get to Last Chance and pay merely inflated prices, instead of the outrageous ones I charge them."

I had to smile, though I was sure I was about to become the object of some outrageous prices myself. She was a shrewd operator.

"How old are you?" I found myself asking, then almost bit my tongue. The last thing a proud and independent child likes to discuss is age. But she surprised me.

"In mere chronological time, eleven Earth years. That's just over six of your years. In real, internal time, of course, I'm ageless."

"Of course. Now about that cycle . . ."

"Of course. But I evaded your earlier question. What I do besides sit here is irrelevant, because while sitting here I am engaged in contemplating eternity. I'm diving into my navel, hoping to learn the true depth of the womb. In short, I'm doing my yoga exercises." She looked thoughtfully out over the water to her pet. "Besides, it's the only pool in a thousand kilometres." She grinned at me and dived flat over the water. She cut it like a knife blade and torpedoed out to her otter, who set up a happy racket of barks.

When she surfaced near the middle of the pool, out by the jets and falls, I called to her.

"What about the cycle?"

She cupped her ear, though she was only about fifteen metres away.

"*I said what about the cycle?*"

"I can't hear you," she mouthed. "You'll have to come out here."

I stepped into the pool, grumbling to myself. I could see that her price included more than just money.

"I can't swim," I warned.

"Don't worry, it won't get much deeper than that." It was up to my chest. I sloshed out until I was on tiptoe, then grabbed at a jutting curlicue on the fountain. I hauled myself up and sat on the wet Venusian marble with water trickling down my legs.

Ember was sitting at the bottom of the waterslide, thrashing her feet in the water. She was leaning flat against the smooth rock. The water that sheeted over the rock made a bow wave at the crown of her head. Beads of water ran off her head feathers. Once again she made me smile. If charm could be sold, she could have been wealthy. What am I talking about? Nobody ever sells anything *but* charm, in one way or another. I got a grip on myself before she tried to sell me the north and south poles. In no time at all I was able to see her as an avaricious, cunning little guttersnipe again.

"One billion Solar Marks per hour, not a penny less," she said from that sweet little mouth.

There was no point in negotiating from an offer like that. "You brought me out here to hear *that*? I'm really disappointed in you. I didn't take you for a tease, I really didn't. I thought we could do business. I – "

"Well, if that offer isn't satisfactory, try this one. Free of charge, except for oxygen and food and water." She waited, threshing the water with her feet.

Of course there would be some teeth in that. In an intuitive leap of truly cosmic scale, a surmise worthy of an Einstein, I saw the string. She saw me make that leap, knew I didn't like where I had landed, and her teeth flashed at me. So once again, and not for the last time, I had to either strangle her or smile at her. I smiled. I don't know how, but she had this knack of making her opponents like her even as she screwed them.

"Are you a believer in love at first sight?" I asked her, hoping to throw her off guard. Not a chance.

"Maudlin wishful thinking, at best," she said. "You have *not* bowled me over, Mister – "

"Kiku."

"Nice. Martian name?"

"I suppose so. I never really thought of it. I'm not rich, Ember."

"Certainly not. You wouldn't have put yourself in my hands if you were."

"Then why are you so attracted to me? Why are you so determined to go with me, when all I want from you is to rent your cycle? If I was that charming, I would have noticed it by now."

"Oh, I don't know," she said, with one eyebrow climbing up her forehead. "There's *something* about you that I find absolutely fascinating. Irresistible, even." She pretended to swoon.

"Want to tell me what it is?"

She shook her head. "Let that be my little secret for now."

I was beginning to suspect she was attracted to me by the shape of my neck – so she could sink her teeth into it and drain my blood. I decided to let it lie. Maybe she'd tell me more in the days ahead. Because it looked like there would be days together, many of them.

"When can you be ready to leave?"

"I packed right after I fixed your eye. Let's get going."

○

Venus is spooky. I thought and thought, and that's the best way I can describe it.

It's spooky because of the way you see it. Your right eye – the one that sees what's called visible light – shows you only a small circle of light that's illuminated by your hand torch. Occasionally there's a glowing spot of molten metal in the distance, but it's far too dim to see by. Your infraeye pierces those shadows and gives you a blurry picture of what lies outside the torchlight, but I would have almost rather been blind.

There's no good way to describe how this dichotomy affects your mind. One eye tells you that everything beyond a certain point is shadowy, while the other shows you what's in those shadows. Ember says that after a while your brain can blend the two pictures as easily as it does for binocular vision. I never reached that point. The whole time I was there I was trying to reconcile the two pictures.

I don't like standing in the bottom of a bowl a thousand kilometres wide. That's what you see. No matter how high you climb or how far you go, you're still standing in the bottom of that bowl. It has something to do with the bending of the light rays by the thick atmosphere, if I understand Ember correctly.

Then there's the sun. When I was there it was nighttime, which means that the sun was a squashed ellipse hanging just above the horizon in the east, where it had set weeks and weeks ago. Don't ask me to explain it. All I know is that the sun never sets on Venus. Never, no matter where you are. It just gets flatter and flatter and wider and wider until it oozes around to the north or south, depending on where you are, becoming a flat, bright line of light until it begins pulling itself back together in the west, where it's going to rise in a few weeks.

Ember says that at the equator it becomes a complete circle for a split second when it's actually directly underfoot. Like the lights of a terrific stadium. All this happens up at the rim of the bowl you're standing in, about ten degrees above the theoretical horizon. It's another refraction effect.

You don't see it in your left eye. Like I said, the clouds keep out virtually all of the visible light. It's in your right eye. The colour is what I got to think of as infrablue.

It's quiet. You begin to miss the sound of your own breathing, and if you think about that too much, you begin to wonder why you *aren't* breathing. You know, of course, except the hindbrain, which never likes it at all. It doesn't matter to the autonomic nervous system that your Venus-lung is dribbling oxygen directly into your bloodstream; those circuits aren't made to understand things; they are primitive and very wary of improvements. So I was plagued by a feeling of suffocation, which was my medulla getting even with me, I guess.

I was also pretty nervous about the temperature and pressure. Silly, I know. Mars would kill me just as dead without a suit, and do it more slowly and painfully into the bargain. If my suit failed here, I doubt if I'd have felt anything. It was just the thought of that incredible pressure being held one millimetre away from my fragile skin by a force field that, physically speaking, isn't even there. Or so Ember told me. She might have been trying to get my goat. I mean, lines of magnetic forces aren't tangible, but they're there, aren't they?

I kept my mind off it. Ember was there and she knew about such things.

What she couldn't adequately explain to me was why a sky-cycle didn't have a motor. I thought about that a lot, sitting on the saddle and pedalling my ass off with nothing to look at but Ember's silver-plated buttocks.

She had a tandem cycle, which meant four seats; two for us and two for our tagalongs. I sat behind Ember, and the tagalongs sat in two seats off to our right. Since they aped our leg movements with exactly the same force we applied, what we had was a four-human-power cycle.

"I can't figure out for the life of me," I said on our first day out, "what would have been so hard about mounting an engine on this thing and using some of the surplus power from our packs."

"Nothing hard about it, lazy," she said, without turning around. "Take my advice as a fledgling medico; this is much better for you. If you *use* the muscles you're wearing, they'll last you a lot longer. It makes you feel healthier and keeps you out of the clutches of money-grubbing medicos. I *know*. Half my work is excising fat from flabby behinds and digging varicose veins out of legs. Even out here, people don't get more than twenty years' use of their legs before they're ready for a trade-in. That's pure waste."

"I think I should have had a trade-in before we left. I'm about done in. Can't we call it a day?"

She tut-tutted, but touched a control and began spilling hot gas from the balloon over our heads. The steering vanes sticking out at our sides tilted, and we started a slow spiral to the ground.

We landed at the bottom of the bowl – my first experience with it, since all my other views of Venus had been from the air where it isn't so noticeable. I stood looking at it and scratching my head while Ember turned on the tent and turned off the balloon.

The Venusians use null fields for just about everything. Rather than try to cope with a technology that must stand up to the temperature and pressure extremes, they coat everything in a null field and let it go at that. The balloon on the cycle was nothing but a standard globular field with a discontinuity at the bottom for the air heater. The cycle body was protected with the same kind of field that Ember and I wore, the kind that follows the surface at a set distance. The tent was a hemispherical field with a flat floor.

It simplified a lot of things. Air locks, for instance. What we did was to simply walk into the tent. Our suit fields vanished as they were absorbed into the tent field. To leave, one need merely walk through the wall again, and the suit would form around you.

I plopped myself down on the floor and tried to turn my hand torch off. To my surprise, I found that it wasn't built to turn off. Ember turned on the campfire and noticed my puzzlement.

"Yes, it is wasteful," she conceded. "There's something in a Venusian that hates to turn out a light. You won't find a light switch on the entire planet. You may not believe this, but I was shocked silly a few years ago when I heard about light switches. The idea had never occurred to me. See what a provincial I am?"

That didn't sound like her. I searched her face for clues to what had brought on such a statement, but I could find nothing. She was sitting in front of the campfire with Malibu on her lap, preening her feathers.

I gestured at the fire, which was a beautifully executed holo of snapping, crackling logs with a heater concealed in the centre of it.

"Isn't that an uncharacteristic touch? Why didn't you bring a fancy house, like the ones in town?"

"I like the fire. I don't like phoney houses."

"Why not?"

She shrugged. She was thinking of other things. I tried another tack.

"Does your mother mind you going into the desert with strangers?"

She shot me a look I couldn't read.

"How should I know? I don't live with her. I'm emancipated. I think she's in Venusburg." I had obviously touched a tender area, so I went cautiously.

"Personality conflicts?"

She shrugged again, not wanting to get into it.

"No. Well, yes, in a way. She wouldn't emigrate from Venus. I wanted to leave and she wanted to stay. Our interests didn't coincide. So we went our own ways. I'm working my way toward passage off-planet."

"How close are you?"

"Closer than you might think." She seemed to be weighing something in her mind, sizing me up. I could hear the gears grind and the cash register bells cling as she studied my face. Then I felt the charm start up again, like the flicking of one of those nonexistent light switches.

"See, I'm as close as I've ever been to getting off Venus. In a few weeks, I'll be there. As soon as we get back with some blast jewels. Because you're going to adopt me."

I think I was getting used to her. I wasn't rocked by that, though it was nothing like what I had expected to hear. I had been thinking vaguely along the lines of blast jewels. She picks some up along with me, sells them, and buys a ticket off-planet, right?

That was silly, of course. She didn't need *me* to get jewels. She was the guide, not I, and it was her cycle. She could get as many jewels as she wanted, and probably already had. This scheme had to have something to do with me, personally, as I had known back in town and forgotten about. There was something she wanted from me.

"That's why you had to go with me? That's the fatal attraction? I don't understand."

"Your passport. I'm in love with your passport. On the blank labelled 'citizenship' it says 'Mars'. Under age it says, oh . . . about seventy-three?" She was within a year, though I keep my appearance at about thirty.

"So, my dear Kiku, you are visiting a planet which is groping its way into the Stone Age. A medieval planet, Mr Kiku, that sets the age of majority at thirteen, a capricious and arbitrary figure, as I'm sure you'll agree. The laws of this planet state that certain rights of free citizens are withheld from minor citizens. Among these are liberty, the pursuit of happiness, and the ability *to get out of the goddam place!*" She startled me with her fury, coming so hard on the heels of her usual amusing glibness. Her fists were clenched. Malibu, sitting in her lap, looked sadly up at his friend, then over to me.

She quickly brightened and bounced up to prepare dinner. She would not respond to my questions. The subject was closed for the day.

○

I was ready to turn back the next day. Have you ever had stiff legs? Probably not; if you go in for that sort of thing – heavy physical labour – you're probably one of those health nuts and keep yourself in shape. I wasn't in shape, and I thought I'd die. For a panicky moment I thought I *was* dying.

Luckily, Ember had anticipated it. She knew I was a desk jockey, and she knew how pitifully underconditioned Martians tend to be. Added to the sedentary life-styles of most modern people, we Martians come off even worse than the majority because Mars's gravity never gives us much of a challenge no matter how hard we try. My leg muscles were like soft noodles.

She gave me an old-fashioned massage and a newfangled injection that killed off the accumulated poisons. In an hour I began to take a flickering interest in the trip. So she loaded me onto the cycle and we started off on another leg of the journey.

There's no way to measure the passage of time. The sun gets flatter and wider, but it's much too slow to see. Sometime that day we passed a tributary of the Reynoldswrap River. It showed up as a bright line in my right eye, as a crusted, sluggish semiglacier in my left. Molten aluminium, I was told. Malibu knew what it was, and barked plaintively for us to stop so he could go for a slide. Ember wouldn't let him.

You can't get lost on Venus, not if you can still see. The river had been visible since we left Prosperity, though I hadn't known what it was. We could still see the town behind us and the mountain range in front of us and even the desert. It was a little way up the slope of the bowl. Ember said that meant it was still about three days' journey away from us. It takes practice to judge distance. Ember kept trying to point out Venusburg, which was several thousand kilometres behind us. She said it was easily visible as a tiny point on a clear day. I never spotted it.

We talked a lot as we pedalled. There was nothing else to do and, besides, she was fun to talk to. She told me more of her plan for getting off Venus and filled my head with her naive ideas of what other planets were like.

It was a subtle selling campaign. We started off with her being the advocate for her crazy plan. At some point it evolved into an assumption. She took it as settled that I would adopt her and take her to Mars with me. I half believed it myself.

O

On the fourth day I began to notice that the bowl was getting higher in front of us. I didn't know what was causing it until Ember called a halt and we hung there in the air. We were facing a solid line of rock that sloped gradually upward to a point about fifty metres higher than we were.

"What's the matter?" I asked, glad of the rest.

"The mountains are higher," she said matter-of-factly. "Let's turn to the right and see if we can find a pass."

"Higher? What are you talking about?"

"Higher. You know, taller, sticking up more than they did the last time I was around, of slightly greater magnitude in elevation, bigger than – "

"I know the definition of higher," I said. "But why? Are you sure?"

"Of course I'm sure. The air heater for the balloon is going flat-out; we're as high as we can go. The last time I came through here, it was plenty to get me across. But not today."

"Why?"

"Condensation. The topography can vary quite a bit here. Certain metals and rocks are molten on Venus. They boil off on a hot day, and they can condense on the mountaintops where it's cooler. Then they melt when it warms and flow back to the valleys."

"You mean you brought me here in the middle of winter?"

She threw me a withering glance.

"You're the one who booked passage for winter. Besides, it's night, and it's not even midnight yet. I hadn't thought the mountains would be this high for another week."

"Can't we get around?"

She surveyed the slope critically.

"There's a permanent pass about five hundred kilometres to the east. But that would take us another week. Do you want to?"

"What's the alternative?"

"Parking the cycle here and going on foot. The desert is just over this range. With any luck we'll see our first jewels today."

I was realising that I knew far too little about Venus to make a good decision. I had finally admitted to myself that I was lucky to have Ember along to keep me out of trouble.

"We'll do what you think best."

"All right. Turn hard left and we'll park."

We tethered the cycle by a long tungsten-alloy rope. The reason for that, I learned, was to prevent it from being buried in case there was more condensation while we were gone. It floated at the end of the cable with its heaters going full blast. And we started up the mountain.

Fifty metres doesn't sound like much. And it's not, on level ground. Try it sometime on a seventy-five degree slope. Luckily for us, Ember had come prepared with alpine equipment. She sank pitons here and there and kept us together with ropes and pulleys. I followed her lead, staying slightly behind her tagalong. It was uncanny how that thing followed her up, placing its feet in precisely the spots where she had stepped. Behind me, my tagalong was doing the same thing. Then there was Malibu, almost running along, racing back to see how we were doing, going to the top and chattering about what was on the other side.

I don't suppose it would have been much for a mountain climber. Personally I'd have preferred to slide on down the mountainside and call it quits. I would have, but Ember just kept going up. I don't think I've ever been so tired as the moment when we reached the top and stood looking over the desert.

Ember pointed ahead of us.

"There's one of the jewels going off now," she said.

"Where?" I asked, barely interested. I could see nothing.

"You missed it. It's down lower. They don't form up this high. Don't worry, you'll see more by and by."

And down we went. This wasn't too hard. Ember set the example by sitting down in a smooth place and letting go. Malibu was close behind her, squealing happily as he bounced and rolled down the slippery rock face. I saw Ember hit a bump and go flying in the air to come down on her head. Her suit was already stiffened. She continued to bounce her way down, frozen in a sitting position.

I followed them down in the same way. I didn't much care for the idea of bouncing around like that, but I cared even less for a slow, painful descent. It wasn't too bad. You don't feel much after your suit freezes in impact mode. It expands slightly away from your skin and becomes harder than metal, cushioning you from anything but the most severe blows that could bounce your brain against your skull and give you internal injuries. We never got going nearly fast enough for that.

Ember helped me up at the bottom after my suit unfroze. She looked like she had enjoyed the ride. I hadn't. One bounce seemed to have impacted my back slightly. I didn't tell her about it, but just started off after her, feeling a pain with each step.

"Where on Mars do you live?" she asked brightly.

"Uh? Oh, at Coprates. That's on the northern slope of the Canyon."

"Yes, I know. Tell me more about it. Where will we live? Do you have a surface apartment, or are you stuck down in the underground? I can hardly wait to see the place."

She was getting on my nerves. Maybe it was just the lower-back pain.

"What makes you think you're going with me?"

"But of course you're taking me back. You said, just – "

"I said nothing of the sort. If I had a recorder I could prove it to you. No, our conversations over the last days have been a series of monologues. You tell me what fun you're going to have when we get to Mars, and I just grunt something. That's because I haven't the heart, or haven't *had* the heart, to tell you what a hare-brained scheme you're talking about."

I think I had finally managed to drive a barb into her. At any rate, she didn't say anything for a while. She was realising that she had overextended herself and had been counting the spoils before the battle was won.

"What's hare-brained about it?" she said at last.

"Just everything."

"No, come on, tell me."

"What makes you think I want a daughter?"

She seemed relieved. "Oh, don't worry about that. I won't be any trouble. As soon as we land, you can file dissolution papers. I won't contest it. In fact, I can sign a binding agreement not to contest anything before you even adopt me. This is strictly a business arrangement, Kiku. You don't have to worry about being a mother to me. I don't need one. I'll – "

"What makes you think it's just a business arrangement to *me*?" I exploded. "Maybe I'm old-fashioned. Maybe I've got funny ideas. But I won't enter into an adoption of convenience. I've already had my one child, and I was a good parent. I won't adopt you just to get you to Mars. That's my final word."

She was studying my face. I think she decided I meant it.

"I can offer you twenty thousand Marks."

I swallowed hard.

"Where did you get that kind of money?"

"I told you I've been soaking the good people of Prosperity. What the hell is there for me to spend it on out here? I've been putting it away for an emergency like this. Up against an unfeeling Neanderthal with funny ideas about right and wrong, who – "

"That's enough of that." I'm ashamed to say that I was tempted. It's unpleasant to find that what you had thought of as moral scruples suddenly seem not quite so important in the face of a stack of money. But I was helped along by my backache and the nasty mood it had given me.

"You think you can buy me. Well, I'm not for sale. I think it's wrong."

"Well *damn* you, Kiku, damn you to hell." She stomped her foot hard on the ground, and her tagalong redoubled the gesture. She was going to go on damning me, but we were blasted by an explosion as her foot hit the ground.

It had been quiet before, as I said. There's no wind, no animals, hardly anything to make a sound on Venus. But when a sound gets going, watch out. That thick atmosphere is murder. I thought my head was going to come off. The sound waves battered against our suits, partially stiffening them. The only thing that saved us from deafness was the millimetre of low-pressure air between the suit field and our eardrums. It cushioned the shock enough that we were left with just a ringing in our ears.

"What was that?" I asked.

Ember sat down on the ground. She hung her head, uninterested in anything but her own disappointment.

"Blast jewel," she said. "Over that way." She pointed, and I could see a dull glowing spot about a kilometre off. There were dozens of smaller points of light – infralight – scattered around the spot.

"You mean you set it off just by stomping the ground?"

She shrugged. "They're unstable. They're full of nitroglycerine, as near as anyone can figure."

"Well, let's go pick up the pieces."

"Go ahead." She was going limp on me. And she stayed that way, no matter how I cajoled her. By the time I finally got her on her feet, the glowing spots were gone, cooled off. We'd never find them now. She wouldn't talk to me as we continued down into the valley. All the rest of the day we were accompanied by distant gunshots.

○

We didn't talk much the next day. She tried several times to reopen the negotiations, but I made it clear that my mind was made up. I pointed out to her that I had rented her cycle and services according to the terms she had set. Absolutely free, she had said, except for consumables, which I had paid for. There had been no mention of adoption. If there had, I assured her, I would have turned her down just as I was doing now. Maybe I even believed it.

That was during the short time, the morning after our argument, when it seemed like she was having no more to do with the trip. She just sat there in the tent while I made breakfast. When it came time to go, she pouted and said she wasn't going looking for blast jewels, that she'd just as soon stay right there or turn around.

After I pointed out our verbal contract, she reluctantly got up. She didn't like it, but honoured her word.

Hunting blast jewels proved to be a big anticlimax. I'd had visions of scouring the countryside for days. Then the exciting moment of finding one. Eureka! I'd have howled. The reality was nothing like that. Here's how you hunt blast jewels: you stomp down hard on the ground, wait a few seconds, then move on and stomp again. When you see and hear an explosion, you simply walk to where it occurred and pick them up. They're scattered all over, lit up in the infrared bands from the heat of the explosion. They might as well have had neon arrows flashing over them. Big adventure.

When we found one, we'd pick it up and pop it into a cooler mounted on our tagalongs. The jewels are formed by the pressure of the explosion, but certain parts of them are volatile at Venus temperatures. These elements will boil out and leave you with a greyish powder in about three hours if you don't cool them down. I don't know why they lasted as long as they did. They were considerably hotter than the air when we picked them up, so I thought they should have melted right away.

Ember said it was the impaction of the crystalline lattice that gave the jewels the temporary strength to outlast the temperature. Things behave differently in the temperature and pressure extremes of Venus. As they cooled off, the lattice was weakened and a progressive decay set in. That's why it was important to get them as soon as possible after the explosion to get unflawed gems.

We spent the whole day at that. Eventually we collected about ten kilos of gems, ranging from pea size up to a few the size of an apple.

I sat beside the campfire and examined them that night. Night by my watch, anyway. Another thing I was beginning to miss was the twenty-five-hour cycle of night and day. And while I was at it, moons. It would have cheered me up considerably to spot Deimos or Phobos that night. But the sun just squatted up there in the horizon, moving slowly to the north in preparation for its transition to the morning sky.

The jewels were beautiful, I'll say that much for them. They were a wine-red colour, tinged with brown. But when the light caught them right, there was no predicting what I might see. Most of the raw gems were coated with a dull substance that hid their full glory. I experimented with chipping some of them. What was left behind when I flaked off the patina was a slippery surface that sparkled even in candlelight. Ember showed me how to suspend them from a string and strike them. Then they would ring like tiny bells, and every once in a while one would shed all its imperfections and emerge as a perfect eight-sided equilateral.

I was cooking for myself that day. Ember had cooked from the first, but she no longer seemed interested in buttering me up.

"I hired on as a guide," she pointed out, with considerable venom. "Webster's defines guide as – "

"I know what a guide is."

" – and it says nothing about cooking. Will you marry me?"

"No." I wasn't even surprised.

"Same reasons?"

"Yes. I won't enter into an agreement like that lightly. Besides, you're too young."

"Legal age is twelve. I'll be twelve in one week."

"That's too young. On Mars you must be fourteen."

"What a dogmatist. You're not kidding, are you? Is it really fourteen?"

That's typical of her lack of knowledge of the place she was trying so hard to get to. I don't know where she got her ideas about Mars. I finally concluded that she made them up whole in her daydreams.

We ate the meal I prepared in silence, toying with our collection of jewels. I estimated that I had about a thousand Marks' worth of uncut stones. And I was getting tired of the Venusian bush. I figured on spending another day collecting, then heading back for the cycle. It would probably be a relief for both of us. Ember could start laying traps for the next stupid tourist to reach town, or even head for Venusburg and try in earnest.

When I thought of that, I wondered why she was still out here. If she had the money to pay the tremendous bribe she had offered me, why wasn't she in town where the tourists were as thick as flies? I was going to ask her that, but she came up to me and sat down very close.

"Would you like to make love?" she asked.

I'd had about enough inducements. I snorted, got up, and walked through the wall of the tent.

Once outside, I regretted it. My back was hurting something terrible, and I belatedly realised that my inflatable mattress would not go through the wall of the tent. If I got it through somehow, it would only burn up. But I couldn't back out after walking out like that. I felt committed. Maybe I couldn't think straight because of the backache; I don't know. Anyway, I picked out a soft-looking spot of ground and lay down.

I can't say it was all that soft.

○

I came awake in the haze of pain. I knew without trying that if I moved I'd get a knife in my back. Naturally I wasn't anxious to try.

My arm was lying on something soft. I moved my head – confirming my suspicions about the knife – and saw that it was Ember. She was asleep, lying on her back. Malibu was curled up in her arm.

She was a silver-plated doll, with her mouth open and a look of relaxed vulnerability on her face. I felt a smile growing on my lips, just like the ones she had coaxed out of me back in Prosperity. I wondered why I'd been treating her so bad. At least it seemed to me that morning that I'd been treating her bad. Sure, she'd used me and tricked me and seemed to want to use me again. But what had she hurt? Who was suffering for it? I couldn't think of anyone at the moment. I resolved to apologise to her when she woke up and try to start over again. Maybe we could even reach some sort of accommodation on this adoption business.

And while I was at it, maybe I could unbend enough to ask her to take a look at my back. I hadn't even mentioned it to her, probably for fear of getting deeper in her debt. I was sure she wouldn't have taken payment for it in cash. She preferred flesh.

I was about to awaken her, but I happened to glance on my

other side. There was something there. I almost didn't recognise it for what it was.

It was three metres away, growing from the cleft of two rocks. It was globular, half a metre across, and glowing a dull reddish colour. It looked like a soft gelatin.

It was a blast jewel, before the blast.

I was afraid to talk, then remembered that talking would not affect the atmosphere around me and could not set off the explosion. I had a radio transmitter in my throat and a receiver in my ear. That's how you talk on Venus; you subvocalise and people can hear you.

Moving very carefully, I reached over and gently touched Ember on the shoulder.

She came awake quietly, stretched, and started to get up.

"Don't move," I said, in what I hoped was a whisper. It's hard to do when you're subvocalising, but I wanted to impress on her that something was wrong.

She became alert, but didn't move.

"Look over to your right. Move very slowly. Don't scrape against the ground or anything. I don't know what to do."

She looked, said nothing.

"You're not alone, Kiku," she finally whispered. "This is one I never heard of."

"How did it happen?"

"It must have formed during the night. No one knows much about how they form or how long it takes. No one's ever been closer to one than about five hundred metres. They always explode before you can get that close. Even the vibrations from the prop of a cycle will set them off before you can get close enough to see them."

"So what do we do?"

She looked at me. It's hard to read expressions on a reflective face, but I think she was scared. I know I was.

"I'd say sit tight."

"How dangerous is this?"

"Brother. I don't know. There's going to be quite a bang when that monster goes off. Our suits will protect us from most of it. But it's going to lift us and accelerate us *very* fast. That kind of sharp acceleration can mess up your insides. I'd say a concussion at the very least."

I gulped. 'Then – "

"Just sit tight. I'm thinking."

So was I. I was frozen there with a hot knife somewhere in my back. I knew I'd have to squirm sometime.

The damn thing was moving.

I blinked, afraid to rub my eyes, and looked again. No, it wasn't. Not on the outside anyway. It was more like the movement you can see inside a living cell beneath a microscope. Internal flows, exchanges of fluids from here to there. I watched it and was hypnotised.

There were worlds in the jewel. There was ancient Barsoom of my childhood fairy tales; there was Middle Earth with brooding castles and sentient forests. The jewel was a window into something unimaginable, a place where there were no questions and no emotions but a vast awareness. It was dark and wet without menace. It was growing, and yet complete as it came into being. It was bigger than this ball of hot mud called Venus and had its roots down in the core of the planet. There was no corner of the universe that it did not reach.

It was aware of me. I felt it touch me and felt no surprise. It examined me in passing but was totally uninterested. I posed no questions for it, whatever it was. It already knew me and had always known me.

I felt an overpowering attraction. The thing was exerting no influence on me; the attraction was a yearning within me. I was reaching for a completion that the jewel possessed and I knew I could never have. Life would always be a series of mysteries for me. For the jewel, there was nothing but awareness. Awareness of everything.

I wrenched my eyes away at the last possible instant. I was covered in sweat, and I knew I'd look back in a moment. It was the most beautiful thing I will ever see.

166

"Kiku, listen to me."

"What?" I remembered Ember as from a huge distance.

"Listen. Wake up. Don't look at that thing."

"Ember, do you see anything? Do you feel something?"

"I see something. I . . . I don't want to talk about it. I can't talk about it. Wake up, Kiku, and don't look back."

I felt like I was already a pillar of salt; so why not look back? I knew that my life would never be quite like it had been. It was like some sort of involuntary religious conversion, like I knew what the universe was for all of a sudden. The universe was a beautiful silk-lined box for the display of the jewel I had just beheld.

"Kiku, that thing should already have gone off. We shouldn't be here. I moved when I woke up. I tried to sneak up on one before and got five hundred metres away from it. I set my foot down soft enough to walk on water and it blew. So this thing can't be here."

"That's nice," I said. "How do we cope with the fact that it *is* here?"

"All right, all right, it is here. But it must not be finished. It must not have enough nitro in it yet to blow up. Maybe we can get away."

"Listen," I said, looking at her with an act of will. "Maybe one of us can get away. Maybe both. But it's more important that you not be injured. If I'm hurt, you can maybe fix me up. If you're hurt, you'll probably die; and if we're both hurt, we're dead."

"Yeah. So?"

"So, I'm the closest to the jewel. You can start backing away from it first, and I'll follow you. I'll shield you from the worst of the blast, if it goes off. How does that sound?"

"Not too good." But she thought it over and could see no flaws in my reasoning. I think she didn't relish being the protected instead of the heroine. Childish, but natural. She proved her maturity by bowing to the inevitable.

"All right. I'll try to get ten metres from it. I'll let you know when I'm there, and you can move back. I think we can survive it at ten metres."

"Twenty."

"But . . . oh, all right. Twenty. Good luck, Kiku. I think I love you." She paused. "Uh, Kiku?"

"What is it? You should get moving. We don't know how long it'll stay stable."

"All right. But I have to say this. My offer last night, the one that got you so angry?"

"Yeah?"

"Well, it wasn't meant as a bribe. I mean, like the twenty thousand Marks. I just . . . well, I don't know much about that yet. I guess it was the wrong time?"

"Yeah, but don't worry about it. Just get moving."

She did, a centimetre at a time. It was lucky that neither of us had to worry about holding our breath. I think the tension would have been unbearable.

And I looked back. I couldn't help it. I was in the sanctuary of a cosmic church when I heard her calling me. I don't know what sort of power she used to reach me where I was. She was crying.

"Kiku, please listen to me."

"Huh? Oh, what is it?"

She sobbed in relief. "Oh, Christ, I've been calling you for an hour. *Please* come on. Over here, I'm back far enough."

My head was foggy. "Oh, Ember, there's no hurry. I want to look at it just another minute. Hang on."

"*No!* If you don't start moving right this minute, I'm coming back and I'll drag you out."

"You can't do . . . Oh. All right, I'm coming." I looked over at her sitting on her knees. Malibu was beside her. The little otter was staring in my direction. I looked at her and took a sliding step, scuttling on my back. My back was not something to think about.

I got two metres back, then three. I had to stop to rest. I looked at the jewel, then back at Ember. It was hard to tell which drew me more strongly. I must have reached a balance point. I could have gone either way.

Then a small silver streak came at me, running as fast as it could go. It reached me and dived across.

"*Malibu!*" Ember screamed. I turned. The otter seemed happier than I had ever seen him, even in the waterslide in town. He leaped, right at the jewel.

○

Regaining consciousness was a very gradual business. There was no dividing line between different states of awareness for two reasons: I was deaf, and I was blind. So I cannot say when I went from dreams to reality; the blend was too uniform, there wasn't enough change to notice.

I don't remember learning that I was deaf and blind. I don't remember learning the hand-spelling language that Ember talked to me with. The first rational moment that I can recall as such was when Ember was telling me her plans to get back to Prosperity.

I told her to do whatever she felt best, that she was in complete control. I was desolated to realise that I was not where I had thought I was. My dreams had been of Barsoom. I thought I had become a blast jewel and had been waiting in a sort of detached ecstasy for the moment of explosion.

She operated on my left eye and managed to restore some vision. I could see things that were a metre from my face, hazily. Everything else was shadows. At least she was able to write things on sheets of paper and hold them up to me to see. It made things quicker. I learned that she was deaf too. And Malibu was dead. Or might be. She had put him in the cooler and thought she might be able to patch him up when she got back. If not, she could always make another otter.

I told her about my back. She was shocked to hear that I had hurt it on the slide down the mountain, but she had sense enough not to scold me about it. It was short work to fix it up. Nothing but a bruised disc, she told me.

It would be tedious to describe all of our trip back. It was difficult, because neither of us knew much about blindness. But I was able to adjust pretty quickly. Being led by the hand was easy enough, and I stumbled only rarely after the first day. On the second day we scaled the mountains, and my tagalong malfunctioned. Ember discarded it and we traded off with hers. We could only do it when I was sitting still, as hers was made for a much shorter person. If I tried to walk with it, it quickly fell behind and jerked me off balance.

Then it was a matter of being set on the cycle and pedalling. There was nothing to do but pedal. I missed the talking we had done on the way out. I missed the blast jewel. I wondered if I'd ever adjust to life without it.

But the memory faded when we arrived back at Prosperity. I don't think the human mind can really contain something of that magnitude. It was slipping away from me by the hour, like a dream fades away in the morning. I found it hard to remember what it was that was so great about the experience. To this day, I can't really tell about it except in riddles. I'm left with shadows. I feel like an earthworm who has been shown a sunset and has no place to store the memory.

Back in town it was a simple matter for Ember to restore our hearing. She just hadn't been carrying any spare eardrums in her first-aid kit.

"It was an oversight," she told me. "Looking back, it seems obvious that the most likely injury from a blast jewel would be burst eardrums. I just didn't think."

"Don't worry about it. You did beautifully."

She grinned at me. "Yes, I did, didn't I?"

The vision was a larger problem. She didn't have any spare eyes and no one in town was willing to sell one of theirs at any price. She gave me one of hers as a temporary measure. She kept her infraeye and took to wearing an eye patch over the other. It made her look bloodthirsty. She told me to buy another at Venusburg, as our blood types weren't much of a match. My body would reject it in about three weeks.

The day came for the weekly departure of the blimp to Last Chance. We were sitting in Ember's workshop, facing each other with our legs crossed and the pile of blast jewels between us.

They looked awful. Oh, they hadn't changed. We had even polished them up until they sparkled three times as much as they had back in the firelight of our tent. But now we could see them for the rotten, yellowed, broken fragments of bone that they were. We had told no one what we had seen out in the Fahrenheit Desert. There was no way to check on it, and all our experience had been purely subjective. Nothing that would stand up in a laboratory. We were the only ones who knew their true nature. Probably we would always remain the only ones. What could we tell anyone?

"What do you think will happen?" I asked.

She looked at me keenly. "I think you already know that."

"Yeah." Whatever they were, however they survived and reproduced, the one fact we knew for sure was that they couldn't survive within a hundred kilometres of a city. Once there had been blast jewels in the very spot where we were sitting. And humans do expand. Once again, we would not know what we were destroying.

I couldn't keep the jewels. I felt like a ghoul. I tried to give them to Ember, but she wouldn't have them either.

"Shouldn't we tell someone?" Ember asked.

"Sure. Tell anyone you want. Don't expect people to start tiptoeing until you can prove something to them. Maybe not even then."

"Well, it looks like I'm going to spend a few more years tiptoeing. I find I just can't bring myself to stomp on the ground."

I was puzzled. "Why? You'll be on Mars. I don't think the vibrations will travel that far."

She stared at me. "What's this?"

There was a brief confusion; then I found myself apologising profusely to her, and she was laughing and telling me what a dirty rat I was, then taking it back and saying I could play that kind of trick on her any time I wanted.

It was a misunderstanding. I honestly thought I had told her about my change of heart while I was deaf and blind. It must have been a dream, because she hadn't gotten it and had assumed the answer was a permanent no. She had said nothing about adoption since the explosion.

"I couldn't bring myself to pester you about it any more, after what you did for me," she said, breathless with excitement. "I owe you a lot, maybe my life. And I used you badly when you first got here."

I denied it, and told her I had thought she was not talking about it because she thought it was in the bag.

"When did you change your mind?" she asked.

I thought back. "At first I thought it was while you were caring for me when I was helpless. Now I can recall when it was. It was shortly after I walked out of the tent for that last night on the ground."

She couldn't find anything to say about that. She just beamed at me. I began to wonder what sort of papers I'd be signing when we got to Venusburg; adoption, or marriage contract.

I didn't worry about it. It's uncertainties like that that make life interesting. We got up together, leaving the pile of jewels on the floor. Walking softly, we hurried out to catch the blimp.

Let's Go to Golgotha!

GARRY KILWORTH

The Time-Travel Agency was the third room along one of the branches of a Banyan building. It was a long way up, and it took Simon Falk a considerable time to reach the pink glass doors. A notice outside read, PAN PACKAGE TOURS OFFER YOU THE REMARKABLE! THIS IS YOUR CHANCE TO SEE THE BATTLE OF MARATHON. THE WARS OF THE ROSES, THE FIRST MANNED SPACE FLIGHT. ABSOLUTELY NO PERSONAL RISK. Simon stared into the interior and then went, reluctantly, it seemed, inside. An assistant slid silently to his side the moment he was in the room, with hands clasped before him in deference to his customer. Perhaps he was requesting aid from above, thought Simon, to get him through his potential sale?

"Can I help you, sir?"

Simon knotted his own fingers behind his back to even the balance and to hint gently that he was not yet ready to buy.

"Just some brochures, please. Can I take some away with me to, er, study at leisure?"

"Certainly, sir." The fingers unravelled themselves and began deftly plucking multi-coloured sheets of paper from the display shelves with the expertise of a seasoned fruit-picker.

"When you and your . . . ?"

"Family," Simon finished for him.

"Precisely!" The words were neat and well cared-for. Trimmed to the correct length and each separated by a time pause fitting for the intended effect. "When you have made your minds up," he

173

continued, "perhaps you will give us a call and we will see what can be arranged. There is no need to come personally for the booking . . ."

Simon wriggled uncomfortably. "I was just on my way home – I know I could have ordered them by mail but my wife is impatient."

"Yes," the salesman smiled silkily. "Um, the Coronation of Elizabeth the First is fully booked, I'm afraid, and the Revolution of Mars has only a limited number of seats available."

"I don't believe we are too interested in those events," said Simon.

"Your first time, sir?"

"Yes, as a matter of fact it is."

"Then may I recommend the Sacking of Carthage? We mingle with the camp followers on a neighbouring slope. However, I must add that it's not for the squeamish."

Simon asked, "Isn't that a little dangerous?"

"Er, no, not as long as you follow our little instructions." The agent wagged a finger playfully. "We've never lost a customer yet."

Simon murmured his thanks and almost ran out of the room. He hated these pre-holiday forays, but he owed his family a vacation and they were going to get it. It had to be one of these time-tours: he could not afford space travel. There was nothing else to do. Earth was a solid block of brick and concrete flourishing with Banyan buildings, and ocean cruises made his children ill. He stepped out of the building and hailed a floater, avoiding the blast of the air purifiers as he crossed the tiled roof to meet it.

Mandy was waiting at the door of their flat in the same mantis-like attitude employed by travel agents.

"Did you get the brochures?"

He sighed a resigned sigh. "Yes, I got them."

She grabbed at the wad. "Wonderful, let me see them. Oh, don't look so depressed, you know you always enjoy it once we get away. A trip through time!" She clutched the brochures to her breast. "I'm going to love every minute of it."

"Well, I hope it'll be up to your expectations," Simon said dryly. "It's going to cost us enough, and my business is not doing as well as it should." He trailed his sentence over to the cocktail cabinet, and made himself a drink.

"Oh, tish,'" she replied. "A holiday will do you good. You'll come back full of fresh ideas and thoroughly relaxed." She turned over some of the brochures in her hands. "We don't want anything too violent – it might upset the children."

Simon gave a snort. "The children would wallow in it. James likes nothing better than the sight of blood and Julie would rather see a space war picture than a live ballet performance."

"Don't be cynical, dear. Anyway, that's all the more reason to get them away," protested Mandy. "They have nothing else to do but play on the rooftops these days."

"Nothing else to do," he cried, overdoing the incredulous tone. "Did I have underground free-play fairgrounds when I was a boy? Did you have . . . ?"

"Oh, don't start that again. When will you understand that children cannot appreciate what they have always had? Let them see how children lived in other ages, other countries." Mandy paused. Then she continued, "We should have shown them before. Perhaps we should take them to Sparta. Did you know that the children of Sparta were placed in military academies at the age of eight and told to steal their food or starve? The crime was getting caught – I wonder what our children would think of the boy that let a fox gnaw on his abdomen rather than let his elders discover he had stolen it, and had hidden it up his smock?" Her blue eyes searched his face for signs of agreement.

"They would probably think he was a damn fool, and so do I,'" Simon replied.

She tried again. "Perhaps we should take them to Rome . . . ?"

"Or Pompeii the day before it erupted – and leave them there."

"Don't be nasty. What about the Holy Land . . ."

". . . at the time of the Crusades," finished twelve-year-old James, who had entered the kitchen eating.

"Not before your dinner, James," complained his mother. "Your father and I will decide where we are going – go and wash your hands. Where's Julie?"

"She's coming."

That evening Simon and Mandy Falk sat at the table poring over brochures and fighting over places, prices and dates until the front door sang softly, telling them that their closest friends were waiting to enter the house. Simon pressed a switch and shortly afterwards Harry and Sarah Tolbutt entered the room.

"Hello, hello, holiday time again?" chirped Harry, unzipping his outerwear suit.

Simon smiled and scratched the bridge of his nose.

"Yep. We can't decide where to go. Or should I say *when* to go? It's a bit confusing."

"If you are talking about time-tours, why don't you come with us? We're going to see the Crucifixion," said Sarah, with a little flick of her head.

"The what!" cried the Falks together.

"The Crucifixion of Christ," said Harry nonchalantly. He became earnest. "You see, we thought the children needed to see exactly what happened so that they had a real understanding of religion and what it means. You know what children are like."

"We know," said Simon in a hollow tone.

Sarah continued. "If they could see exactly how Jesus died to save us – or our souls or whatever it was that he saved – it might have a profound effect on them. At least, we hope it will."

Simon began mixing the drinks.

"Isn't it a bit sacrilegious?" he said quietly. "I mean, after all . . ."

Harry spoke again. "Well, I suppose on the surface it does seem a bit ghoulish and bloodthirsty, but as long as one goes with the right attitude I think it is all right. As long as one bears in mind what one is there for."

Mandy said, "Do you know, that is exactly what I was thinking before you came over? Wasn't I, Simon?"

"Yes, I'm a mind-reader," he winked at Harry. Mandy ignored him. "We are drawing too far away from the things that matter in life, like religion."

"You've not mentioned going to church in ten years," scoffed Simon.

Mandy dismissed this remark with a flick of her hand. "That's not important," she retorted. "A pack of old men droning out of the scriptures is not religion. I want to see the real thing – I think we should go, Simon."

Thus it was decided by Mandy and Sarah. Simon, his family and their friends were going to see the Crucifixion, at modest package tour prices, of course.

O

Pan Time-Tours Limited had its offices in Southend High Square. The Falks and the Tolbutts shared a floater to the pre-tour lecture to economise on the fare. The day was unusually bright for the season and in the floater, protected from the fresh sea breeze, they were warm and excited. Simon always felt good on a day when the sun managed to cut its way through the layers of cloud and he could see it twinkling on the giant floating platform that launched the starships high above the sky. He had never been into space. Simon Falk was secretly a confirmed homebody.

They reached the small lecture hall and took seats inside. Simon looked around him.

"There's quite a few people here," he whispered to Harry. "Do you think they are all on our tour?"

"Must be," said Harry. "There's no other lecture booked for today."

"Can I have your attention, please?" A young, serious-looking clergyman stood on the small rostrum before them. The murmuring died down. The vicar was a short man with old-fashioned glass spectacles. It was an affectation of the clergy. His glasses flashed like metal discs in the sunlight that fell in stripes down the east side of the hall.

"First of all, welcome to Pan Time-Tours. I am one of your Preparation Officers and I am here to give you advice on what to expect and how you must conduct yourselves." He smiled. "We do not lay down any rules, but it is important you should know how to act because on this tour, as on many others, you will be mixing with the locals. You must be inconspicuous – this is the primary role."

One or two hands shot up, but the clergyman waved them down.

"Now, I know a lot of you will have questions, but I must ask you to be patient. We will give you time at the termination of the lecture to get your queries answered. Many of them will probably be dealt with as the lecture continues. We have done this all before."

He looked up and smiled again. The sunlight from the window struck his left cheek, smearing it with holy gold, and the audience settled comfortably in their soft chairs.

"You will all be issued with the appropriate clothing before you embark and everyone will go through our treatment room to ensure that their outward appearance does not clash with that of the natives. This is a perfectly harmless process and is easily reversible on return from your holiday. We can't have any giant Nordic blondes standing out like poorly disguised Vikings at a Ramadan feast. A few days before the trip you will all be invited to visit our language laboratory, where you will be taught Hebrew by the knowledge-injection principle during one afternoon. As you probably know, the knowledge will only last about a month before it disappears completely from your brains. We can't stuff it in in two or three hours and expect it to remain there, otherwise we would all be brilliant."

He gave a soft snigger.

"Can't I be a Roman soldier?" a spotty-faced youth shouted from behind Simon.

The clergyman reproved the caller with a stern finger and said gravely, "Sir, I did warn you not to ask questions until the end. You will be given ample opportunity then. However, I will give you a reply because I was shortly coming to the importance of being Hebrews. The tour needs to stay together. A Roman soldier or two tagging along behind civilians will not look right, and besides, occupation troops have commitments – they might be recalled to barracks at short notice. You might be stopped for dirty buttons or something – a soldier is too vulnerable. Apart from all this, soldiers act in a particular fashion and have gestures and phrases peculiar to their profession – we would be sure to give ourselves away. Take it from me that we need to go as civilians."

"I don't want to be a Jew," muttered James. Simon nudged him to be quiet.

The speaker continued. "Now, this last part is most important – and I shall understand if any of you wish to drop out. If you do – only at this juncture, mind you – your deposit money will be refunded. If any of you are thrown in prison for any reason, we might not be able to get you out in time – that is, before you disappear into the bowels of a slave galley or end up at the bottom of the stoning pit."

There was a loud shuffling of feet and muttering of voices from his audience, and he waited with bowed head until it had ceased.

"There is no risk," he continued, "providing you do exactly as you are told. I cannot stress the importance of this too much. You know what happened and how it happened. We will arrive on the day that Pilate asks the inhabitants of Jerusalem whom he should set free, as the citizens are permitted to grant amnesty to one prisoner over the Feast of the Passover. When the crowd begins to shout 'Barabbas', as we know it must, then you must shout it too. You must not appear to be different in any way from the rest of the citizens. This is vitally important. You have to appear to be in agreement with the rest of the crowd. You must jeer at Christ and shake your fists as he drags the cross through the streets. You must remember that communities in those times were not very large, and if a small section of people is silent the others will begin to wonder why and will question you. You will be sure to give yourselves away under stress – not because you are idiots but because you are clever. People in those times were simple. They followed the ring-leaders, and they will regard anyone who does not with great suspicion. It is far more difficult to think and speak with simplicity under pressure than it is the reverse, so do as I say and everyone will be perfectly safe. It may be distasteful and even repugnant to your nature, but it is a necessity. When they nail up the sign 'Jesus of Nazareth – King of the Jews', you must laugh. Those that remain awestruck while the rest of the crowd are dancing and prancing, screaming and shouting, will only draw attention to themselves by their silence. I repeat, it is for your own safety. Now, are there any questions?"

The sermon was at an end. Only two childless couples asked for a refund of their deposit.

"How could they do that?" asked Julie for about the fifth time, just before they left for Jerusalem. "How could they crucify him? His own people. The same people that cheered and threw palm leaves before his feet such a short time before. It's like giving someone a ticker-tape parade and then hanging him."

"I don't suppose that is unknown either," replied Simon.

The children, after their initial reluctance to enjoy the pre-holiday plans, had settled down to the idea and had been studying their Bibles.

"Don't forget what the man said, they were a very simple people."

Simon was pleased with Julie. She was going with the right objectives in mind: to study the people who had executed Christ and to attempt to analyse their motives.

Julie went on, "I can't believe they *had* to do it. I know Christ had to die to save us all from sin but . . ."

"It was mankind that was to blame. You must think in general terms. You can't blame individual nations like the Romans or the Jews."

"Well, I still think it is terrible, they way they treated him."

Yes, Simon was well pleased with Julie. He was not too sure about James yet. James was a deeper one than Julie and had to be plumbed over a longer period of time than had been available.

The treatment room, as promised, was painless, and the journey itself was almost a delight. It left you with a slightly dizzy feeling but if you kept your eyes closed the sensation was that of sliding down a seemingly endless helter-skelter. There really was nothing to it. When Simon opened his eyes he found himself sitting on warm sand beside a narrow goat track. The others were in the positions they had held inside the time room. They all climbed to their feet and made their way along the goat track towards the town that shimmered in the heat in the distance. The sun pressed hot on the backs of their necks and Simon put an arm round James to stop him from stumbling. None of them were used to walking on uneven ground covered in sharp stones. Simon felt sorry for some of the older members of the party.

The courier entered the town first. He was recognisable by his matted hair, rags and the ancient staff he carried, but no one was to speak to him, except in dire emergency. The walk was a long one and the rough smocks were uncomfortable. Several children were beginning to complain of the heat and that their skins were sore where the cloth was rubbing, but there was a general atmosphere of excitement pervading the adults. At least we look authentic enough, thought Simon. The smocks and sandals were genuine, bought on a previous trip by a Tour Preparation Officer. Some of the members had elected to go barefoot at the request of the firm. Their feet had been hardened during the process in the treatment room. Nevertheless, thought Simon, they will be raw by the time we go back. Presumably Pan Time-Tours relied on the suffering of Christ to overawe the visitors and make them ashamed of their own trivial problems. A dog ran in and out of their legs, barking, as they trailed down a narrow dusty street. Their first meeting with one of the locals. Simon glanced at Mandy. Her new brown eyes flashed at him, and she looked very beautiful in a gypsyish sort of way.

"Glad you came?" she whispered in Hebrew.

"I don't know yet," he said in all seriousness.

Finally they passed between some hard mud dwellings and out into a square in the middle of the town.

"Just in time," said the courier. "Spread out, everyone."

The mob was dense, but Harry procured a clear place just inside the periphery of the crowd. A tall, thin man with an intelligent face was addressing the people from the steps of a stone building He looked harassed and a little ill. He was speaking in Latin.

"What is he saying?" whispered Simon to Harry, who had studied the classics in his youth.

"He is asking us to choose the one to go free," answered Harry. "You know, you've read the book."

"Oh," said Simon.

The crowd shuffled but remained silent. A fly settled on the end of Simon's perspiring nose and he flicked it away impatiently. God, it was hot, he thought. The Roman repeated his previous sentence. Suddenly, as if he had just comprehended the question, James cried out "Barabbas!" in a high voice. He had been day-dreaming, and the question, as did many questions in Latin in the classroom at school, had taken him off his guard. The sound echoed over the hard baked square, and James looked a little frightened at his outburst Then the mutterings in the crowd began, and soon everyone was yelling.

"Barabbas! Barabbas!"

Simon felt relieved that the shouting had started. He had been startled by his son's yell and was afraid that attention had been drawn to them. No one was looking at them, however.

"What did you do that for?" he hissed under the uproar.

James was nervous and tense.

"I'm sorry. I thought we were supposed to. He asked us and the man said . . . I don't know."

"Never mind," intervened Harry. "It would have happened anyway. You just jumped the gun, that's all. Don't do it again, though, or we may be in trouble."

James looked miserable, but Simon let it go at that. There was no sense in causing a scene, and what was done was done. They stood for about an hour in the square, with none of them quite sure what was happening, and then Julie said she felt sick. Simon and Mandy took her behind one of the strawbrick houses, leaving James with Harry and Sarah and their children.

"It must be the heat," said Mandy after a while. "It's getting at me a bit too. Couldn't we sit down somewhere in the shade?"

She looked down the narrow street for somewhere to rest but there was nothing in view. Then, having an idea, she walked over to one of the houses and looked in from the open doorway. A Hebrew family was sitting on stools in the middle of the room with their hands clasped in front of them. The old man of the group raised his eyes inquiringly. It was cool in the doorway, but it was obvious that she was intruding on something very private.

"Sorry," said Mandy, and stepped back into the street. The heat from the ground came up through the soles of her sandals again and she walked on to the next house. It was also occupied: so was the next, and the next. She returned to where Simon and Julie stood.

"There's something funny here," she whispered to Simon when she reached him. "The houses have people in them."

"So?" said Simon in an irritated tone.

"Well, one would think they would be out on a day like today. Why aren't they watching Christ pull his cross through the streets? All the other inhabitants are."

"Perhaps they are . . . Well, I don't know. What's the point?" Then he looked thoughtful. "You know, you have something there. Let's check a few more of the houses."

They went from house to house, through dozens of streets, peering into doorways, looking through curtains until they knew they had covered a large portion of the town. Enough to know that there was something terribly wrong. The realisation of what that wrong was began to sink in very rapidly, and no matter how hard Simon's mind tried to reject it or concoct excuses to cover it, the awful thought remained. Julie followed her agitated parents, not understanding and obviously unwell.

"I want a drink," she finally complained.

"Well, you can't have one," snapped Mandy. "The water isn't fit to drink. It's got all sorts of germs in it."

"These people are all right," Julie sniffed to deaf ears.

Simon felt a hot wave of air pass over his face. His eyes were sore, his mouth felt dry, and the dust was mixing with the sweat on his feet to form a slimy grime between his toes. His physical discomfort, however, was nothing compared to his mental stress. He felt very afraid.

"Doesn't it strike you as peculiar that the crowd was so large?" he asked, wiping his brow with his sleeve at the same time.

Mandy's voice was taut. "Well, it has been boosted by tours from the future. There's more than one agency, don't forget."

Simon was visibly trembling now. "There are dozens of agencies," he cried. "And all the inhabitants of this town are in their houses, praying. Quickly, we've got to find Harry and the others."

Simon grabbed Julie and swung her on to his back. They ran through the streets with the perspiration dripping from their eyebrows and their eyes stinging with the salt and dust. In the distance they could hear the crowd chanting and jeering; they could hear the shrieks of laughter and high-pitched catcalls. It was an ugly, frightening sound, like the screaming of monkeys as a lion pads beneath their trees. It was the forced laughter of hyenas that circle the lion's den at a safe distance as the lord lies, unconcerned, in the warm sun. Then, suddenly, there was silence.

Simon slowed, gasping for breath. He could see the rut made by the corner of the cross snaking along the street and disappearing into the distance. A shudder went through him.

"My God," he sobbed to his wife, "we've killed him."

A sandal slipped from his foot as he ran but he disregarded it. He felt none of the sharp stones that cut the soles and heels of his feet.

The pair of them stumbled on, following the tell-tale mark in the dust, until they reached the crowd. The faces were all turned in one direction and wore expressions of shocked sympathy. Simon did not dare look towards the crosses. He knew he would faint if he did, and he had seen the shadows out of the corner of his eye. It was enough. They found Harry and Sarah and the children on the edge of the crowd, as silent and watchful as the others. Sarah's cheeks were blotched with white and Harry's mouth was half-open.

"Harry," choked Simon, as quickly as his emotion would allow, "Harry, we've got to get him down."

Hany's stunned mind took time to register the fact that Simon was with them once more. He did not take his eyes from the man on the centre cross.

Licking his lips, he replied helplessly, "Can't do it, Simon. It's got to happen, you know. This is the way it is, but, my God, I wish we had never come. He looked at me, you know. I'll never forget his eyes as long as I live. They were so . . ." he paused to find a word, ". . . so deep."

Simon was frantic. "Harry. Harry. Look at the crowd! Look around you! There are no Jews here. No natives. The only ones here are us. The holiday-makers. Do you realise the enormity of what we've done? The whole guilt of mankind rests on our shoulders."

He was sobbing violently now. "We've crucified the Son of God, and we're going to do it next tour, and the next and the next . . ."

"For ever and ever, time without end, amen," finished Harry, humbly.

Useful Phrases
for the Tourist
JOANNA RUSS

THE LOCRINE: peninsule and surrounding regions. High
   Lokrinnen.

X 437894 = II

Reasonably Earthlike (see companion audio tapes and translitera-
   tions)

For physiology, ecology, religion and customs, Wu and Fabricant,
   Prague, 2355, Vol. 2 *The Locrine, Useful Knowledge for the
   Tourist*, q.v.

AT THE HOTEL:

That is my companion. It is not intended as a tip.

I will call the manager.

This cannot be my room because I cannot breathe ammonia.

I will be most comfortable between temperatures of 290 and 303
   degrees Kelvin.

Waitress, this meal is still alive.

AT THE PARTY:

Is that you?

Is that all of you? How much (many) of you is (are) there?

I am happy to meet your clone.

Interstellar amity demands that we make some physical display at
   this point, but I beg to be excused.

Are you toxic?

Are you edible? I am not edible.

We humans do not regenerate.
My companion is not edible.
That is my ear.
I am toxic.
Is that how you copulate?
Is this intended to be erotic?
Thank you very much.
Please explain.
Do you turn colours?
Are you pregnant?
I shall leave the room.
Can't we just be friends?
Take me to the Earth Consulate immediately.
Although I am very flattered by your kind offer, I cannot accompany you to the mating pits, as I am viviparous.

IN THE HOSPITAL:
No!
My eating orifice is not at that end of my body.
I would rather do it myself.
Please do not let the atmosphere in (out) as I will be most uncomfortable.
I do not eat lead.
Placing the thermometer there will yield little or no useful information.

SIGHTSEEING:
You are not my guide. My guide was bipedal.
Earth people do not do that.
Oh, what a jolly fine natatorium (mating perch, arranged spectacle, involuntary phenomenon)!
At what hour does the lovelorn princess fling herself into the flaming volcano? May we participate?
That is not demonstrable.
That is hardly likely.
This is ridiculous.

I have seen much better examples of that.

Please direct me to the nearest sentient mammal.

Take me to the Earth Consulate without delay.

AT THE THEATRE:

Is that amusing?

I am sorry; I did not mean to be offensive.

I did not intend to sit on you. I did not realise that you were in this seat.

Could you deform yourself a little lower?

My eyes are sensitive only to light of the wavelengths 3000–7000Å.

Am I imagining this?

Am I supposed to imagine this?

Should I be perturbed by the water on the floor?

Where is the exit?

Help!

This is great art.

My religious convictions prevent me from joining in the performance.

I do not feel well.

I feel very sick.

I do not eat living food.

Is this supposed to be erotic?

May I take this home with me?

Is this part of the performance?

Stop touching me.

Sir or madam, that is mine. (extrinsic)

Sir or madam, that is mine. (intrinsic)

I wish to visit the waste-reclamation units.

Have you finished?

May I begin?

You are in my way.

Under no circumstances.

If you do not stop that, I will call the attendant.

That is forbidden by my religion.

Sir or madam, this is a private unit.
Sir and madam, this is a private unit.

COMPLIMENTS:
You are more than before.
Your hair is false.
If you uncover your feet, I will faint.
There is no room.
You will undoubtedly be here tomorrow.

INSULTS:
You are just the same.
There are more of you than previously.
Your fingers are showing.
How clean you are!
You are clean, but animated.

GENERAL:
Take me to the Earth Consulate.
Direct me to the Earth Consulate.
The Earth Consulate will hear of this.
This is no way to treat a visitor.
Please direct me to my hotel.
At what time does the moon rise? Is there a moon?
Is it a full moon? Take me to the Earth Consulate immediately.
May I have the second volume of Wu and Fabricant, entitled
    Physiology, Ecology, Religion and Customs of the Locrine?
    Price is no object.
Something has just gone amiss with my vehicle.
I am dying.

Trips

ROBERT SILVERBERG

*Does this path have a heart? All paths are the same: they
lead nowhere. They are paths going through the bush, or
into the bush. In my own life I could say I have traversed
long, long paths, but I am not anywhere . . . Does this path
have a heart? If it does, the path is good; if it doesn't, it is
of no use. Both paths lead nowhere; but one has a heart,
the other doesn't. One makes for a joyful journey; as long
as you follow it, you are one with it. The other will make
you curse your life.*

— The Teachings of Don Juan

1.

The second place you come to – the first having proved unsatis-
factory, for one reason and another – is a city which could almost
be San Francisco. Perhaps it is, sitting out there on the peninsula
between the ocean and the bay, white buildings clambering over
improbably steep hills. It occupies the place in your psychic space
that San Francisco has always occupied, although you don't really
know yet what this city calls itself. Perhaps you'll find out before
long.

You go forward. What you feel first is the strangeness of the
familiar, and then the utter heartless familiarity of the strange. For
example the automobiles, and there are plenty of them, are all
halftracks: low sleek sexy sedans that have the flashy Detroit
styling, the usual chrome, the usual streamlining, the low-raked

windows all agleam, but there are only two wheels, both of them in front, with a pair of tread-belts circling endlessly in back. Is this good design for city use? Who knows? Somebody evidently thinks so, here. And then the newspapers: the format is the same, narrow columns, gaudy screaming headlines, miles of black type on coarse greyish-white paper, but the names and the places have been changed. You scan the front page of a newspaper in the window of a curbside vending machine. Big photo of Chairman DeGrasse, serving as host at a reception for the Patagonian Ambassador. An account of the tribal massacres in the highlands of Dzungaria. Details of the solitude epidemic that is devastating Persepolis. When the halftracks stall on the hillsides, which is often, the other drivers ring silvery chimes, politely venting their impatience. Men who look like Navahos chant what sound like sutras in the intersections. The traffic lights are blue and orange. Clothing tends toward the prosaic, greys and dark blues, but the cut and slope of men's jackets has an angular, formal eighteenth-century look, verging on pomposity. You pick up a bright coin that lies in the street: it is vaguely metallic but rubbery, as if you could compress it between your fingers, and its thick edges bear incuse lettering: TO GOD WE OWE OUR SWORDS. On the next block a squat two-storey building is ablaze, and agitated clerks do a desperate dance. The fire engine is glossy green and its pump looks like a diabolical cannon embellished with sweeping flanges; it spouts a glistening yellow foam that eats the flames and, oxidising, runs off down the gutter, a trickle of sluggish blue fluid. Everyone wears eyeglasses here, *everyone*. At a sidewalk café, pale waitresses offer mugs of boiling-hot milk into which the silent tight-faced patrons put cinnamon, mustard and what seems to be Tabasco sauce. You offer your coin and try a sample, imitating what they do, and everyone bursts into laughter. The girl behind the counter pushes a thick stack of paper currency at you by way of change: UNITED FEDERAL COLUMBIAN REPUBLIC, each bill declares. GOOD FOR ONE EXCHANGE. Illegible signatures. Portrait of early leader of the republic, so famous that they give him no label of identification, bewigged, wall-eyed, ecstatic. You sip your milk, blowing gently. A light scum begins to form on its speckled surface. Sirens start to wail. About you, the other milk-drinkers stir uneasily. A parade is coming. Trumpets, drums, far-off chanting. Look! Four naked boys carry an open brocaded litter on which there sits an immense block of ice, a great frosted cube, mysterious, impenetrable. "Patagonia!" the onlookers cry sadly. The word is wrenched from them: "Patagonia!" Next, marching by himself, a mitred bishop advances, all in green, curtsying to the crowd, tossing hearty blessings as though they were flowers. "Forget your sins! Cancel your debts! All is made new! All is good!" You shiver and peer intently into his eyes as he passes you, hoping that he will single you out for an embrace. He is terribly tall but white-haired and fragile, somehow, despite his agility and energy. He reminds you of Norman, your wife's older brother, and perhaps he *is* Norman, the Norman of this place, and you wonder if he can give you news of Elizabeth, the Elizabeth of this place, but you say nothing and he goes by. And then comes a tremendous wooden scaffold on wheels, a true juggernaut, at the summit of which rests a polished statue carved out of gleaming black stone: a human figure, male, plump, arms intricately folded, face complacent. The statue emanates a sense of vast Sumerian calm. The face is that of Chairman DeGrasse. "He'll die in the first blizzard," murmurs a man to your left. Another, turning suddenly, says with great force, "No, it's going to be done the proper way. He'll last until the time of the accidents, just as he's supposed to. I'll bet on that." Instantly they are nose to nose, glaring, and then they are wagering – a tense complicated ritual involving slapping of palms, interchanges of slips of paper, formal voiding of spittle, hysterical appeals to witnesses. The emotional climate here seems a trifle too intense. You decide to move along. Warily you leave the café, looking in all directions.

2.

Before you began your travels you were told how essential it was to define your intended role. Were you going to be a tourist, or an explorer, or an infiltrator? Those are the choices that confront anyone arriving at a new place. Each bears its special risks.

To opt for being a tourist is to choose the easiest but most contemptible path; ultimately it's the most dangerous one, too, in a certain sense. You have to accept the built-in epithets that go with the part: they will think of you as a *foolish* tourist, an *ignorant* tourist, a *vulgar* tourist, a *mere* tourist. Do you want to be considered mere? Are you able to accept that? Is that really your preferred self-image – baffled, bewildered, led about by the nose? You'll sign up for packaged tours, you'll carry guidebooks and cameras, you'll go to the cathedral and the museums and the marketplace, and you'll remain always on the outside of things, seeing a great deal, experiencing nothing. What a waste! You will be diminished by the very travelling that you thought would expand you. Tourism hollows and parches you. All places become one: a hotel, a smiling swarthy sunglassed guide, a bus, a plaza, a fountain, a marketplace, a museum, a cathedral. You are transformed into a feeble shrivelled thing made out of glued-together travel folders; you are naked but for your visas; the sum of your life's adventures is a box of left-over small change from many indistinguishable lands.

To be an explorer is to make the *macho* choice. You swagger in, bent on conquest, for isn't any discovery a kind of conquest? Your existential position, like that of any mere tourist, lies outside the heart of things, but you are unashamed of that; and while tourists are essentially passive the explorer's role is active; an explorer intends to grasp that heart, take possession, squeeze. In the explorer's role you consciously cloak yourself in the trappings of power: self-assurance, thick bankroll, stack of credit cards. You capitalise on the glamour of being a stranger. Your curiosity is invincible; you ask unabashed questions about the most intimate things, never for an instant relinquishing eye-contact. You open locked doors and flash bright lights into curtained rooms. You are Magellan; you are Malinowski; you are Captain Cook. You will gain much, but – ah, here is the price! – you will always be feared and hated, you will never be permitted to attain the true core. Nor is superficiality the worst peril. Remember that Magellan and Captain Cook left their bones on tropic beaches. Sometimes the natives lose patience with explorers.

The infiltrator, though? His is at once the most difficult role and the most rewarding one. Will it be yours? Consider. You'll have to get right with it when you reach your destination, instantly learn the regulations, find your way around like an old hand, discover the location of shops and freeways and hotels, figure out the units of currency, the rules of social intercourse – all of this knowledge mastered surreptitiously, through observation alone, while moving about silently, camouflaged, *never asking for help*. You must become a part of the world you have entered, and the way to do it is to encourage a general assumption that you already are a part of it, have always been a part of it. Wherever you land, you need to recognise that life has been going on for millions of years, life goes on there steadily, with you or without you; you are the intrusive one, and if you don't want to feel intrusive you'd better learn fast how to fit in. Of course it isn't easy. The infiltrator doesn't have the privilege of buying stability by acting dumb. You won't be able to say, "How much does it cost to ride on the cable-car?" You won't be able to say, "I'm from somewhere else, and this is the kind of money I carry, dollars quarters pennies halves nickels, is any of it legal tender here?" You don't dare identify yourself in any way as an outsider. If you don't get the idioms or the accent right, you can tell them you grew up out of town, but that's as much as you can reveal. The truth is your eternal secret, even when you're in trouble, *especially* when you're in trouble. When your back's to the wall you won't have time to say, "Look, I wasn't born in this universe at all, you see, I came zipping in from some other place, so pardon me, forgive me, excuse me, pity me." No, no, no, you can't do that. They won't believe you, and even if they do, they'll make it all the worse for you once they know. If you want to infiltrate, Cameron, you've got to fake it all the way. Jaunty smile, steely even gaze. And you have to infiltrate. You know that, don't you? You don't really have any choice.

Infiltrating has its dangers too. The rough part comes when they find you out, and they always do find you out. Then they'll react bitterly against your deception, they'll lash out in blind rage. If you're lucky, you'll be gone before they learn your sweaty little secret. Before they discover the discarded phrasebook hidden in the boarding-house room, before they stumble on the torn-off pages of your private journal. They'll find you out. They always do. But by then you'll be somewhere else, you hope, beyond the reach of their anger and their sorrow, beyond their reach, beyond their reach.

3.

Suppose I show you, for Exhibit A, Cameron reacting to an extraordinary situation. You can test your own resilience by trying to picture yourself in his position. There has been a sensation in Cameron's mind very much like that of the extinction of the cosmos: a thunderclap, everything going black, a blankness, a total absence. Followed by the return of light, flowing inward upon him like high tide on the celestial shore, a surging stream of brightness moving with inexorable certainty. He stands flat-footed, dumbfounded, high on a bare hillside in warm early-hour sunlight. The house – redwood timbers, picture window, driftwood sculptures, paintings, books, records, refrigerator, gallon jugs of red wine, carpets, tiles, avocado plants in wooden tubs, carport, car, driveway – is gone. The neighbouring houses are gone. The winding street is gone. The eucalyptus forest that ought to be behind him, rising toward the crest of the hill, is gone. Downslope there is no Oakland, there is no Berkeley, only a scattering of crude squatters' shacks running raggedly along unpaved switchbacks toward the pure blue bay. Across the water there is no Bay Bridge; on the far shore there is no San Francisco. The Golden Gate Bridge does not span the gap between the city and the Marin headland. Cameron is astonished, not that he didn't expect something like this, but that the transformation is so complete, so absolute. If you don't want your world any more, the old man had said, you can just drop it, can't you? Let go of it, let it drop. Can't you? Of course you can. And so Cameron has let go of it. He's in another place entirely, now. Wherever this place is, it isn't home. The sprawling Bay Area cities and towns aren't here, never were. Goodbye, San Leandro, San Marco, El Cerrito, Walnut Creek. He sees a landscape of gentle bare hills, rolling meadows, the dry brown grass of summer; the scarring hand of man is evident only occasionally. He begins to adapt. This is what he must have wanted, after all, and though he has been jarred by the shock of transition he is recovering quickly, he is settling in, he feels already that he could belong here. He will explore this unfamiliar world and if he finds it good he will discover a niche for himself. The air is sweet. The sky is cloudless. Has he really gone to some new place, or is he still in the old place and has everything else that was there simply gone away? Easy. He has gone. Everything else has gone. The cosmos has entered into a transitional phase. Nothing's stable any more. From this moment onward, Cameron's existence is a conditional matter, subject to ready alteration. What did the old man say? Go wherever you like. Define your world as you would like it to be, and go there, and if you discover that you don't care for this or don't need that, why, go somewhere else. It's all trips, this universe. What else is there? There isn't anything but trips. Just trips. So here you are, friend. New frameworks! New patterns! New!

4.

There is a sound to his left, the crackling of dry brush under foot, and Cameron turns, looking straight into the morning sun, and sees a man on horseback approaching him. He is tall, slender, about Cameron's own height and build, it seems, but perhaps a shade broader through the shoulders. His hair, like Cameron's, is golden, but it is much longer, descending in a straight flow to his shoulders and tumbling onto his chest. He has a soft full curling beard, untrimmed but tidy. He wears a wide-brimmed hat, buckskin chaps, and a light fringed jacket of tawny leather. Because of the sunlight Cameron has difficulty at first making out his features, but after a moment his eyes adjust and he sees that the other's face is very much like his own, thin lips, jutting high-bridged nose, clefted chin, cool blue eyes below heavy brows. Of course. Your face is my face. You and I, I and you, drawn to the same place at the same time across the many worlds. Cameron had not expected this, but now that it has happened it seems to have been inevitable.

They look at each other. Neither speaks. During that silent moment Cameron invents a scene for them. He imagines the other dismounting, inspecting him in wonder, walking around him, peering into his face, studying it, frowning, shaking his head, finally grinning and saying:

– I'll be damned. I never knew I had a twin brother. But here you are. It's just like looking in the mirror.

– We aren't twins.

– We've got the same face. Same everything. Trim away a little hair and nobody could tell me from you, you from me. If we aren't twins, what are we?

– We're closer than brothers.

– I don't follow your meaning, friend.

– This is how it is. I'm you. You're me. One soul, one identity. What's your name?

– Cameron.

– Of course. First name?

– Kit.

– That's short for Christopher, isn't it? My name is Cameron too. Chris. Short for Christopher. I tell you, we're one and the same person, out of two different worlds. Closer than brothers. Closer than anything.

None of this is said, however. Instead the man in the leather clothing rides slowly toward Cameron, pauses, gives him a long incurious stare, and says simply, "Morning. Nice day." And continues onward.

"Wait," Cameron says.

The man halts. Looks back. "What?"

Never ask for help. Fake it all the way. Jaunty smile, steely even gaze.

198

Yes. Cameron remembers all that. Somehow, though, infiltration seems easier to bring off in a city. You can blend into the background there. More difficult here, exposed as you are against the stark unpeopled landscape. Cameron says, as casually as he can, using what he hopes is a colourless neutral accent, "I've been travelling out from inland. Came a long way."

"Umm. Didn't think you were from around here. Your clothes."

"Inland clothes."

"The way you talk. Different. So?"

"New to these parts. Wondered if you could tell me a place I could hire a room till I got settled."

"You come all this way on foot?"

"Had a mule. Lost him back in the valley. Lost everything I had with me."

"Umm. Indians cutting up again. You give them a little gin, they go crazy." The other smiles faintly; then the smile fades and he retreats into impassivity, sitting motionless with hands on thighs, face a mask of patience that seems merely to be a thin covering for impatience or worse.

– Indians? –

"They gave me a rough time," Cameron says, getting into the fantasy of it.

"Umm."

"Cleaned me out, let me go."

"Umm. Umm."

Cameron feels his sense of a shared identity with this man lessening. There is no way of engaging him. I am you, you are I, and yet you take no notice of the strange fact that I wear your face and body, you seem to show no interest in me at all. Or else you hide your interest amazingly well.

Cameron says, "You know where I can get lodging?"

"Nothing much around here. Not many settlers this side of the bay, I guess."

"I'm strong. I can do most any kind of work. Maybe you could use – "

"Umm. No." Cold dismissal glitters in the frosty eyes. Cameron wonders how often people in the world of his former life saw such a look in his own. A tug on the reins. Your time is up, stranger. The horse swings around and begins picking its way daintily along the path.

Desperately Cameron calls, "One thing more!"

"Umm?"

"Is your name Cameron?"

A flicker of interest. "Might be."

"Christopher Cameron. Kit. Chris. That you?"

"Kit." The other's eyes drill into his own. The mouth compresses until the lips are invisible: not a scowl but a speculative, pensive movement. There is tension in the way the other man grasps his reins. For the first time Cameron feels that he has made contact. "Kit Cameron, yes. Why?"

"Your wife," Cameron says. "Her name Elizabeth?"

The tension increases. The other Cameron is cloaked in explosive silence. Something terrible is building within him. Then, unexpectedly, the tension snaps. The other man spits, scowls, slumps in his saddle. "My woman's dead," he mutters. "Say, who the hell are you? What do you want with me?"

"I'm – I'm – " Cameron falters. He is overwhelmed by fear and pity. A bad start, a lamentable start. He trembles. He had not thought it would be anything like this. With an effort he masters himself. Fiercely he says, "I've got to know. Was her name Elizabeth?" For an answer the horseman whacks his heels savagely against his mount's ribs and gallops away, fleeing as though he has had an encounter with Satan.

5.

Go, the old man said. You know the score. This is how it is: everything's random, nothing's fixed unless we want it to be, and even then the system isn't as stable as we think it is. So go. Go. Go, he said, and, of course, hearing something like that, Cameron went. What else could he do, once he had his freedom, but abandon his native universe and try a different one? Notice that I didn't say a better one, just a different one. Or two or three or five different ones. It was a gamble, certainly. He might lose everything that mattered to him, and gain nothing worth having. But what of it? Every day is full of gambles like that: you stake your life whenever you open a door. You never know what's heading your way, not ever, and still you choose to play the game. How can a man be expected to become all he's capable of becoming if he spends his whole life pacing up and down the same courtyard? Go. Make your voyages. Time forks, again and again and again. New universes split off at each instant of decision. Left turn, right turn, honk your horn, jump the traffic light, hit your gas, hit your brake, every action spawns whole galaxies of possibility. We move through a soup of infinities. If repressing a sneeze generates an alternative continuum, what, then, are the consequences of the truly major acts, the assassinations and inseminations, the conversions, the renunciations? Go. And as you travel, mull these thoughts constantly. Part of the game is discerning the precipitating factors that shaped the worlds you visit. What's the story here? Dirt roads, donkey-carts, hand-sewn clothes. No Industrial Revolution, is that it? The steam-engine man – what was his name, Savery, Newcomen, Watt? – smothered in his cradle? No mines, no factories, no assembly lines, no dark Satanic mills. That must be it. The air is so pure here: you can tell by that, it's a simpler era. Very good, Cameron. You see the patterns swiftly. But now try somewhere else. Your own self has rejected you here; besides, this place has no Elizabeth. Close your eyes. Summon the lightning.

6.

The parade has reached a disturbing level of frenzy. Marchers and floats now occupy the side streets as well as the main boulevard, and there is no way to escape from their demonic enthusiasm. Streamers cascade from office windows and gigantic photographs of Chairman DeGrasse have sprouted on every wall, suddenly, like dark infestations of lichen. A boy presses close against Cameron, extends a clenched fist, opens his fingers: on his palm rests a glittering jewelled case, egg-shaped, thumbnail-sized. "Spores from

Patagonia," he says. "Let me have ten exchanges and they're yours." Politely Cameron declines. A woman in a blue and orange frock tugs at his arm and says urgently, "All the rumours are true, you know. They've just been confirmed. What are you going to do about that? What are you going to *do?*" Cameron shrugs and smiles and disengages himself. A man with gleaming buttons asks, "Are you enjoying the festival? I've sold everything and I'm going to move to the highway next Godsday." Cameron nods and murmurs congratulations, hoping congratulations are in order. He turns a corner and confronts, once more, the bishop who looks like Elizabeth's brother, who *is*, he concludes, indeed Elizabeth's brother. "Forget your sins!" he is crying still. "Cancel your debts!" Cameron thrusts his head between two plump girls at the curb and attempts to call to him, but his voice fails, nothing coming forth but a hoarse wordless rasp, and the bishop moves on. Moving on is a good idea, Cameron tells himself. This place exhausts him. He has come to it too soon, and its manic tonality is more than he wants to handle. He finds a quiet alleyway and presses his cheek against a cool brick wall, and stands there breathing deeply until he is calm enough to depart. All right. Onward.

7.

Empty grasslands spread to the horizon. This could be the Gobi steppe. Cameron sees neither cities nor towns nor even villages, just six or seven squat black tents pitched in a loose circle in the saddle between two low grey-green hummocks, a few hundred yards from where he stands. He looks beyond, across the gently folded land, and spies dark animal figures at the limits of his range of vision: about a dozen horses, close together, muzzle to muzzle, flank to flank, horses with riders. Or perhaps they are a congregation of centaurs. Anything is possible. He decides, though, that they are Indians, a war party of young braves, maybe, camping in these desolate plains. They see him. Quite likely they saw him some while before he noticed them. Casually they break out of their grouping, wheel, ride in his direction.

He awaits them. Why should he flee? Where could he hide? Their pace accelerates from trot to canter, from canter to wild gallop; now they plunge toward him with fluid ferocity and a terrifying eagerness. They wear open leather jackets and rough rawhide leggings; they carry lances, bows, battle-axes, long curved swords; they ride small, agile horses, hardly more than ponies, tireless packets of energy. They surround him, pulling up, the fierce little steeds rearing and whinnying; they peer at him, point, laugh, exchange harsh derisive comments in a mysterious language. Then, solemnly, they begin to ride slowly in a wide circle around him. They are flat-faced, small-nosed, bearded, with broad, prominent cheekbones; the crowns of their heads are shaven but long black hair streams down over their ears and the napes of their necks. Heavy folds in the upper lids give their eyes a slanted look. Their skins are copper-coloured but with an underlying golden tinge, as though these are not Indians at all but – what? Japanese? A samurai corps? No, probably not Japanese. But not Indians either.

They continue to circle him, gradually moving more swiftly. They chatter to one another and occasionally hurl what sound like questions at him. They seem fascinated by him, but also contemptuous. In a sudden demonstration of horsemanship one of them cuts from the circular formation and, goading his horse to an instant gallop, streaks past Cameron, leaning down to jab a finger into his forearm. Then another does it, and another, streaking back and forth across the circle, poking him, plucking at his hair, tweaking him, nearly running him down. They draw their swords and swish them through the air just above his head. They menace him, or pretend to, with their lances. Throughout it all they laugh. He stands perfectly still. This ordeal, he suspects, is a test of his courage. Which he passes, eventually. The lunatic galloping ceases; they rein in, and several of them dismount.

They are little men, chest-high to him but thicker through the chest and shoulders than he is. One unships a leather pouch and offers it to him with an unmistakable gesture: take, drink. Cameron sips cautiously. It is a thick greyish fluid, both sweet and sour. Fermented milk? He gags; winces, forces himself to sip again; they watch him closely. The second taste isn't so bad. He takes a third more willingly and gravely returns the pouch. The warriors laugh, not derisively now but more in applause, and the man who had given him the pouch slaps Cameron's shoulder admiringly. He tosses the pouch back to Cameron. Then he leaps to his saddle, and abruptly they all take off. Mongols, Cameron realises. The sons of Genghis Khan; riding to the horizon. A worldwide empire? Yes, and this must be the wild west for them, the frontier, where the young men enact their rites of passage. Back in Europe, after seven centuries of Mongol dominance, they have become citified, domesticated, sippers of wine, theatregoers, cultivators of gardens, but here they follow the ways of their all-conquering forefathers. Cameron shrugs. Nothing for him here. He takes a last sip of the milk and drops the pouch into the tall grass. Onward.

8.

No grass grows here. He sees the stumps of buildings, the black-ened trunks of dead trees, mounds of broken tile and brick. The smell of death is in the air. All the bridges are down. Fog rolls in off the bay, dense and greasy, and becomes a screen on which images come alive. These ruins are inhabited. Figures move about. They are the living dead. Looking into the thick mist he sees a vision of the shock wave, he recoils as alpha particles shower his skin. He beholds the survivors emerging from their shattered houses, straggling into the smouldering streets, naked, stunned, their bodies charred, their eyes glazed, some of them with their hair on fire. The walking dead. No one speaks. No one asks why this has happened. He is watching a silent movie. The apocalyptic fire has touched the ground here; the land itself is burning. Blue phosphorescent flames rise from the earth. The final judgment, the day of wrath. Now he hears a dread music beginning, a dead-march, all cellos and basses, the dark notes coming at wide intervals: ooom ooom ooom ooom ooom. And then the tempo picks up, the music becomes a danse macabre, syncopated, lively, the timbre still dark, the rhythms funereal: ooom ooom ooom-de-ooom de-ooom de-ooom de-ooom-de-ooom, jerky, chaotic, wildly gay. The distorted melody of the Ode to Joy lurks somewhere in the ragged strands of sound. The dying victims stretch their fleshless hands toward him. He shakes his head. What service can I do for you? Guilt assails him. He is a tourist in the land of their grief. Their eyes reproach him. He would embrace them, but he fears they will crumble at his touch, and he lets the procession go past him without doing anything to cross the gulf between himself and them. "Elizabeth?" he murmurs. "Norman?" They have no faces, only eyes. "What can I do? I can't do anything for you." Not even tears will come. He looks away. Though I speak with the tongues of men and of angels, and have not charity, I am become as sounding brass, or a tinkling cymbal. And though I have the gift of prophecy, and understand all mysteries, and all knowledge; and though I have all faith, so that I could remove mountains, and have not charity, I am nothing. But this world is beyond the reach of love. He looks away. The sun appears. The fog burns off. The visions fade. He sees only the dead land, the ashes, the ruins. All right. Here we have no continuing city, but we seek one to come. Onward. Onward.

9.

And now, after this series of brief, disconcerting intermediate stops, Cameron has come to a city that is San Francisco beyond doubt, not some other city on San Francisco's site but a true San Francisco, a recognisable San Francisco. He pops into it atop Russian Hill, at the very crest, on a dazzling, brilliant, cloudless day. To his left, below, lies Fisherman's Wharf; ahead of him rises the Coit Tower, yes, and he can see the Ferry Building and the Bay Bridge. Familiar landmarks – but how strange all the rest seems! Where is the eye-stabbing Transamerica pyramid? Where is the colossal sombre stalk of the Bank of America? The strangeness, he realises, derives not so much from substitutions as from absences. The big Embarcadero developments are not there, nor the Chinatown Holiday Inn, nor the miserable tentacles of the elevated freeways, nor, apparently, anything else that was constructed in the last twenty years. This is the old short-shanked San Francisco of his boyhood, a sparkling miniature city, un-Manhattanised, skylineless. Surely he has returned to the place he knew in the sleepy 1950s, the tranquil Eisenhower years.

He heads downhill, searching for a newspaper box. He finds one at the corner of Hyde and North Point, a bright yellow metal rectangle. San Francisco *Chronicle*, ten cents. Ten cents? Is that the right price for 1954? One Roosevelt dime goes into the slot. The paper, he finds, is dated Tuesday, August 19, 1975. In what Cameron still thinks of, with some irony now, as the real world, the world that has been receding rapidly from him all day in a series of discontinuous jumps, it is also Tuesday, the 19th of August, 1975. So he has not gone backward in time at all; he has come to a San Francisco where time has seemingly been standing still. Why? In vertigo he eyes the front page.

A three-column headline declares:

FUEHRER ARRIVES IN WASHINGTON

Under it, to the left, a photograph or three men, smiling broadly, positively beaming at one another. The caption identifies them as President Kennedy, Fuehrer Goering and Ambassador Togarashi of Japan, meeting in the White House rose garden. Cameron closes his eyes. Using no data other than the headline and the caption, he attempts to concoct a plausible speculation. This is a world, he decides, in which the Axis must have won the war. The United States is a German fiefdom. There are no high-rise buildings in San Francisco because the American economy, shattered by defeat, has not yet in thirty years of peace returned to a level where it can afford to erect them, or perhaps because American venture capital, prodded by the financial ministers of the Third Reich – (Hjalmar Schacht? The name drifts out of the swampy recesses of memory) – now tends to flow toward Europe. But how could it have happened? Cameron remembers the war years clearly, the tremendous surge of patriotism, the vast mobilisation, the great national effort. Rosie the Riveter. Lucky Strike

Green Goes To War. Let's Remember Pearl Harbor, As We Did
The Alamo. He doesn't see any way the Germans might have
brought America to her knees. Except one. The bomb, he thinks,
the bomb, the Nazis get the bomb in 1940 and Wernher von
Braun invents a transatlantic rocket and New York and
Washington are nuked one night and that's it, we've been pushed
beyond the resources of patriotism, we cave in and surrender
within a week. And so –

He studies the photograph. President Kennedy, grinning,
standing between Reichsfuehrer Goering and a suave youthful-
looking Japanese. Kennedy? Ted? No, this is Jack, the very same
Jack who, looking jowly, heavy bags under his eyes, deep creases
in his face – he must be almost sixty years old, nearing the end of
what is probably his second term of office. Jacqueline waiting
none too patiently for him upstairs. Get done with your Japs and
Nazis, love, and let's have a few drinkies together before the con-
cert. Yes. John-John and Caroline somewhere on the premises
too, the nation's darlings, models for young people everywhere.
Yes. And Goering? Indeed, the very same Goering who. Well into
his eighties, monstrously fat, chin upon chin, multitudes of chins,
vast bemedalled bosom, little mischievous eyes glittering with a
long lifetime's cheery recollections of gratified lusts. How happy
he looks! And how amiable! It was always impossible to hate
Goering the way one loathed Goebbels, say, or Himmler or
Streicher; Goering had charm, the outrageous charm of a monstre
sacre, of a Nero, of a Caligula, and here he is alive in the 1970s,
a mountain of immortal flesh, having survived Adolf to become –
Cameron assumes – Second Fuehrer and to be received in pomp
at the White House, no less. Perhaps a state banquet tomorrow
night, rollmops, sauerbraten, kassler rippchen, koenigsberger
klopse, washed down with flagons of Bernkasteler Doktor 69,
Schloss Johannisberg 71, or does the Fuehrer prefer beer? We
have the finest lagers on tap, Löwenbrau, Würzburger Hofbrau –

But wait. Something rings false in Cameron's historical con-
struct. He is unable to find in John F. Kennedy those depths of
opportunism that would allow him to serve as puppet President of

a Nazi-ruled America, taking orders from some slick-haired hard-eyed gauleiter and hopping obediently when the Fuehrer comes to town. Bomb or no bomb, there would have been a diehard underground resistance movement, decades of guerrilla warfare, bitter hatred of the German oppressor and of all collaborators. No surrender, then. The Axis has won the war, but the United States has retained its autonomy. Cameron revises his speculations. Suppose, he tells himself, Hitler in this universe did not break his pact with Stalin and invade Russia in the summer of 1941, but led his forces across the Channel instead to wipe out Britain. And the Japanese left Pearl Harbor alone, so the United States never was drawn into the war, which was over in fairly short order – say, by September of 1942. The Germans now rule Europe from Cornwall to the Urals, and the Japanese have the whole Pacific west of Hawaii; the United States, lost in dreamy neutrality, is an isolated nation, a giant Portugal, economically stagnant, largely cut off from world trade. There are no skyscrapers in San Francisco because no one sees reason to build anything in this country. Yes? Is this how it is?

He seats himself on the stoop of a house and explores his newspaper. This world has a stock market, albeit a sluggish one: the Dow-Jones Industrials stand at 354.61. Some of the listings are familiar – IBM, AT&T, General Motors – but many are not. Litton, Syntex and Polaroid all are missing; so is Xerox, but he finds its primordial predecessor, Haloid, in the quotations. There are two baseball leagues, each with eight clubs; the Boston Braves have moved to Milwaukee but otherwise the table of teams could have come straight out of the 1940s. Brooklyn is leading in the National League, Philadelphia in the American. In the news section he finds recognisable names: New York has a Senator Rockefeller, Massachusetts has a Senator Kennedy. (Robert, apparently. He is currently in Italy. Yesterday he toured the majestic Tomb of Mussolini near the Colosseum, today he has an audience with Pope Benedict.) An airline advertisement invites San Franciscans to go to New York via TWA's glorious new Starliners, now only twelve hours with just a brief stop in

Chicago. The accompanying sketch indicates that they have about reached the DC-4 level here, or is that a DC-6, with all those propellers? The foreign news is tame and sketchy: not a word about Israel vs. the Arabs, the squabbling republics of Africa, the People's Republic of China, or the war in South America. Cameron assumes that the only surviving Jews are those of New York and Los Angeles, that Africa is one immense German colonial tract with a few patches under Italian rule, that China is governed by the Japanese, not by the heirs of Chairman Mao, and that the South American nations are torpid and unaggressive. Yes? Reading this newspaper is the strangest experience this voyage has given him so far, for the pages *look* right, the tone of the writing *feels* right, there is the insistent texture of unarguable reality about the whole paper, and yet everything is subtly off, everything has undergone a slight shift along the spectrum of events. The newspaper has the quality of a dream, but he has never known a dream to have such overwhelming substantive density.

He folds the paper under his arm and strolls toward the bay. A block from the waterfront he finds a branch of the Bank of America – some things withstand all permutations – and goes inside to change some money. There are risks, but he is curious. The teller unhesitatingly takes his five-dollar bill and hands him four singles and a little stack of coins. The singles are unremarkable, and Lincoln, Jefferson and Washington occupy their familiar places on the cent, nickel and quarter; but the dime shows Ben Franklin and the fifty-cent piece bears the features of a heartylooking man, youngish, full-faced, bushy-haired, whom Cameron is unable to identify at all.

On the next corner eastward he comes to a public library. Now he can confirm his guesses. An almanac! Yes, and how odd the list of Presidents looks. Roosevelt, he learns, retired in poor health in 1940, and that, so far as he can discover, is the point of divergence between this world and his. The rest follows predictably enough. Wendell Willkie, defeating John Nance Garner in the 1940 election, maintains a policy of strict neutrality while

– yes, it was as he had imagined – the Germans and Japanese quickly conquer most of the world. Willkie dies in office during the 1944 Presidential campaign – aha! That's Willkie on the half dollar! – and is briefly succeeded by Vice President McNary, who does not want the Presidency; a hastily recalled Republican convention nominates Robert Taft. Two terms then for Taft, who beats James Byrnes, and two for Thomas Dewey, and then in 1960 the long Republican era is ended at last by Senator Lyndon Johnson of Texas. Johnson's running mate – it is an amusing reversal, Cameron thinks – is Senator John F. Kennedy of Massachusetts. After the traditional two terms, Johnson steps down and Vice President Kennedy wins the 1968 Presidential election. He has been re-elected in 1972, naturally; in this placid world incumbents always win. There is, of course, no UN here; there has been no Korean War, no movement of colonial liberation, no exploration of space. The almanac tells Cameron that Hitler lived until 1960, Mussolini until 1958. The world seems to have adapted remarkably readily to Axis rule, although a German army of occupation is still stationed in England.

He is tempted to go on and on, comparing histories, learning the transmuted destinies of such figures as Hubert Humphrey, Dwight Eisenhower, Harry Truman, Nikita Khruschchev, Lee Harvey Oswald, Juan Peron. But suddenly a more intimate curiosity flowers in him. In a hallway alcove he consults the telephone book. There is one directory covering both Alameda and Contra Costa counties, and it is a much more slender volume than the directory which in his world covers Oakland alone. There are two dozen Cameron listings, but none at his address, and no Christophers or Elizabeths or any plausible permutations of those names. On a hunch he looks in the San Francisco book. Nothing promising there either; but then he checks Elizabeth under her maiden name, Dudley, and yes, there is an Elizabeth Dudley at the familiar old address on Laguna. The discovery causes him to tremble. He rummages in his pocket, finds his Ben Franklin dime, drops it in the slot. He listens. There's the dial tone. He makes the call.

10.

The apartment, what he can see of it by peering past her shoulder, looks much as he remembers it: well-worn couches and chairs upholstered in burgundy and dark green, stark whitewashed walls, elaborate sculptures – her own – of grey driftwood, huge ferns in hanging containers. To behold these objects in these surroundings wrenches powerfully at his sense of time and place and afflicts him with an almost unbearable nostalgia. The last time he was here, if indeed he has ever been 'here' in any sense, was in 1969; but the memories are vivid, and what he sees corresponds so closely to what he recalls that he feels transported to that earlier era. She stands in the doorway, studying him with cool curiosity tinged with unmistakable suspicion. She wears unexpectedly ordinary clothes, a loose-fitting embroidered white blouse and a short, pleated blue skirt, and her golden hair looks dull and carelessly combed, but surely she is the same woman from whom he parted this morning, the same woman with whom he has shared his life these past seven years, a beautiful woman, a tall woman, nearly as tall as he – on some occasions taller, it has seemed – with a serene smile and steady green eyes and smooth, taut skin. "Yes?" she says uncertainly. "Are you the man who phoned?"

"Yes. Chris Cameron." He searches her face for some flicker of recognition. "You don't know me? Not at all?"

"Not at all. Should I know you?"

"Perhaps. Probably not. It's hard to say."

"Have we once met? Is that it?"

"I'm not sure how I'm going to explain my relationship to you."

"So you said when you called. Your *relationship* to me? How can strangers have had a relationship?"

"It's complicated. May I come in?"

She laughs nervously, as though caught in some embarrassing faux pas. "Of course," she says, not without giving him a quick appraisal, making a rapid estimate of risk. The apartment is in fact almost exactly as he knew it, except that there is no stereo phonograph, only a bulky archaic Victrola, and her record collection is surprisingly scanty, and there are rather fewer books than his Elizabeth would have had. They confront one another stiffly. He is as uneasy over this encounter as she is, and finally it is she who seeks some kind of social lubricant, suggesting that they have a little wine. She offers him red or white.

"Red, please," he says.

She goes to a low sideboard and takes out two cheap, clumsy-looking tumblers. Then, effortlessly, she lifts a gallon jug of wine from the floor and begins to unscrew its cap. "You were awfully mysterious on the phone," she says, "and you're still being mysterious now. What brings you here? Do we have mutual friends?"

"I think it wouldn't be untruthful to say that we do. At least in a manner of speaking."

"Your own manner of speaking is remarkably roundabout, Mr Cameron."

"I can't help that right now. And call me Chris, please." As she pours the wine he watches her closely, thinking of that other Elizabeth, *his* Elizabeth, thinking how well he knows her body, the supple play of muscles in her back, the sleek texture of her skin, the firmness of her flesh, and he flashes instantly to their strange, absurdly romantic meeting years ago, that June when he had gone off alone into the Sierra high country for a week of backpacking and, following heaps of stones that he had wrongly taken to be trail-markers, had come to a place well off the path, a private place, a cool dark glacial lake rimmed by brilliant patches of late-lying snow, and had begun to make camp, and had become suddenly aware of someone else's pack thirty yards away, and a pile of discarded clothing on the shore, and then had seen her, swimming just beyond a pine-tipped point, heading toward land, rising like Venus from the water, naked, noticing him, startled by his presence, apprehensive for a moment but then immediately making the best of it, relaxing, smiling, standing unashamed shin-deep in the chilly shallows and inviting him to join her for a swim. These recollections of that first contact and all that ensued excite him terribly, for this person before him is at once the Elizabeth he loves, familiar, joined to him by the bond of shared experience, and also someone new, a complete stranger, from whom he can draw fresh inputs, that jolting gift of novelty which his Elizabeth can never again offer him. He stares at her shoulders and back with fierce, intense hunger; she turns toward him with the glasses of wine in her hands, and, before he can mask that wild gleam of desire, she receives it with full force. The impact is immediate. She recoils. She is not the Elizabeth of the Sierra lake; she seems unable to handle such a level of unexpected erotic voltage. Jerkily she thrusts the wine at him, her hands shaking so that she spills a little on her sleeve. He takes the glass and backs away, a bit dazed by his own frenzied upwelling of emotion. With an effort he calms himself. There is a long moment of awkward silence while they drink. The psychic atmosphere grows less torrid; a certain mood of remote, businesslike courtesy develops between them.

After the second glass of wine she says, "Now. How do you know me and what do you want from me?"

Briefly he closes his eyes. What can he tell her? How can he explain? He has rehearsed no strategies. Already he has managed to alarm her with a single unguarded glance; what effect would a confession of apparent madness have? But he has never used strategies with Elizabeth, has never resorted to any tactics except the tactic of utter candidness. And this is Elizabeth. Slowly he says. "In another existence you and I are married, Elizabeth. We live in the Oakland hills and we're extraordinarily happy together."

"Another existence?"

"In a world apart from this, a world where history took a different course a generation ago, where the Axis lost the war, where John Kennedy was President in 1963 and was killed by an assassin, where you and I met beside a lake in the Sierra and fell in love. There's an infinity of worlds, Elizabeth, side by side, worlds in which all possible variations of every possible event take place. Worlds in which you and I are married happily, in which you and I have been married and divorced, in which you and I don't exist, in which you exist and I don't, in which we meet and loathe one another, in which – in which – do you see, Elizabeth, there's a world for everything, and I've been travelling from world to world. I've seen nothing but wilderness where San Francisco ought to be, and I've met Mongol horsemen in the East Bay hills, and I've seen this whole area devastated by atomic warfare, and – does this sound insane to you, Elizabeth?"

"Just a little." She smiles. The old Elizabeth, cool, judicious, performing one of her specialties, the conditional acceptance of the unbelievable for the sake of some amusing conversation. "But go on. You've been jumping from world to world. I won't even bother to ask you how. What are you running away from?"

"I've never seen it that way. I'm running *toward*."

"Toward what?"

"An infinity of worlds. An endless range of possible experience."

"That's a lot to swallow. Isn't one world enough for you to explore?"

"Evidently not."

"You had all infinity," she says. "Yet you chose to come to me. Presumably I'm the one point of familiarity for you in this otherwise strange world. Why come here? What's the point of your wanderings, if you seek the familiar? If all you wanted to do was find your way back to your Elizabeth, why did you leave her in the first place? Are you as happy with her as you claim to be?"

"I can be happy with her and still desire her in other guises."

"You sound driven."

"No," he says. "No more driven than Faust. I believe in searching as a way of life. Not searching *for*, just searching. And it's impossible to stop. To stop is to die, Elizabeth. Look at Faust, going on and on, going to Helen of Troy herself, experiencing everything the world has to offer, and always seeking more. When Faust finally cries out, *This is it, this is what I've been looking for, this is where I choose to stop*, Mephistopheles wins his bet."

"But that was Faust's moment of supreme happiness."

"True. When he attains it, though, he loses his soul to the devil, remember?"

"So you go on, on and on, world after world, seeking you know not what, just seeking, unable to stop. And yet you claim you're not driven."

He shakes his head. "Machines are driven. Animals are driven. I'm an autonomous human being operating out of free will. I don't make this journey because I have to, but because I want to."

"Or because you think you ought to want to."

"I'm motivated by feelings, not by intellectual calculations and preconceptions."

"That sounds very carefully thought out," she tells him. He is stung by her words, and looks away, down into his empty glass. She indicates that he should help himself to the wine. "I'm sorry," she says, her tone softening a little.

He says, "At any rate, I was in the library and there was a telephone directory and I found you. This is where you used to live in my world, too, before we were married." He hesitates. "Do you mind if I ask – "

"What?"

"You're not married?"

"No. I live alone. And like it."

"You always were independent-minded."

"You talk as though you know me so well."

"I've been married to you for seven years."

"No. Not to me. Never to me. You don't know me at all."

He nods. "You're right. I don't really know you, Elizabeth, however much I think I do. But I want to. I feel drawn to you as strongly as I was to the other Elizabeth, that day in the mountains. It's always best right at the beginning, when two strangers reach toward one another, when the spark leaps the gap – " Tenderly he says, "May I spend the night here?"

"No."

Somehow the refusal comes as no surprise. He says, "You once gave me a different answer when I asked you that."

"Not I. Someone else."

"I'm sorry. It's so hard for me to keep you and her distinct in my mind, Elizabeth. But please don't turn me away. I've come so far to be with you."

"You came uninvited. Besides, I'd feel so strange with you – knowing you were thinking of her, comparing me with her, measuring our differences, our points of similarities – "

"What makes you think I would?"

"You would."

"I don't think that's sufficient reason for sending me away."

"I'll give you another," she says. Her eyes sparkle mischievously. "I never let myself get involved with married men."

She is teasing him now. He says, laughing, confident that she is beginning to yield, "That's the damndest far-fetched excuse I've ever heard, Elizabeth!"

"Is it? I feel a great kinship with her. She has all my sympathies. Why should I help you deceive her?"

"Deceive? What an old-fashioned word! Do you think she'd object? She never expected me to be chaste on this trip. She'd be flattered and delighted to know that I went looking for you here. She'd be eager to hear about everything that went on between us. How could she possibly be hurt by knowing that I had been with you, when you and she are – "

"Nevertheless, I'd like you to leave. Please."

"You haven't given me one convincing reason."

"I don't need to."

"I love you. I want to spend the night with you."

"You love someone else who resembles me," she replies. "I keep telling you that. In any case, I don't love you. I don't find you attractive, I'm afraid."

"Oh. She does, but you – don't. I see. How do you find me, then? Ugly? Overbearing? Repellent?"

"I find you disturbing," she says. "A little frightening. Much too intense, much too controlled, perhaps dangerous. You aren't my type. I'm probably not yours. Remember, I'm not the Elizabeth you met by that mountain lake. Perhaps I'd be happier if I were, but I'm not. I wish you had never come here. Now: please go. Please."

11.

Onward. This place is all gleaming towers and airy bridges, a glistening fantasy of a city. High overhead float glassy bubbles, silent airborne passenger vehicles, containing two or three people apiece who sprawl in postures of elegant relaxation. Bronzed young boys and girls lie naked beside soaring fountains spewing turquoise-and-scarlet foam. Giant orchids burst in tropical voluptuousness from the walls of colossal hotels. Small mechanical birds wheel and dart in the soft air like golden bullets, emitting sweet pinging sounds. From the tips of the tallest buildings comes a darker music, a ground-bass of swelling hundred-cycle notes oscillating around an insistent central rumble. This is a world two centuries ahead of his, at the least. He could never infiltrate here. He could never even be a tourist. The only role available to him is that of visiting savage, Jemmy Button among the Londoners, and what, after all, was Jemmy Button's fate? Not a happy one. Patagonia! Patagonia! Thees ticket eet ees no longer good here, sor. Coloured rays dance in the sky, red, green, blue, exploding, showering the city with transcendental images. Cameron smiles. He will not let himself be overwhelmed, though this place is more confusing than the world of the halftrack automobiles. Jauntily he plants himself at the centre of a small park between two lanes of flowing noiseless traffic. It is a formal garden lush with toothy orange-fronded ferns and thorny skyrockets of looping cactus. Lovers stroll past him arm in arm, offering one another swigs from glossy sweat-beaded green flasks that look like tubes of polished jade. Delicately they dangle blue grapes before each other's lips, playfully they smile, arch their necks, take the bait with eager pounces; then they laugh, embrace, tumble into the dense moist grass, which stirs and sways and emits gentle thrumming melodies. This place pleases him. He wanders through the garden, thinking of Elizabeth, thinking of springtime, and, coming ultimately to a sinuous brook in which the city's tallest towers are reflected as inverted needles, he kneels to drink. The water is cool, sweet, tart, much like young wine. A moment after it touches his lips a mechanism rises from the spongy earth, five slender brassy columns, three with eye-sensors sprouting on all sides, one marked with a pattern of dark gridwork, one bearing an arrangement of winking coloured lights. Out of the gridwork come ominous words in an unfathomable language. This is some kind of police machine, demanding his credentials: that much is clear. "I'm sorry," he says. "I can't understand what you're saying." Other machines are extruding themselves from trees, from the bed of the stream, from the hearts of the sturdiest ferns. "It's all right," he says. "I don't mean any harm. Just give me a chance to learn the language and I promise to become a useful citizen." One of the machines sprays him with a fine azure mist. Another drives a tiny needle into his forearm and extracts a droplet of blood. A crowd is gathering. They point, snicker, wink. The music of the building-tops has become higher in pitch, more sinister in texture; it shakes the balmy air and threatens him in a personal way. "Let me stay," Cameron begs, but the music is shoving him, pushing him with a flat irresistible hand, inexorably squeezing him out of this world. He is too primitive for them. He is too coarse, he carries too many obsolete microbes. Very well. If that's what they want, he'll leave, not out of fear, not because they've succeeded in intimidating him, but out of courtesy alone. In a flamboyant way he bids them farewell, bowing with a flourish worthy of Raleigh, blowing a kiss to the five-columned machine, smiling, even doing a little dance. Farewell. Farewell. The music rises to a wild crescendo. He hears celestial trumpets and distant thunder. Farewell. Onward.

12.

Here some kind of oriental marketplace has sprung up, foul-smelling, cluttered, medieval. Swarthy old men, white-bearded, in thick grey robes, sit patiently behind open burlap sacks of spices and grains. Lepers and cripples roam everywhere, begging importunately. Slender long-legged men wearing only tight loincloths and jingling dangling earrings of bright copper stalk through the crowd on solitary orbits, buying nothing, saying nothing; their skins are dark red, their faces are gaunt, their

solemn features are finely modelled. They carry themselves like
Inca princes. Perhaps they *are* Inca princes. In the haggle and
babble of the market Cameron hears no recognisable tongue
spoken. He sees the flash of gold as transactions are completed.
The women balance immense burdens on their heads and show
brilliant teeth when they smile. They favour patchwork skirts
that cover their ankles, but they leave their breasts bare. Several
of them glance provocatively at Cameron but he dares not return
their quick dazzling probes until he knows what is permissible
here. On the far side of the squalid plaza he catches sight of a
woman who might well be Elizabeth; her back is to him, but he
would know those strong shoulders anywhere, that erect stance,
that cascade of unbound golden hair. He starts toward her, sliding with difficulty between the close-packed marketgoers.
When he is still halfway across the marketplace from her he
notices a man at her side, tall, a man of his own height and build.
He wears a loose black robe and a dark scarf covers the lower
half of his face. His eyes are grim and sullen and a terrible cica-
trice, wide and glaringly crosshatched with stitchmarks, runs
along his left cheek up to his hairline. The man whispers something to the woman who might be Elizabeth; she nods and turns,
so that Cameron now is able to see her face, and yes, the woman
does seem to be Elizabeth, but she bears a matching scar, angry
and hideous, up the right side of her face. Cameron gasps. The
scar-faced man suddenly points and shouts. Cameron senses
motion to one side, and swings around just in time to see a short
thickbodied man come rushing toward him wildly waving a
scimitar. For an instant Cameron sees the scene as though in a
photograph: he has time to make a leisurely examination of his
attacker's oily beard, his hooked hairy-nostriled nose, his yellowed teeth, the cheap glassy-looking inlaid stones on the haft
of the scimitar. Then the frightful blade descends, while the
assassin screams abuse at Cameron in what might be Arabic. It
is a sorry welcome. Cameron cannot prolong this investigation.
An instant before the scimitar cuts him in two he takes himself
elsewhere, with regret.

13.

Onward. To a place where there is no solidity, where the planet itself has vanished, so that he swims through space, falling peacefully, going from nowhere to nowhere. He is surrounded by a brilliant green light that emanates from every point at once, like a message from the fabric of the universe. In great tranquillity he drops through this cheerful glow for days on end, or what seems like days on end, drifting, banking, checking his course with small motions of his elbows or knees. It makes no difference where he goes; everything here is like everything else here. The green glow supports and sustains and nourishes him, but it makes him restless. He plays with it. Out of its lambent substance he succeeds in shaping images, faces, abstract patterns; he conjures up Elizabeth for himself, he evokes his own sharp features, he fills the heavens with a legion of marching Chinese in tapered straw hats, he obliterates them with forceful diagonal lines, he causes a river of silver to stream across the firmament and discharge its glittering burden down a mountainside a thousand miles high. He spins. He floats. He glides. He releases all his fantasies. This is total freedom, here in this unworldly place. But it is not enough. He grows weary of emptiness. He grows weary of serenity. He has drained this place of all it has to offer, too soon, too soon. He is not sure whether the failure is in himself or in the place, but he feels he must leave. Therefore: onward.

14.

Terrified peasants run shrieking as he materialises in their midst. This is some sort of farming village along the eastern shore of the bay: neat green fields, a cluster of low wicker huts radiating from a central plaza, naked children toddling and crying, a busy subpopulation of goats and geese and chickens. It is midday; Cameron sees the bright gleam of water in the irrigation ditches. These people work hard. They have scattered at his approach, but now they creep back warily, crouching, ready to take off again if he performs any more miracles. This is another of those bucolic worlds in which San Francisco has not happened, but he is unable to identify these settlers, nor can he isolate the chain of events that brought them here. They are not Indians, nor Chinese, nor Peruvians; they have a European look about them, somehow Slavic, but what would Slavs be doing in California? Russian farmers, maybe, colonising by way of Siberia? There is some plausibility in that – their dark complexions, their heavy facial structure, their squat powerful bodies – but they seem oddly primitive, haft-naked, in furry leggings or less, as though they are no subjects of the Tsar but rather Scythians or Cimmerians transplanted from the prehistoric marshes of the Vistula.

"Don't be frightened," he tells them, holding his upraised outspread arms toward them. They do seem less fearful of him now, timidly approaching, staring with big dark eyes. "I won't harm you. I'd just like to visit with you." They murmur. A woman boldly shoves a child forward, a girl of about five, bare, with black greasy ringlets, and Cameron scoops her up, caresses her, tickles her, lightly sets her down. Instantly the whole tribe is around him, no longer afraid; they touch his arm, they kneel, they stroke his shins. A boy brings him a wooden bowl of porridge. An old woman gives him a mug of sweet wine, a kind of mead. A slender girl drapes a stole of auburn fur over his shoulders. They dance, they chant; their fear has turned into love; he is their honoured guest. He is more than that: he is a god. They take him to an unoccupied hut, the largest in the village. Piously they bring him offerings of incense and acorns. When it grows dark they build an immense bonfire in the plaza, so that he wonders in vague concern if they will feast on him when they are done honouring him, but they feast on slaughtered cattle instead, and yield to him the choicest pieces, and afterward they stand by his door, singing discordant, energetic hymns. That night three girls of the tribe, no doubt the fairest virgins available, are sent to him, and in the morning he finds his threshold heaped with newly plucked blossoms. Later two tribal artisans, one lame and the other blind, set to work with stone adzes and chisels, hewing an immense and remarkably accurate likeness of him out of a redwood stump that has been mounted at the plaza's centre.

So he has been deified. He has a quick Faustian vision of himself living among these diligent people, teaching them advanced methods of agriculture, leading them eventually into technology, into modern hygiene, into all the contemporary advantages without the contemporary abominations. Guiding them toward the light, moulding them, creating them. This world, this village, would be a good place for him to stop his transit of the infinities, if stopping were desirable: god, prophet, king of a placid realm, teacher, inculcator of civilisation, a purpose to his existence at last. But there *is* no place to stop. He knows that. Transforming happy primitive farmers into sophisticated twentieth-century agriculturalists is ultimately as useless a pastime as training fleas to jump through hoops. It is tempting to live as a god, but even divinity will pall, and it is dangerous to become attached to an unreal satisfaction, dangerous to become attached at all. The journey, not the arrival, matters. Always.

So Cameron does godhood for a little while. He finds it pleasant and fulfilling. He savours the rewards until he senses that the rewards are becoming too important to him. He makes his formal renunciation of his godhead. Then: onward.

15.

And this place he recognises. His street, his house, his garden, his green car in the carport, Elizabeth's yellow one parked out front. Home again, so soon? He hadn't expected that; but every leap he has made, he knows, must in some way have been a product of deliberate choice, and evidently whatever hidden mechanism within him that has directed these voyages has chosen to bring him home again. All right, touch base. Digest your travels, examine them, allow your experiences to work their alchemy on you: you need to stand still a moment for that. Afterward you can always leave again. He slides his key into the door.

Elizabeth has one of the Mozart quartets on the phonograph. She sits curled up in the livingroom window-seat, leafing through a magazine. It is late afternoon and the San Francisco skyline, clearly visible across the bay through the big window, is haloed by the brilliant retreating sunlight. There are freshly cut flowers in the little crystal bowl on the redwood-burl table: the fragrance of gardenias and jasmine dances past him. Unhurriedly she looks up, brings her eyes into line with his, dazzles him with the warmth of her smile, and says, "Well, hello!"

"Hello, Elizabeth."

She comes to him. "I didn't expect you back this quickly, Chris. I don't know if I expected you to come back at all, as a matter of fact."

"This quickly? How long have I been gone, for you?"

"Tuesday morning to Thursday afternoon. Two and a half days." She eyes his coarse new beard, his ragged, sun-bleached shirt. "It's been longer for you, hasn't it?"

"Weeks and weeks. I'm not sure how long. I was in eight or nine different places, and I stayed in the last one quite some time. They were villagers, farmers, some primitive Slavonic tribe living down by the bay. I was their god, but I got bored with it."

"You always did get bored so easily," she says, and laughs, and takes his hands in hers and pulls him toward her. She brushes her lips lightly against him, a peck, a play-kiss, their usual first greeting, and then they kiss more passionately, bodies pressing close, tongue seeking tongue. He feels a pounding in his chest, the old inextinguishable throb. When they release each other he steps back, a little dizzied, and says, "I missed you, Elizabeth. I didn't know how much I'd miss you until I was somewhere else and aware that I might never find you again."

"Did you seriously worry about that?"

"Very much."

"I never doubted we'd be together again, one way or another. Infinity's such a big place, darling. You'd find your way back to me, or to someone very much like me. And someone very much like you would find his way to me, if you didn't. How many Chris Camerons do you think there are, on the move between worlds right now? A thousand? A trillion trillion?" She turns toward the sideboard and says, without breaking the flow of her words, "Would

223

you like some wine?" and begins to pour from a half-empty jug of red. "Tell me where you've been," she says.

He comes up behind her and rests his hands on her shoulders, and draws them down the back of her silk blouse to her waist, holding her there, kissing the nape of her neck. He says, "To a world where there was an atomic war here, and to one where there still were Indian raiders out by Livermore, and one that was all fantastic robots and futuristic helicopters, and one where Johnson was President before Kennedy and Kennedy is alive and President now, and one where – oh, I'll give you all the details later. I need a chance to unwind first." He releases her and kisses the tip of her earlobe and takes one of the glasses from her, and they salute each other and drink, draining the wine quickly. "It's so good to be home," he says softly. "Good to have gone where I went, good to be back." She fills his glass again. The familiar domestic ritual: red wine is their special drink, cheap red wine out of gallon jugs. A sacrament, more dear to him than the burnt offerings of his recent subjects. Halfway through the second glass he says, "Come. Let's go inside."

The bed has fresh linens on it, cool, inviting. There are three thick books on the nighttable: she's set up for some heavy reading in his absence. Cut flowers in here, too, fragrance everywhere. Their clothes drop away. She touches his beard and chuckles at the roughness, and he kisses the smooth cool place along the inside of her thigh and draws his cheek lightly across it, sandpapering her lovingly, and then she pulls him to her and their bodies slide together and he enters her. Everything thereafter happens quickly, much too quickly; he has been long absent from her, if not she from him, and now her presence excites him, there is a strangeness about her body, her movements, and it hastens him to his ecstasy. He feels a mild pang of regret, but no more: he'll make it up to her soon enough, they both know that. They drift into a sleepy embrace, neither of them speaking, and eventually uncoil into tender new passion, and this time all is as it should be. Afterward they doze. A spectacular sunset blazes over the city when he opens his eyes. They rise, they take a shower together, much giggling, much playfulness. "Let's go across the bay for a fancy dinner tonight," he suggests. "Trianon, Blue Fox, Ernie's, anywhere. You name it. I feel like celebrating."

"So do I, Chris."

"It's good to be home again."

"It's good to have you here," she tells him. She looks for her purse. "How soon do you think you'll be heading out again? Not that I mean to rush you, but – "

"You know I'm not going to be staying?"

"Of course I know."

"Yes. You would." She had never questioned his going. They both tried to be responsive to each other's needs; they had always regarded one another as equal partners, free to do as they wished. "I can't say how long I'll stay. Probably not long. Coming home this soon was really an accident, you know. I just planned to go on and on and world after world, and I never programmed my next jump, at least not consciously. I simply leaped. And the last leap deposited me on my own doorstep, somehow, so I let myself into the house. And there you were to welcome me home."

She presses his hand between hers. Almost sadly she says, "You aren't home, Chris."

"What?"

He hears the sound of the front door opening. Footsteps in the hallway.

"You aren't home," she says.

Confusion seizes him. He thinks of all that has passed between them this evening.

"Elizabeth?" calls a deep voice from the livingroom.

"In here, darling. I have company!"

"Oh? Who?" A man enters the bedroom, halts, grins. He is clean-shaven and dressed in the clothes Cameron had worn on Tuesday; otherwise they could be twins. "Hey, hello!" he says warmly, extending his hand.

Elizabeth says, "He comes from a place that must be very much like this one. He's been here since five o'clock, and we were just going out for dinner. Have you been having an interesting time?"

"Very," the other Cameron says. "I'll tell you all about it later. Go on, don't let me keep you."

"You could join us for dinner," Cameron suggests helplessly.

"That's all right. I've just eaten. Breast of passenger pigeon – they aren't extinct everywhere. I wish I could have brought some home for the freezer. So you two go and enjoy. I'll see you later. Both of you, I hope. Will you be staying with us? We've got notes to compare, you and I."

16.

He rises just before dawn, in a marvellous foggy stillness. The Camerons have been wonderfully hospitable, but he must be moving along. He scrawls a thank-you note and slips it under their bedroom door. *Let's get together again some day. Somewhere. Somehow.* They want him as a houseguest for a week or two, but no, he feels like a bit of an intruder here, and anyway the universe is waiting for him. He has to go. The journey, not the arrival, matters, for what else is there but trips? Departing is unexpectedly painful, but he knows the mood will pass. He closes his eyes. He breaks his moorings. He gives himself up to his sublime restlessness. Onward. Onward. *Goodbye, Elizabeth. Goodbye, Chris.* I'll see you both again. Onward.

All Tomorrow's Parties

PAUL J. McAULEY

And with exactly a year left before the end of the century-long gathering of her clade, she went to Paris with her current lover, racing ahead of midnight and the beginning of the New Year. Paris! The Premier Quartier: the early Twentieth Century. Fireworks bursting in great flowers above the night-black Seine, and a brawling carnival which under a multi-coloured rain of confetti filled every street from the Quai du Louvre to the Arc de Triomphe.

Escorted by her lover (they had been hunting big game in the Pleistocene era taiga of Siberia; he still wore his safari suit, and a Springfield rifle was slung over his shoulder), she crossed to the Palaeolithic oak woods of the Ile de la Cité. In the middle of the great stone circle naked druids with blue-stained skins beat huge drums under flaring torchs, while holographic ghosts swung above the electric lights of the Twentieth Century shore, a fleet of luminous clouds dancing in the sky. Her attentive lover identified them for her, leaning against her shoulder so she could sight along his arm. He was exactly her height, with piercing blue eyes and a salt-and-pepper beard.

An astronaut. A gene pirate. Emperor Victoria. Mickey Mouse.

"What is a mouse?"

He pointed. "That one, the black-skinned creature with the circular ears."

She leaned against his solid human warmth. "For an animal, it seems very much like a person. Was it a product of the gene wars?"

"It is a famous icon of the country where I was born. My countrymen preferred creatures of the imagination to those of the real world. It is why they produced so few good authors."

"But you were a good author."

"I was not bad, except at the end. Something bad always happened to all good writers from my country. Sometimes slowly, sometimes quickly, but without exception."

"What is it carrying?"

"A light sabre. It is an imaginary weapon that is authentic for the period. They were obsessed with weapons and divisions. They saw the world as a struggle of good against evil. That was how wars could be called good, except by those who fought in them."

She didn't argue. Her lover, a partial, had been modelled on a particular Twentieth Century writer, and had direct access to the appropriate records in the Library. Although she had been born just at the end of the Twentieth Century, she had long ago forgotten everything about it.

Behind them, the drums reached a frenzied climax and fell silent. The sacrificial victim writhed on the heel stone and the chief druid lifted the still beating heart above his head in triumph. Blood that looked black in the torchlight ran down his arms.

The spectators beyond the circle clapped or toasted each other. One man was trying to persuade his companion to fuck on the altar. They were invisible to the druids, who were merely puppets lending local colour to the scene.

"I'm getting tired of this," she said.

"Of course. We could go to Cuba. The ocean fishing there is good. Or to Afrique, to hunt lions. I think I liked that best, but after a while I could no longer do it. That was one of the things that destroyed my writing."

"I'm getting tired of you," she said, and her lover bowed and walked away.

She was getting tired of everything.

She had been getting tired of everything for longer than she could remember. What was the point of living forever if you did nothing new? Despite all her hopes, this *faux* Earth, populated by two billion puppets and partials, and ten million of her clade, had failed to revive her.

In one more year, the fleet of spaceships would disperse; the sun, an ordinary G2 star she had moved by the pressure of its own light upon gravity tethered reflective sails, would go supernova; nothing would be saved but the store of information which the Library had collected and collated. She had not yet accessed any of that. Perhaps that would save her.

She returned to the carnival, stayed there three days. But despite use of various intoxicants she could not quite lose herself in it, could not escape the feeling that she had failed after all. This was supposed to be a great congress of her own selves, a place to share and exchange memories that spanned five million years and the entire Galaxy. But it seemed to her that the millions of her selves simply wanted to forget what they were, to lose themselves in the pleasures of the flesh. Of course, many had assumed bodies for the first time to attend the gathering; one could perhaps excuse them, for this carnival was to them a genuine farewell to flesh they would abandon at the end of the year.

On the third day she was sitting in cold dawn light at a green café table in the Jardin des Tuileries, by the great fountain. Someone was sculpting the clouds through which the sun was rising. The café was crowded with guests, partials and puppets, androids and animals – even a silver gynoid, its face a smooth oval mirror. The air buzzed with the tiny machines which attended the guests; in one case, a swirling cloud of gnat-sized beads *was* a guest. After almost a century in costume, the guests were reverting to type.

She sipped a citron pressé, listened to the idle chatter. The party in Paris would break up soon. The revellers would disperse to other parts of the Earth. Except for a clean-up crew, the puppets, partials and all the rest would be returned to store. At another table, a youthful version of her erstwhile lover was talking to an older man with brown hair brushed back from his high forehead and pale blue eyes magnified by the thick lenses of his spectacles.

"The lions, Jim. Go to Afrique and listen to the lions roar at night. There is no sound like it."

"Ah, and I would love that, but Nora would not stand it. She needs the comforts of civilisation. Besides, the thing we must not forget is that I would not be able to see the lions. Instead I think we will drink some more of this fine white wine and you will tell me about them."

"Aw hell, I could bring you a living lion if you like," the younger man said. "I could describe him to you and you could touch him and smell him until you got the idea." He was quite unaware that there were two lions right there in the park, accompanying a naked girl child whose feet, with pigeon's wings at the ankles, did not quite touch the ground.

Did these puppets come here every day, and recreate a conversation millions of years dead for the delectation of the guests? Was each day to them the same day? Suddenly, she felt as if a cold wind was blowing through her, as if she was raised up high and naked upon the pinnacle of the mountain of her millions of years.

"You confuse the true and the real," someone said. A man's voice, soft, lisping. She looked around but could not see who amongst the amazing people and creatures might have said such a thing, the truest realest thing she had heard for . . . how long? She could not remember how long.

She left, and went to New Orleans.

Where it was night, and raining, a soft warm rain falling in the lamplit streets. It was the Twentieth Century here, too. They were cooking crawfish under the mimosa trees at every intersection of the brick paved streets, and burning the Maid of New Orleans over Lake Pontchartrain. The Maid hung up there in the black night sky – wrapped in oiled silks and shining like a star, with the blue-white wheel of the Galaxy a backdrop that spanned the horizon – then flamed like a comet and plunged into the black water while cornet bands played *Laissez le Bon Temps Rouler*.

She fell in with a trio of guests whose originals were all less than a thousand years old. They were students of the Rediscovery, they said, although it was not quite clear what the Rediscovery was. They wore green ("For Earth," one said, although she thought that odd because most of the Earth was blue), and drank a mild psychotropic called absinthe, bitter white stuff poured into water over a sugar cube held in silver tongs. They were interested in the origins of the clade, which amused her greatly, because of course she was its origin, going amongst the copies and clones disguised as her own self. But even if they made her feel every one of her five million years, she liked their innocence, their energy, their openness.

She strolled with her new friends through the great orrery at the waterfront. Its display of the lost natural wonders of the Galaxy was derived from records and memories guests had deposited in the Library, and changed every day. She was listening to the three students discuss the possibility that humans had not originally come from the Earth when someone went past and said loudly, looking right at her, "None of them look like you, but they are just like you all the same. All obsessed with the past because they are trapped in it."

A tall man with a black, spade-shaped beard and black eyes that looked at her with infinite amusement. The same soft, lisping voice she had heard in the café in Paris. He winked and plunged into the heart of the white-hot whirlpool of the accretion disc of the black hole of Sigma Draconis 2, which drew matter from the photosphere of its companion blue-white giant – before the reconstruction, it had been one of the wonders of the Galaxy. She followed, but he was gone.

She looked for him everywhere in New Orleans, and fell in with a woman who before the gathering had lived in the water vapour zone of a gas giant, running a tourist business for those who could afford to download themselves into the ganglia of living blimps a kilometre across. The woman's name was Rapha; she had ruled the worlds of a hundred stars once, but had given that up long before she had answered the call for the gathering.

"I was a man when I had my empire," Rapha said, "but I gave that up too. When you've done everything, what's left but to party?"

She had always been a woman, she thought. And for two million years she had ruled an empire of a million worlds – for all she knew, the copy she had left behind ruled there still. But she didn't tell Rapha that. No one knew who she was, on all the Earth. She said, "Then let's party until the end of the world."

She knew that it wouldn't work – she had already tried everything, in every combination – but because she didn't care if it worked or not, perhaps this time it would.

They raised hell in New Orleans, and went to Antarctica.

It was raining in Antarctica, too.

It had been raining for a century, ever since the world had been made.

Statite sails hung in stationary orbit, reflecting sunlight so that the swamps and cycad forests and volcanic mountain ranges of the South Pole were in perpetual day. The hunting lodge was on a floating island a hundred metres above the tops of the giant ferns, close to the edge of a shallow viridescent lake. A flock of delicate, dappled *Dromiceiomimus* squealed and splashed in the shallows; great dragonflies flitted through the rainy middle air; at the misty horizon the perfect cones of three volcanoes sent up threads of smoke into the sagging clouds.

She and Rapha rode bubbles in wild loops above the forests, chasing dinosaurs or goading dinosaurs to chase them. Then they plunged into one of the volcanoes and caused it to erupt, and one of the hunters overrode the bubbles and brought them back and politely asked them to stop.

The lake and the forest were covered in a mantle of volcanic ash. The sky was milky with ash.

"The guests are amused, but they will not be amused for ever. It is the hunting that is important here. If I may suggest other areas where you might find enjoyment . . ."

He was a slightly younger version of her last lover. A little less salt in his beard; a little more spring in his step.

She said, "How many of you have I made?"

But he didn't understand the question.

They went to Thebes (and some of the hunting party went with them), where they ran naked and screaming through the streets, toppling the statues of the gods. They went to Greenland, and broke the rainbow bridge of Valhalla and fought the trolls and ran again, laughing, with Odin's thunder about their ears. Went to Troy, and set fire to the wooden horse before the Greeks could climb inside it.

None of it mattered. The machines would repair everything; the puppets would resume their roles. Troy would fall again the next night, on schedule.

"Let's go to Golgotha," Rapha said, wild-eyed, very drunk.

This was in a bar of some Christian-era American town. Outside, a couple of the men were roaring up and down the main street on motorcycles, weaving in and out of the slow-moving, candy-coloured cars. Two cops watched indulgently.

"Or Afrique," Rapha said. "We could hunt man-apes."

"I've done it before," someone said. He didn't have a name, but some kind of number. He was part of a clone. His shaved head was horribly scarred; one of his eyes was mechanical. He said, "You hunt them with spears or slings. They're pretty smart, for man-apes. I got killed twice."

Someone came into the bar. Tall, saturnine, black eyes, a spade-shaped beard. At once, she asked her machines if he was a partial or a guest, but the question confused them. She asked them if there were any strangers in the world, and at once they told her that there were the servants and those of her clade, but no strangers.

He said softly, "Are you having a good time?"

"Who are you?"

"Perhaps I'm the one who whispers in your ear, 'Remember that you are mortal.' Are you mortal, Angel?"

No one in the world should know her name. Her true name.

Danger, danger, someone sang in the background of the song that was playing on the jukebox. *Danger*, burbled the coffee pot on the heater behind the counter of the bar.

She said, "I made you, then."

"Oh no. Not me. You made all of this. Even all of the guests, in one way or another. But not me. We can't talk here. Try the one place which has any use in this *faux* world. There's something there I'm going to take, and when I've done that I'll wait for you."

"Who are you? What do you want?"

"Perhaps I want to kill you." He smiled. "And perhaps you want to die. It's one thing you have not tried yet."

He walked away, and when she started after him Rapha got in the way. Rapha hadn't seen the man. She said the others wanted to go to Hy Brasil.

"The gene wars," Rapha said. "That's where we started to become what we are. And then – I don't know, but it doesn't matter. We're going to party to the end of the world. When the sun explodes, I'm going to ride the shock wave as far as I can. I'm not going back. There's a lot of us who aren't going back. Why should we? We went to get copied and woke up here, thousands of years later, thousands of light years away. What's to go back for? Wait! Where are you going?"

"I don't know," she said, and walked out.

The man had scared her. He had touched the doubt which had made her organise the gathering. She wanted a place to hide so that she could think about that before she confronted him.

Most of the North American continent was, in one form or another, modelled after the Third Millennium of the Christian Era. She took a car (a red Dodge as big as a boat, with fins and chrome trim) and drove to Dallas, where she was attacked by tribes of horsemen near the glittering slag of the wrecked city. She took up with a warlord for a while, poisoned all his wives, grew bored and seduced his son, who murdered his father and began a civil war. She went south on horseback through the alien flower jungles which had conquered Earth after humanity had more or less abandoned it, then caught a *pneumatique* all the way down the spine of Florida to Key West.

A version of her last lover lived there, too. She saw him in a bar by the beach two weeks later. There were three main drugs in Key West: cigarettes, heroin and alcohol. She had tried them all, decided she liked alcohol best. It helped you forget yourself in an odd, dissociative way that was both pleasant and disturbing. Perhaps she should have spent more of her long life drunk.

This version of her lover liked alcohol, too. He was both lumbering but shy, pretending not to notice the people who looked at him while he drank several complicated cocktails. He had thickened at the waist; his beard was white and full. His eyes, webbed by wrinkles, were still piercingly blue, but his gaze was vague and troubled. She eavesdropped while he talked with the barkeep. She wanted to find out how the brash man who had to constantly prove himself against the world had turned out.

Badly, it seemed. The world was unforgiving, and his powers were fading.

"I lost her, Carlos," he told the barkeep. He meant his muse. "She's run out on me, the bitch."

"Now, Papa, you know that is not true," the young barkeep said. "I read your article in *Life* just last week."

"It was shit, Carlos. I can fake it well enough, but I can't do the good stuff any more. I need some quiet, and all day I get tourists trying to take my picture and spooking the cats. When I was younger I could work all day in a café, but now I need . . . hell, I don't know what I need. She's a bitch, Carlos. She only loves the young." Later, he said, "I keep dreaming of lions. One of the long white beaches in Afrique where the lions come down at dusk. They play there like cats, and I want to get to them, but I can't."

But Carlos was attending to another customer. Only she heard the old man. Later, after he had gone, she talked with Carlos herself. He was a puppet, and couldn't understand, but it didn't matter.

"All this was a bad idea," she said. She meant the bar, Key West, the Pacific Ocean, the world. "Do you want to know how it started?"

"Of course, ma'am. And may I bring you another drink?"

"I think I have had enough. You stay there and listen. Millions of years ago, while all of what would become humanity lived on the nine worlds and thousand worldlets around a single star in the Sky Hunter arm of the Galaxy, there was a religion which taught that individuals need never die. It was this religion which first drove humanity from star to star in the Galaxy. Individuals copied their personalities into computers, or cloned themselves, or spread their personalities through flocks of birds, or fish, or amongst hive insects. But there was one flaw in this religion. After millions of years, many of its followers were no longer human in form or in thought, except that they could trace back, generation upon generation, their descent from a single human ancestor. They had become transcendents, and each individual transcendent had become a clade, or an alliance, of millions of different minds. Mine is merely one of many, but it is one of the oldest, and one of the largest.

"I brought us here to unite us all in shared experiences. It isn't possible that one of us could have seen every wonder in the Galaxy, visit every world. There are a hundred billion stars in the Galaxy. It takes a year or two to explore the worlds of each star, and then there is the travel between the stars. But there are ten million of us here. Clones, copies, descendants of clones and copies. Many of us have done nothing but explore. We have not seen everything, but we have seen most of it. I thought that we could pool all our information, that it would result in . . . something. A new religion, godhead. Something new, something *different*. But it seems that most just want to party, and I wonder how much I have changed, for they are so little like me. Many of them say that they will not return, that they will stay here until the sun ends it all. Some have joined in the war in China – a few even refuse regeneration. Mostly, though, they want to party."

"There are parties every night, ma'am," the barkeep said. "That's Key West for you."

"Someone was following me, but I lost him. I think he was tracing me through the travel net, but I used contemporary transport to get here. He frightened me and I ran away, but perhaps he is what I need. I think I will find him. What month is this?"

"June, ma'am. Very hot, even for June. It means a bad hurricane season."

"It will get hotter," she said, thinking of the machine ticking away in the core of the sun.

And went to Tibet, where the Library was.

For some reason, the high plateau had been constructed as a replica of part of Mars. She had given her servants a lot of discretion when building the Earth; it pleased her to be surprised, although it did not happen very often.

She had arrived at the top of one of the rugged massifs that defined the edge of the vast basin. There was a shrine here, a mani eye painted on a stone pillar, a heap of stones swamped with skeins of red and blue and white and yellow prayer flags ravelling in the cold wind. The scarp dropped away steeply to talus slopes and the flood lava of the basin's floor, a smooth, lightly cratered red plain mantled with fleets of barchan dunes. Directly below, nestling amongst birches at the foot of the scarp's sheer cliff, was the bone-white Library.

She took a day to descend the winding path. Now and then pilgrims climbed past her. Many shuffled on their knees, eyes lifted to the sky; a few fell face-forward at each step, standing up and starting again at the point where their hands touched the ground. All whirled prayer wheels and muttered their personal mantra as they climbed, and few spared her more than a glance, although at noon while she sat under a gnarled juniper one old man came to her and shared his heel of dry black bread and stringy dried yak meat. She learned from him that the pilgrims were not puppets, as she had thought, but were guests searching for enlightenment. That was so funny and so sad she did not know what to think about it.

The Library was a replica of the White Palace of the Potala. It had been a place of quiet order and contemplation, where all the stories that the clade had told each other, all the memories that they had downloaded or exchanged, had been collected and collated.

Now it was a battleground.

Saffron-robed monks armed with weaponry from a thousand different eras were fighting against man-shaped black androids. Bodies of men and machines were sprawled on the great steps; smoke billowed from the topmost ranks of the narrow windows; red and green energy beams flickered against the pink sky.

237

She walked through the carnage untouched. Nothing in this world could touch her. Only perhaps the man who was waiting for her, sitting cross-legged beneath the great golden Buddha, which a stray shot from some energy weapon had decapitated and half-melted to slag. On either side, hundreds of candles floated in great bowls filled with water; their lights shivered and flickered from the vibration of heavy weaponry.

The man did not open his eyes as she approached, but he said softly, "I already have what I need. These foolish monks are defending a lost cause. You should stop them."

"It is what they have to do. They can't destroy us, of course, but I could destroy you."

"Guests can't harm other guests," he said calmly. "It is one of the rules."

"I am not a guest. Nor, I think, are you."

She told her machines to remove him. Nothing happened.

He opened his eyes. He said, "Your machines are invisible to the puppets and partials you created to populate this fantasy world. I am invisible to the machines. I do not draw my energy from the world grid, but from elsewhere."

And then he leaped at her, striking with formal moves millions of years old. The Angry Grasshopper, the Rearing Horse, the Snapping Mantis. Each move, magnified by convergent energies, could have killed her, evaporated her body, melted her machines.

But she allowed her body to respond, countering his attacks. She had thought that she might welcome death; instead, she was amused and exhilarated by the fury of her response. The habit of living was deeply ingrained; now it had found a focus.

Striking attitudes, tangling in a flurry of blows and counter-blows, they moved through the battleground of the Library, through its gardens, moved down the long talus slope at the foot of the massif in a storm of dust and shattered stones.

At the edge of a lake which filled a small, perfectly circular crater, she finally tired of defensive moves and went on the attack. The Striking Eagle, the Plunging Dragon, the Springing Tiger Who Defends Her Cubs. He countered in turn. Stray energies boiled the lake dry. The dry ground shook, split open in a mosaic of plates. Gradually, a curtain of dust was raised above the land, obscuring the setting sun and the green face of the Moon, which was rising above the mountains.

They broke apart at last. They stood in the centre of a vast crater of vitrified rock. Their clothes hung in tatters about their bodies. It was night, now. Halfway up the scarp of the massif, small lightnings flashed where the monks still defended the Library.

"Who are you?" she said again. "Did I create you?"

"I'm closer to you than anyone else in this strange mad world," he said.

That gave her pause. All the guests, clones or copies or replicants, were of her direct genetic lineage.

She said, "Are you my death?"

As if in answer, he attacked again. But she fought back as forcefully as before, and when he broke off, she saw that he was sweating.

"I am stronger than you thought," she said.

He took out a small black cube from his tattered tunic. He said, "I have what I need. I have the memory core of the Library. Everything anyone who came here placed on record is here."

"Then why do you want to kill me?"

"Because you are the original. I thought it would be fitting, after I stole this."

She laughed. "You foolish man! Do you think we rely on a single physical location, a single master copy? It is the right of everyone in the clade to carry away the memories of everyone else. Why else are we gathered here?"

"I am not of your clade." He tossed the cube into the air, caught it, tucked it away. "I will use this knowledge against you. Against all of you. I have all your secrets."

"You say you are closer to me than a brother, yet you do not belong to the clade. You want to use our memories to destroy us." She had a sudden insight. "Is this war, then?"

He bowed. He was near naked, lit by the green light of the

Moon and the dimming glow of the slag that stretched away in every direction. "Bravo," he said. "But it has already begun. Perhaps it is even over by now; after all, we are twenty thousand light years above the plane of the Galactic disc, thirty five thousand light years from the hub of your Empire. It will take you that long to return. And if the war is not over, then this will finish it."

She was astonished. Then she laughed. "What an imagination I have!"

He bowed again, and said softly, "You made this world from your imagination, but you did not imagine me."

And he went somewhere else.

Her machines could not tell her where he had gone; she called upon all the machines in the world, but he was no longer on the Earth. Nor was he amongst the fleet of ships which had carried the guests – in suspended animation, as frozen embryos, as codes triply engraved in gold – to the world she had created for the gathering.

There were only two other places he could be, and she did not think he could have gone to the sun. If he had, then he would have triggered the machine at the core, and destroyed her and everyone else in the subsequent supernova.

So she went to the Moon.

She arrived on the farside. The energies he had used against her suggested that he had his own machines, and she did not think that he would have hidden in full view of the Earth.

The machines which she had instructed to recreate the Earth for the one hundred years of the gathering had recreated the Moon, too, so that the oceans of the Earth would have the necessary tides; it had been easier than tangling gravithic resonances to produce the same effect. It had taken little extra effort to recreate the forests which had cloaked the Moon for a million years, between the first faltering footsteps and the abandonment of the Earth.

It was towards the end of the long Lunar night. All around, blue firs soared up for hundreds of metres, cloaked in wide fans of needles that in the cold and the dark had drooped down to protect the scaly trunks. The grey rocks were coated in thin snow, and frozen lichens crunched underfoot. Her machines scattered in every direction, quick as thought. She sat down on top of a big rough boulder and waited.

It was very quiet. The sky was dominated by the triple-armed pinwheel of the Galaxy. It was so big that when she looked at one edge she could not see the other. The Arm of the Warrior rose high above the arch of the Arm of the Hunter; the Arm of the Archer curved in the opposite direction, below the close horizon. Star clusters made long chains of concentrated light through the milky haze of the galactic arms. There were lines and threads and globes and clouds of stars, all fading into a general misty radiance dissected by dark lanes which barred the arms at regular intervals. The core was knitted from thin shells of stars in tidy orbits concentrically packed around the great globular clusters of the heart stars, like layers of glittering tissue wrapped around a heap of jewels.

Every star had been touched by humankind. Existing stars had been moved or destroyed; millions of new stars and planetary systems had been created by collapsing dust clouds. A garden of stars, regulated, ordered, tidied. The Library held memories of every star, every planet, every wonder of the old untamed Galaxy. She was beginning to realise that the gathering was not the start of something new, but the end of five million years of Galactic colonisation.

After a long time, the machines came back, and she went where they told her.

It was hidden within a steep-sided crater, a castle or maze of crystal vanes that rose in serried ranks from deep roots within the crust, where they collected and focused tidal energy. He was at its heart, busily folding together a small spacecraft. The energy of the vanes had been greatly depleted by the fight, and he was trying to concentrate the remainder in the motor of the spacecraft. He was preparing to leave.

Her machines rose up and began to spin, locking in resonance with the vanes and bleeding off their store of energy. The

241

machines began to glow as she bounded down the steep smooth slope towards the floor of the crater, red-hot, white-hot, as hot as the core of the sun, for that was where they were diverting the energy stored in the vanes.

Violet threads flicked up, but the machines simply absorbed that energy too. Their stark white light flooded the crater, bleaching the ranks of crystal vanes.

She walked through the traps and tricks of the defences, pulled him from his fragile craft and took him up in a bubble of air to the neutral point between the Moon and the Earth.

"Tell me," she said. "Tell me why you came here. Tell me about the war."

He was surprisingly calm. He said, "I am a first generation clone, but I am on the side of humanity, not the transcendents. Transcendent clades are a danger to all of the variety within and between the civilisations in the Galaxy. At last the merely human races have risen against them. I am just one weapon in the greatest war ever fought."

"You are my flesh. You are of my clade."

"I am a secret agent. I was made from a single cell stolen from you several hundred years before you set off for this fake Earth and the gathering of your clade. I arrived only two years ago, grew my power source, came down to steal the memory core and kill you. Although I failed to kill you before, we are no longer in the place where you draw your power. Now – "

After a moment in which nothing happened, he screamed in frustration and despair. She pitied him. Pitied all those who had bent their lives to produce this poor vessel, this failed moment, although all the power, the intrigues and desperate schemes his presence implied were as remote from her as the politics of a termite nest.

She said, "Your power source is not destroyed, but my machines take all its energy. Why did your masters think us dangerous?"

"Because you would fill the Galaxy with your own kind. Because you would end human evolution. Because you will not accept that the Universe is greater than you can ever be. Because you refuse to die, and death is a necessary part of evolution."

She laughed. "Silly little man! Why would we accept limits? We are only doing what humanity has always done. We use science to master nature just as man-apes changed their way of thinking by making tools and using fire. Humanity has always striven to become more than it is, to grow spiritually and morally and intellectually, to go up to the edge and step over it."

For the first time in a million years, those sentiments did not taste of ashes. By trying to destroy her, he had shown her what her life was worth.

He said, "But you do not change. That is why you are so dangerous. You and the other clades of transhumans have stopped humanity evolving. You would fill the Galaxy with copies of a dozen individuals who are so scared of physical death that they will do any strange and terrible thing to themselves to survive."

He gestured at the blue-white globe that hung beneath their feet, small and vulnerable against the vast blackness between galaxies.

"Look at your Earth! Humanity left it four million years ago, yet you chose to recreate it for this gathering. You had a million years of human history on Earth to choose from, and four and a half billion years of the history of the planet itself, and yet almost half of your creation is given over to a single century."

"It is the century where we became what we are," she said, remembering Rapha. "It is the century when it became possible to become transhuman, when humanity made the first steps beyond the surface of a single planet."

"It is the century you were born in. You would freeze all history if you could, an eternity of the same thoughts thought by the same people. You deny all possibilities but your own self."

He drew himself up, defiant to the last. He said, "My ship will carry the memory core home without me. You take all, and give nothing. I give my life, and I give you this."

He held up something as complex and infolded as the throat of an orchid. It was a vacuum fluctuation, a hole in reality that when inflated would remove them from the Universe. She looked away at once – the image was already burned in her brain – and threw him into the core of the sun. He did not even have a chance to scream.

Alone in her bubble of air, she studied the wheel of the Galaxy, the ordered pattern of braids and clusters. Light was so slow. It took a hundred thousand years to cross from one edge of the Galaxy to the other. Had the war against her empire, and the empires of all the other transcendents, already ended? Had it already changed the Galaxy, stirred the stars into new patterns? She would not know until she returned, and that would take thirty-five thousand years.

But she did not have to return. In the other direction was the limitless Universe, a hundred billion galaxies. She hung there a long time, watching little smudges of ancient light resolve out of the darkness. Empires of stars wherever she looked, wonders without end.

We will fight the war, she thought, and we shall win, and we will go on for ever and ever.

And went down, found the bar near the beach. She would wait until the old man came in, and buy him a drink, and talk to him about his dream of the lions.

Notes on Contributors

BRIAN W. ALDISS (b. 1925), an enthusiastic traveller, is one of the monuments of science fiction and fantasy, and indeed of British letters. His vast *Helliconia* trilogy is a triumph of modern sf, and his body of work is without equal in its humane, witty, knowing urbanity. It is almost impossible to believe, such is the freshness of his work, that he was born just five years later than those classic sf pioneers Isaac Asimov, Ray Bradbury and Frank Herbert.

STEPHEN DEDMAN (b. 1959) has recently emerged as one of the most lively and diverse new sf stylists, both in his native Australia and in the USA. His first novel, *The Art of Arrow Cutting*, was published in 1997. He has been an actor, tutor, experimental subject, manager of an sf bookshop and used dinosaur salesman.

GREG EGAN (b. 1961), another Australian, in less than a decade created a body of short and long fiction of such probing ingenuity that it is fair to regard him as the most important current sf writer in English. His novels *Permutation City*, *Distress* and *Diaspora*, and the stories collected in *Axiomatic*, virtually defined sf's cutting edge in the late 1990s.

LISA GOLDSTEIN (b. 1953), an American, writes powerfully in what critic John Clute aptly calls 'a style which treats sf and fantasy material through a magic-realist looking-glass'. Notable books include *The Red Magician* (a 1982 American Book Award winner), *The Dream Years* and the collection *Travellers in Magic*.

GARRY KILWORTH (b. 1941) won the Gollancz/Sunday Times sf short story contest with his first story, 'Let's Go to Golgotha!' He has published many sf novels and shorter works, and most recently a Polynesian fantasy trilogy, *The Navigator Kings*, charting in epic form the myths and legends of the Oceanians in their struggle to conquer the Pacific: *The Roof of Voyaging*, *The Princely Flower* and *Land of Mists*.

PAUL J. McAULEY (b. 1955) holds a PhD in botany and is one of the new breed of highly literate and scientifically informed sf writers fostered by the British magazine *Interzone*. His superb novels include *Eternal Light* and *Fairyland*, which won both the Arthur C. Clarke and the John Campbell Memorial jury awards.

JOANNA RUSS (b. 1937) is one of the generation of astonishingly inventive American feminist writers who reinvigorated sf in the 1970s, notable for her exquisite writing, her sardonic wit and her fine rage. Her best novel, transgressive and technically astonishing for its time, is *The Female Man*, one of the key texts in feminist sf.

ROBERT SILVERBERG (b. 1935) has written an astonishing number of sf and fantasy short stories and novels, many of them prize-winners. Recently he has abandoned science fiction in favour of fantasy, which is the field's loss. 'Trips' is the definitive story on the theme of travel between alternative universes.

JOHN VARLEY (b. 1947), like Greg Egan today and Robert Heinlein in the 1940s, defined a moment in sf's exuberant development. A run of extraordinary and pleasing short stories in the 1970s re-created the exciting pleasures of a richly 'lived-in' future universe. Recently he has been working in Hollywood, but a new sf novel is eagerly anticipated.

GENE WOLFE (b. 1931), along with Aldiss, Ursula Le Guin and a handful of other writers, is one of the contenders for sf's laurel as finest wordsmith. His fiction these days tends to the monumental – the four (or perhaps five) volumes of *The Book of the New Sun*, and another tetralogy, recently completed, *The Book of the Long Sun*. His short stories are especially rewarding: dense, teasing, colourful, fluent.

Acknowledgements

Lonely Planet Publications is grateful for permission to include the following copyright material:

BRIAN W. ALDISS, 'The Difficulties Involved in Photographing Nix Olympica'. Copyright © 1986 by Brian Aldiss; first appeared in *Isaac Asimov's Science Fiction Magazine*.

STEPHEN DEDMAN, 'Tourist Trade'. Copyright © 1996 by Stephen Dedman; first appeared in *Science Fiction Age*.

GREG EGAN, 'Yeyuka'. Copyright © 1997 by Greg Egan; first appeared in *Meanjin*.

LISA GOLDSTEIN, 'Tourists'. Copyright © 1985 by Lisa Goldstein; first appeared in *Isaac Asimov's Science Fiction Magazine*.

GARRY KILWORTH, 'Let's Go to Golgotha!' Copyright © 1975 by Garry Kilworth; first appeared in *Gollancz/Sunday Times Best SF Stories*.

PAUL J. McAULEY, 'All Tomorrow's Parties'. Copyright © 1997 by Paul McAuley; first appeared in *Interzone 119*.

JOANNA RUSS, 'Useful Phrases for the Tourist'. Copyright © 1972 by Joanna Russ; first appeared in *Universe 2*, ed. Terry Carr. Reprinted by permission of Ellen Levine Literary Agency.

LONELY PLANET JOURNEYS

JOURNEYS is a unique collection of travel writing – published by the company that understands travel better than anyone else.

It is a series for anyone who has ever experienced – or dreamed of – the magical moment when they encountered a strange culture or saw a place for the first time. They are tales to read while you're planning a trip, while you're on the road or while you're in an armchair, in front of a fire.

These outstanding titles explore our planet through the eyes of a diverse group of international writers. JOURNEYS books catch the spirit of a place, illuminate a culture, recount an adventure, or introduce a fascinating way of life. They always entertain, and always enrich the experience of travel.

'Lively, intelligent and varied . . . an important contribution to travel literature' – *Age (Melbourne)*

BRIEF ENCOUNTERS
Stories of Love, Sex & Travel
edited by Michelle de Kretser

Love affairs on the road, passionate holiday flings, disastrous pick-ups, erotic encounters . . . In this seductive collection of stories, 22 authors from around the world write about travel romances. A tourist in Peru falls for her handsome guide; a writer explores the ambiguities of his relationship with a Japanese woman; a beautiful young man on a train proposes marriage . . . Combining fiction and reportage, *Brief Encounters* is must-have reading – for everyone who has dreamt of escape with that perfect stranger.

Includes stories by Pico Iyer, Mary Morris, Emily Perkins, Mona Simpson, Lisa St Aubin de Terán, Paul Theroux and Sara Wheeler.

DRIVE THRU AMERICA
Sean Condon

If you've ever wanted to drive across the US but couldn't find the time (or afford the gas), *Drive Thru America* is perfect for you.

In his search for American myths and realities – along with comfort, cable TV and good, reasonably priced coffee – Sean Condon paints a hilarious road-portrait of the USA.

'entertaining and laugh-out-loud funny'
– Alex Wilber, Travel editor, Amazon.com

SEAN & DAVID'S LONG DRIVE
Sean Condon

Sean and David are young townies who have rarely strayed beyond city limits. One day, for no good reason, they set out to discover their homeland, and what follows is a wildly entertaining adventure that covers half of Australia.

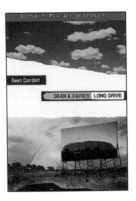

'a hilariously detailed log of two burned out friends' *– Rolling Stone*

'a definitive Generation X road epic ... a wonderful read' *– Globe & Mail*

MALI BLUES
Traveling to an African Beat
Lieve Joris (translated by Sam Garrett)

Drought, rebel uprisings, ethnic conflict: these are the predominant images of West Africa. But as Lieve Joris travels in Senegal, Mauritania and Mali, she meets survivors, fascinating individuals charting new ways of living between tradition and modernity. With her remarkable gift for drawing out people's stories, Joris brilliantly captures the rhythms of a world that refuses to give in.

THE GATES OF DAMASCUS
Lieve Joris (translated by Sam Garrett)

This best-selling book is a beautifully drawn portrait of day-to-day life in modern Syria. Through her intimate contact with local people, Lieve Joris draws us into the fascinating world that lies behind the gates of Damascus. Hala's husband is a political prisoner, jailed for his opposition to the Assad regime; through the author's friendship with Hala we see how Syrian politics impacts on the lives of ordinary people.

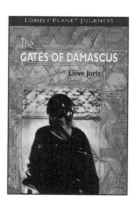

'she has expanded the boundaries of travel writing'
– Times Literary Supplement

GREEN DREAMS
Travels in Central America
Stephen Benz

On the Amazon, in Costa Rica, Honduras and on the Mayan trail from Guatemala to Mexico, Stephen Benz describes his encounters with water, mud, insects and other wildlife – and not least with the ecotourists themselves. With witty insights into the phenomenon of modern travel, *Green Dreams* discusses the paradox at the heart of cultural and 'green' tourism.

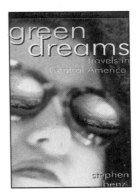

Provocative and absorbing reading.

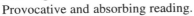

FULL CIRCLE
A South American Journey
Luis Sepúlveda (translated by Chris Andrews)

'A journey without a fixed itinerary' in the company of Chilean writer Luis Sepúlveda. Extravagant characters and extraordinary situations are memorably evoked: gauchos organising a tournament of lies, a scheming heiress on the lookout for a husband, a pilot with a corpse on board his plane . . . Part autobiography, part travel memoir, *Full Circle* brings us the distinctive voice of one of South America's most compelling writers.

WINNER 1996 Astrolabe – Etonnants Voyageurs award for the best work of travel literature published in France.